new Strategies for Free Children:

Child Abuse Prevention for Elementary School Children

A Leader's Manual of
The Child Assault Prevention Projects

by
Sally J. Cooper, Executive Director
The National Assault Prevention Center

Editor: Jan Brittan
Designer: Susan Sheaffer Curtis
Photographer: Karen Colbert

published by

NAPC

The National Assault Prevention Center
Box 02005, Columbus, Ohio 43202
(614) 291-2540

©1991 by the National Assault Prevention Center. All rights reserved. Pages 134, 135, 142, 144 and the Appendices may be duplicated without permission for use in Child Assault Prevention (CAP) services. For permission to reprint, adapt, or translate other materials, write to:

Editor, National Assault Prevention Center
Box 02005
Columbus, Ohio 43202

Library of Congress Cataloging in Publication Data

LB 91-062365

ISBN 1-880326-49-3

This manual was made possible, in part, through a grant from the Ohio Children's Trust Fund, Ohio Department of Human Services, and does not necessarily represent the views of the Ohio Children's Trust Fund or the Ohio Department of Human Services.

Acknowledgments

Many people have helped to make this book and the work of the Child Assault Prevention Project possible.

Maureen Crossmaker, Dave Nibert, Deb Schipper, and Teri Wehausen cofounded NAPC with me, and gave generously of themselves in so doing.

Laura Kagy Fitch, another cofounder of NAPC, gave me the greatest pleasure in working with her for nine years. Her contributions to CAP and to me personally, as a colleague and friend, are numerous and impressive.

Ellie Kuehn Kaastra, Kate Kain, Rich Snowdon, Vivian Chavez, Pat Stanislaski, Marilyn Williams, Cheryl Mota, Yuri Morita, and Lisa Weintraub, veterans in the International CAP Network, made this work more joyful than I had a right to expect. Nevalyn Nevil, Sharon Austin, Carmen Wojtanowski, Rich Stoff, Bill Bell, Laurie Stein, Gayle Channing, and Bill Habig rendered services to the Board of Trustees of NAPC beyond the call of duty.

Kyle Hoffman, Bill Chittenden, Jane Cooper, Margie Mapes, Dave Nibert, Frayda Turkel, and Sally Dine Fitch have made me a better person, and CAP a better project.

Dave Nibert deserves credit for the entire chapter on research on the CAP model, which was preceded by invaluable work for NAPC. The manuscript was reviewed by Rich Snowdon, CAP Training Center of California; Kate Madson, Licking County Ohio CAP Project; Danialle Rose-Joseph, Cheyenne River Sioux Tribe CAP Project; Starr Potts, Massachusetts Regional CAP Training Center; Cyndee Boyvey-Brown, Portia Gonzales-McDade, Sally Bulford, Anna Marcel de Hermanas, Neal Semel, Quin Ferguson, and Lynda Barnett, the fine staff of NAPC; Sally Dine Fitch, formerly program director of NAPC; Pat Stanislaski, Marilyn Williams, and Cheryl Mota, New Jersey Regional CAP Training Center; Evelyn Gill, Charlotte Corgliana, Cheryl McCullough, Cathy Bell, Susan Connolly, and Joan Montenari, New Jersey CAP statewide network; and Lisa Weintraub, Leona Heillig, and David Singleton, Montreal Assault Prevention Center. I hope I have done justice to your considerable and insightful input.

Quin Ferguson, who runs NAPC quietly and efficiently, has added greatly to my joy and my sanity over the last six years.

I owe the children, parents, teachers, and professionals in the field who have rewarded my work with their experiences and knowledge my deepest appreciation.

Thanks to Yvonne Lutter and Cathy Phelps, my coauthors for the first edition of *Strategies*. It held up well. I hope this revision proves to be as durable.

Thanks to Anne Paulle, Sarah McKinley, Margaret Dilley, Cathy Beard-Henry, and the other members of Women Against Rape, who, in 1978, founded the CAP Project. Thirteen years later, it still represents one of the finest prevention programs in the world by anyone's estimation.

The Columbus Foundation, Ms Foundation for Women, Ohio Department of Human Services, Ohio Children's Trust Fund, Leo Yassenoff Foundation, Columbus Public Schools, Gund Foundation, and L.J. Skaggs and Mary C. Skaggs Foundation have provided affirmation and financial support for CAP and NAPC.

Thanks to Mitch Truesdell, principal of Beck Street Elementary School, and the teachers, parents, and children of Beck, whose beautiful faces grace many of these pages. We got your good side.

I thank Karen D. Colbert for her artistry in photography, Jan Brittan for copy editing, and Susan S. Curtis for the design of the manual. Also, Pam Nowicki of Letter Perfect Graphics, who typeset this manual, Lynne Bonenberger, who proofread it, and Anchor Press, who printed it, have my deepest appreciation.

I continue to believe that life was meant to be a joyous lesson, not a painful passage. This is what we have worked for and, even though our work is not over yet, the network of people you have influenced with your contributions to the field grows ever larger and stronger.

Thank you all,

Sally Cooper, author
May 1991

Table of Contents

Acknowledgments   iii

Chapter 1 Introduction
Children in a Violent Society   3
Violence and Social Justice   4
Working With CAP   5
The CAP Manual   5
    "Victim" vs. "Survivor"
    Continuing Education
References   6

Chapter 2 Our History
The Origin of CAP   9
Nationwide CAP Development   11
International CAP Development   12
The Future of CAP   12

Chapter 3 From Victimization to Empowerment
Introduction   15
    Empowerment
    Multiculturalism
Myths About Rape   16
The Evolution of CAP and Empowerment Theory   17
Rape Prevention Strategies   17
    Traditional Theories
    Feminist Theory and Empowerment
Child Assault Prevention Strategies   19
    Information
    Empowerment
    Support
References   24

Chapter 4 Child Abuse: An Overview
Introduction   27
    Secrecy
    Recognizing Diversity
    Children's Status
Defining Child Abuse   28
    Physical Abuse
    Sexual Abuse
    Neglect
    Emotional Maltreatment
    Ritualized Abuse
    Munchausen Syndrome by Proxy
Child-on-Child Violence   36
Implications of Abuse   37
The Need for Prevention   38
References   38

Chapter 5 Presenting the Children's Workshops

Introduction	43
Developmental Levels	43
Choosing Workshop Facilitators	44
Self-Selection	
Diversity	
A Decade of Experience	45
Women and Men Working Together	46
The Curriculum	46
Observers in the Classroom	
Modifications for Young Children	
Curriculum Adaptations	48
Curriculum Goals by Grade Level	49
Preparing for the Children's Workshop	49
Workshop Script	52
Introduction	
Children's Rights	
Introduce the "Bully" Role-Play	
Introduce the "Stranger" Role-Play	
Introduce the "Known Adult" Role-Play	
Introduce the Teacher Role-Play	
Discussion	
Primary Facilitator's Outline	78

Chapter 6 Presenting the Adult Workshops

Introduction	85
Parent Participation	85
Teacher/Staff In-Services	
Community Education	87
Logistics and Program Content	87
Materials Needed for Adult Presentations	
Shared Components of the Adult Workshops	
Conducting the Adult Workshop	90
Introduction	
Sexual Assault and Prevention	90
Child Assault and Prevention	91
Child Abuse	
Traditional Prevention Strategies	
Factors in Children's Vulnerability	
The Children's Workshop	95
The "Bully" Role-Play	
The "Stranger" Role-Play	
The "Uncle Harry" Role-Play	
Recognizing Child Abuse	99
Physical Symptoms	
Activity and Habit Clues	
Responding to Children	
Rights and Responsibilities	
Tips for Adult Workshops	103
Parents Role in Prevention	
Acting in the Community's Interest	
In-Home Prevention Activities	
Commonly Asked Questions in the Adult Workshops	105
References	108

Chapter 7 Responding to Children

Talk Time	111
Reviewing CAP Concepts	111
Identifying the Abused Child	111
Clues to Possible Abuse	
Physical Symptoms	
Symptoms of Sexual Abuse	
Activity and Habit Clues	
Educational Concerns	115
Emotional Indicators	115
Helping Children in Crisis	116
Confidentiality	117
Understanding Crisis Intervention	117
Listening	
Comfort	
Power and Control	118
Steps in Effective Crisis Intervention	
Guidelines for Talking with Children	121
Affirm Innocence	
Believe the Child	
Assess Safety	
Validate Feelings	
Be Honest	
Find Out What the Child Wants	
Use the Child's Language	
Listen — Don't Interrogate	
Special Considerations	125
Separation/Divorce	
Spanking	
Battering	
Drug and Alcohol Abuse	
Reporting Child Abuse	127
Dual Reporting	
Community Networking	
Advocacy	
Linkage with Protective Services	
References	129

Chapter 8 Creating, Implementing, and Running a CAP Project

Introduction	133
Determining Your CAP Territory	133
Beginning	
Finding Facilitators	
Diversity	
Interviewing	
Volunteers	
Facilitator Responsibilities	136
Preventing Burnout	
Establishing Services	138
Logistics and Scheduling	
Review Time	
Permission Slips	

Coordinating a Project	141
Requirements	
Evaluations and Exit Interviews	
Disclosures of Abuse	
School Responsibilities	
NonProfit Status	145
Insurance for CAP Projects	145
Fundraising	146
CAP Brochure	
Fundraising Events	
Conferences and Seminars	
Risks	
Grants	147
Budgeting	147
Salaries	
Benefits	
Program Supplies	149
Direct Program Expenses	
Costs of Doing Business	
Direct and Indirect Costs	
Finalizing the Budget	

Chapter 9 CAP Program Evaluation

Introduction	155
Evaluating Your Project	155
Formative Evaluation	155
Formative Design 1: Evaluating Program Implementation	
Formative Evaluation 2: Descriptive Statistics	
Summative Evaluation	156
Summative Design 1: Measurement of School Personnel's Perceptions of Program Effectiveness	
Summative Type 2: Measurement of Teacher/Parent Knowledge Acquisition	
Summative Type 3: Student Evaluations	
Evaluation Performed by Non-CAP Personnel	160
Review of the Literature	161
Research on CAP	161
The CAP Preschool Model	
The CAP Special Needs Model	
The TeenCAP Model	
Research on Other Prevention Programs	164
Summary of Major Findings	167
Constructive Information Gained from Research	167
References	168

Chapter 10 Working Together: NAPC and You

What's in the CAP Name?	173
What It Means to Call Yourself a CAP Project	
"Safe, Strong, and Free"	
Your Responsibilities to NAPC	175
Designing a Logo	
Media Relations	
Communication	

Appendix A

Appendix B

Appendix C

Bibliography   211

1
Introduction

Whether you bought this book, borrowed it from a friend, or checked it out of the library, you did so because you are one of the growing number of people who recognize that child abuse is a serious problem.

But many people don't. Even though child abuse has been the subject of public discussion for some years now, even though it seems that you can't read the paper or turn on your television set without hearing about it, many people still deny the reality and the scope of the problem.

That denial is part of the problem. Denial that child abuse happens much too often in our society, or denial that it is serious and traumatic, has terrible implications. It means that prevention, intervention, and therapeutic services operate with too few dollars and too little public outrage over a problem that deserves much more of both. It means that abuse can continue for generations with multiple victims and multiple offenders, without detection or intervention. It means that people — real people — must suffer rather than recover. And it means that most children will never learn the information, strategies, and skills that could prevent their own victimization.

Children in a Violent Society

Every day children in the United States witness unbelievable violence on television. The big blue tube is captivating, exciting, and thrilling, and holds the attention of the typical young person, aged 5–11, for an average of 30 hours each week.[1] Unfortunately, violence on television isn't perceived as horrific, or despicable, or shocking. It is merely entertainment. Consider the following:

- By the time children are 14 years old they will have witnessed 13,000 murders on television.[2] According to the National Coalition on Television Violence, by the time they are 18 they will have witnessed more than 250,000 violent acts.[3]

- Of all types of television programming, cartoons are the single most violent, with 22 acts of violence per hour, or one every three minutes.[4]

- Forty-six percent of all music videos contain violent actions or suggestions of violence.[5]

- Eighty percent of all television programs contain violence. A typical program contains five violent acts.[6]

A growing body of research suggests that children are affected by television violence. The National Victim Center's newsletter, *Crime, Safety and You,* quotes former U.S. Surgeon General C. Everett Koop: "Children especially become desensitized to violent interpersonal conflict and, when seeing another child being hurt, will tend not to do the thing that civilization requires to be done — step in and protect the victim. Instead they will watch, as if this, too, were dramatized entertainment."[7]

The National Victim Center's newsletter also reports that children exposed to television violence may conclude that:

- Problems can be solved through violence or the threat of violence
- The use of violence and physical strength is rewarded
- White people are better than nonwhite people
- Boys are more important than girls

We must convince children that violence is a poor way to solve problems, and that it isn't fun or exciting. In the face of a daily diet of violence, this is a difficult message to teach. CAP is one such effort, never meant to stand alone nor meant to be a panacea. It should be one of many efforts that each community undertakes. Crisis nurseries, parent education classes, and specific training for high-risk parents such as teens are also needed.

Child abuse prevention activities alone will not eliminate violence from our families or our neighborhoods. Children also need to be taught communication skills, effective problem-solving techniques, ways to handle conflict without fists or loss of rights, and self-esteem. Each community must actively teach against racism, sexism, ageism, and ableism. We must teach cooperation, rather than dominance and submission. We must teach civic involvement, rather than apathy, and we must all respect difference, rather than fear it. Teaching children these values will turn them away from aggression as well as victimization.

Violence and Social Justice

When you study violence, you find that behind its ugly myths is the even uglier truth that child abuse cases are not isolated incidents. All kinds of violence against all people are connected. A battered woman, for example, has much in common with a battered child or a "bashed" gay man. The commonality is powerlessness in the face of domination and hatred, second-class citizenship, and objectification. When a women, a child, or a gay man is battered, each is seen by the batterer as less than human. At the moment when he or she strikes, or rapes, or otherwise violates another human being, the abuser has lost sight of that other person's humanity.

You will find a lot of discussion in this book on racism, sexism, ageism, ableism, classism, and homophobia. This is not because we are unsure of our purpose or because we are mixing our agendas. Violence in our society is inextricably tied to second-class citizenship. It is no coincidence that women, children, people of diverse national origin or race, people with disabilities, gay men, and lesbians are subject to a striking amount of violence. Violence is an expression of power and supremacy, and anyone in our society who is seen as less powerful or subordinate is vulnerable to assault.

This is why the anti-violence movement is committed to all movements for civil rights. It is our belief — indeed our philosophy — that the amount of violence in our society will decrease in direct proportion to the elimination of hatred based on bigotry and fear. We are part of a global awareness that embraces rather than fears cultural differences.

Although this book was written with the hope that whoever reads it will find a way to offer prevention services to their community, it was also written with greater hopes in mind. Humankind can do better by its children. The way we treat children is disgraceful. Poverty, homelessness, disease, and hunger are facts of life for too many children. Perhaps if enough of us become outraged enough, and if through this outrage we succeed in raising the status of children, we will succeed in preventing more than just abuse.

This analysis of violence may not be comfortable for you. You may have picked up this book intending only to address the abuse of children in your community. Many people say that if they succeed in preventing just one child from being abused, then their efforts are worthwhile. We argue that you should aspire to much more. Helping one child is a noble cause. But in a nation where more than two million children are abused, where children are the single poorest group of citizens, where health care and prenatal care are privileges rather than rights, helping one child is not enough.

Working With CAP

This work is not for everyone. Although there are many survivors who work for CAP Projects, there are also many who become aware that this work is too hard on them. It can bring up memories and feelings that are difficult to deal with in a professional setting. Even nonsurvivors can have trouble working in the classroom. Talking to children who have been hurt may not be possible for you.

When you decide whether this work is for you, please do so with the children in mind. Evaluate whether you can commit yourself to the everyday focus on abuse. Although it is true that we concentrate on prevention, we meet many young victims. They disclose, often in painful detail, the graphic truths of their experiences, reaching out to CAP professionals for support and assistance. Part of our job is to listen, to believe, and to help them. If you work for CAP, you work for the kids.

The CAP Manual

We have designed this book with chapter headings and subheadings that will help you locate the information you need quickly. It is important for you to use this information to consider whether you want to become involved in a CAP Project. There are chapters on the actual children's and adult's workshops, a comprehensive overview of evaluations of our project, and a chapter on creating and implementing a project. There is also basic information about how to identify a child who may have been abused, how to report cases of abuse, and what you can do to help the child. The Appendices include forms that will help you do all of these.

An entire chapter is devoted to the theory of empowerment upon which all our work rests. Understanding this theory is critical to your success. We believe that the only way to truly help children is to empower them, and their adult community, to stop abuse. We hope that you find empowerment for yourself on these pages as well.

"Victim" vs. "Survivor"

Throughout this manual, we use the word *victim* to refer to someone who is currently being assaulted, one for whom victimization is still happening. The term *survivor* refers to a person who was assaulted at any time in the past. Kathleen Barry first advocated use of the word "survivor" in *Female Sexual Slavery*. Since then, anti-violence groups across the country have adopted this word to pay homage to the person who has lived through a dangerous, life-threatening experience. It emphasizes respect, dignity, strength, and courage. The label "victim" often conveys helplessness; it perpetuates the powerlessness felt at the time of the attack. Recognizing the abuse and its effect on one's self can be a long and painful process. By calling people who have been assaulted "survivors," we affirm belief in their ability to live with the experience and become stronger in spite of it.

Continuing Education

This manual is only the beginning of your knowledge base if you choose to create a project or work with an existing one. The field is expanding rapidly and there is much more information than can possibly be included in one manual. You must become familiar with the field in general. If you want to build your project into a respected and credible organization in your community, you must read the works of researchers, survivors, therapists, and attorneys.

So the journey only begins here. The Bibliography will help you move beyond this manual.

References

1. D. P. Demers, *Breaking Your Child's TV Addiction: A Guide for Parents* (Minneapolis, MN: Marquette Books, 1989), 28.
2. Demers, 36.
3. "Violence as Entertainment," National Victim Center, 1, no. 3 (August 1990).
4. Demers, 37.
5. "Musicvideo Violence," *Response* (Summer 1985): 26.
6. Demers, 36–37.
7. "Violence as Entertainment."

2
Our History

It hardly seems possible that at the writing of this manual the Child Assault Prevention (CAP) Project is 12 years old. CAP is almost a teenager, and will be, by the time you hold this new manual in your hands.

So much has happened over the years. We've had lots of successes and failures that have caused countless celebrations and many tears. When we began this work in 1978, only silence met our birth; the abuse of children was a secret in the United States. And we have truly helped to change the world.

In the short space of 12 years, the child abuse prevention movement has played a significant role in making child abuse, and child sexual assault in particular, a major public issue. We have reached millions of parents, teachers, and children with factual information to replace the myths and half-truths that were prevalent among professional and lay people alike. Stories we have collected over the years show that we have saved some children's lives and prevented many children from being physically or sexually abused. We have listened to thousands of children tell, for the first time, their personal stories of abuse, because we helped them believe that they had a right to live free from abuse. We've taught thousands of teacher/staff in-service workshops, resulting in a growing work force of teachers who are better able to recognize abuse and more comfortable in reporting it. We've listened to countless parents describe their own childhood abuse or that of their children, and shown them a path to recovery. We've held hands with many, in joy and in anguish.

We have changed, too. We are people who believe that we can do something about escalating reports of abuse. We know that we can teach techniques to reduce both victimization and aggression. In a field immersed in despair, we have found reason to hope.

We have developed friendships across nations and continents. Our network of CAP Projects has grown to more than 240 in 36 states and eight nations. Our materials have been offered in seven languages to children with many types of disabilities and from many different cultures. We are a network of friends teaching empowerment to adults and children, and figuring out how to empower ourselves. We are young and old; we are college-educated and working-class; we are male and female; we are from different races, religions, and ethnic backgrounds; and we work together, struggle together, and learn from each other.

The Origin of CAP

Our history began in Columbus, Ohio, in 1978, in an organization called Women Against Rape (WAR). Women Against Rape ran a 24-hour rape crisis center and provided rape prevention services for adult women. One day the group received a phone call from a parochial elementary school teacher. The teacher explained that a second grader had been raped, and the other children had overheard stories about the rape that were frightening them. Parents and teachers reported fear being expressed by the children and noticed changes in behavior such as bed-wetting and crying for no apparent reason.

When the teacher asked whether Women Against Rape could try to help the children regain their sense of safety, WAR said, "Yes." But they realized that they had no idea how to proceed. They had addressed adults and teens, but they had never spoken to children about abuse and how to prevent it. However, many good programs get started because someone says "yes" in the face of a need, and worries later about how to do it.

At this time, Women Against Rape was in the midst of a major research-demonstration project on rape prevention, funded by the National Institute of Mental Health. Nevertheless, the pioneering women, committed to a class of second graders, took the time to research the facts on child abuse. They spoke with child development specialists, therapists, medical professionals, parents, educators, even professionals from the theatre. They spent hours exploring theory and developing the ancestor of the CAP program we know today. After months of research and development they took the program into the classroom, where they listened to and watched the children's reactions. The children were hungry for information, and glad to meet caring adults who would talk with them honestly about their fears. The women saw in just this one school the power of the program, the need for prevention, and the ability of the children to learn.

At that time the CAP curriculum did not have a program for parents, self-defense, the definition of tattling, crisis intervention, the fourth teacher role-play, or many other components of the program today. Those would come from the children and from presenting the program again and again. It was enough to see that the elements WAR had developed were effective.

Women Against Rape began to apply for grants to offer the program to children in other schools.

After a frustrating year of rejection letters, the Columbus Foundation and the Ms Foundation of New York each responded with a $10,000 grant for pilot workshops in eight schools. Thus, CAP was founded. The curriculum developed and changed as children taught us what to say and how to say it. For the first time, we had money to survive for a year, access into eight schools that were impressed by our success in the parochial school, and our first success stories. In fact, the first success story we ever heard was included in an article we wrote for Ms magazine, published in the April 1984 issue.

> Twelve-year-old Tanya and her eight-year-old brother Marcus were walking home from school together. Two adolescent boys attacked them and tried to drag Tanya off the sidewalk and into a yard. Without hesitation both kids started shouting a deep, guttural self-defense yell while Tanya kicked and fought to get loose. The young attackers ran away.
>
> Tanya and Marcus escaped harm because they had participated in a Child Assault Prevention (CAP) workshop in Columbus, Ohio, the summer before. Though shaken by the attempted assault, they had learned real skills that changed the outcome of a dangerous situation just as clearly as teaching children how to cross streets prevents many pedestrian accidents.

Tanya and Marcus were the first children we heard about who had actually used the information we taught to prevent assault. They were not the last. Success stories became commonplace and proved that CAP worked long before formal research into its effectiveness was conducted.

Throughout 1980 and 1981 we continued to conduct classroom workshops and parent and teacher in-service training in and around our city. Word of mouth from principal to principal and teacher to teacher ensured that requests for services were always greater than our funding allowed. This continues to be a reality for many CAP Projects today.

Nationwide CAP Development

In 1980 Sandra Butler (author of *Conspiracy of Silence*) came to Columbus as keynote speaker at a conference on sexual abuse. Sandy's book was the first to look at incest and other types of child sexual assault from a true victim-centered and respectful perspective. The copies in our office were ragged and torn from repeated use. At that same conference we were presenting a workshop, and Sandy came and sat in the front row. She immediately became a believer in our empowerment approach to prevention, and as she traveled around the country, she often talked about the CAP Project in Columbus. Letters from communities all over the United States began to pour in. People in rural and urban areas all around the country wanted to know if we would teach them how to set up a CAP Project in their community.

Our first trip was to California in 1981. The Bay Area had experienced a number of publicized assaults against children, and advocates were looking for a prevention program that empowered and respected children. Rural Marysville, Ohio, was next; a group of mothers were concerned about child abuse and wanted to help children and their community at large.

In 1983, as a result of increasing requests for trainings nationwide, funds were sought to produce a training manual that would help communities create a CAP Project. *Strategies for Free Children* was published by CAP in 1983. More than 12,000 copies have been sold in all 50 states and in many other nations.

In September 1984 "CBS Morning News" featured CAP and child abuse prevention. Suddenly the post office was delivering our mail in huge postal sacks, mail which we took months to answer. This might seem like wonderful news, and it was. But we didn't have funding for a national program. We were barely meeting our bills every month; it took some real ingenuity and sacrifices to pay the postage as we went — reluctantly — national.

Since 1984 we've ventured beyond the elementary model. The CAP Training Center of California wrote the first preschool model, which we revised and adopted for national use, and TeenCAP was created in 1984. There are also models for children with hearing impairments, multiple disabilities, and mental retardation.

In 1985 we created the National Assault Prevention Center, separating from Women Against Rape. We were clearly stretching their purpose beyond local rape prevention efforts, so it was agreed that we would create an organization that fit our growing body of work.

NAPC's mission is to create a safer world for everyone. We develop, pilot, evaluate, and disseminate programs and information that empower people to increase their own safety and the safety of others.

Although CAP is the largest and most well-known division of NAPC, we also have an adult division, the Assault Prevention Training (APT)

Project, which works to prevent the abuse of older people and adults with disabilities. As with CAP, requests for services exceed the funding base. Adults with disabilities and older people are also increasingly vulnerable to abuse. We believe that everyone has the right to live free from abuse; as this becomes a more widely shared belief and priority, funding is sure to increase.

International CAP Development

In July 1985 we traveled to the U.N. Decade for Women Conference in Nairobi, Kenya, and presented CAP to a standing-room-only audience of African, Asian, and European women. This experience gave us our first personal glimpse at child violence in nations beyond North America. Women at that historic workshop overwhelmingly acknowledged child abuse as a major social problem in their own nations and were excited about the hope of prevention.

We also began doing research into the causes and consequences of violence and methods for effective prevention. Although others had evaluated our programs, we had not; and so we began to confirm scientifically our successes and analyze our weaknesses. This process allowed us to revise our programs as we learned how to be more effective.

In 1986 we visited Holland, West Germany, and Ireland, and our first European projects were born. Costa Rica requested a CAP training in 1988, as did the Grand Bahama Islands. CAP was being conducted in diverse communities with great success. We felt both affirmed and overwhelmed by requests, which continued to increase.

The Future of CAP

Today we estimate that more than one million elementary children have attended at least one CAP workshop at their school. The network of projects grows annually. Massachusetts, New Jersey, Ohio, California, and Rhode Island have statewide networks, and Quebec has a French-speaking network of projects. (See Chapter 10, "Working Together: NAPC and You.")

Our board and staff have contributed their very best, always with the optimism that prevention brings to us personally and to our communities. Communities with CAP Projects are sustained by the hope and energies of grass roots efforts.

NAPC is spending a lot of time considering the future. What should NAPC be doing in the year 2000? What will communities be coping with? What will they need? What issues will we face in the next decade, and what solutions will NAPC offer? What will CAP Projects be working on in the year 2000? How will their role change as the prevention of child abuse becomes a greater priority? How can we guarantee access to prevention information for all children? How will we fund our services if resources for human services continue to shrink?

As we contemplate these issues we will be sharing our thoughts with you and inviting your contributions. We will create our future together. That's the way empowerment works.

3
From Victimization to Empowerment

Introduction

Philosophy means the "theory or logical analysis of the principles underlying conduct, thought, and the nature of the universe."[1] Each of us has philosophies that determine our conduct or thoughts in different situations.

For instance, many people recycle glass, aluminum, and paper because their analysis of the earth's needs requires them to take active steps to protect it: our philosophy has changed our conduct. You may choose not to drink and drive because you have determined this conduct to be unsafe for you and others. You may wear a seat belt when you drive. You may eat less red meat and more fish, and exercise regularly. You may read to your children and limit their television viewing. You may volunteer your time and donate to causes of your choice. These choices are tied to your philosophy about "the nature of the universe."

Empowerment

Child Assault Prevention has an underlying philosophy as well. This philosophy arises directly from the feminist anti-violence movement, which analyzed rape, battering, and other forms of violence against women and developed principles to combat them. CAP is based on an *empowerment* philosophy — the belief that all people have the right to information, skills, and strategies with which they gain control of their lives.

This CAP philosophy underlies the activities of each CAP Project around the world. It is the fundamental principle upon which we act. Your understanding and agreement with this philosophy is critical to your ability to help children and to prevent violence. It is important for you to analyze this philosophy carefully and thoroughly to determine whether you agree. If you do find this a theory in which you can believe, this work was meant for you.

Multiculturalism

The empowerment theory behind the CAP Project requires us to interrupt racism, sexism, ageism, ableism, and homophobia when we confront them because we see how these practices affect safety for each of us. However, it is not enough simply to respect diversity; we must also provide safety for its expression. Therefore, another foundation of CAP philosophy is cultural competence — the need for our programs to work equally well with African, Asian, Native American, Hispanic, and European American children, children with and without disabilities, or immigrant and native-born children.

This means that the leadership of our programs must accommodate culturally diverse staff to evaluate and revise programs to meet the specific needs of all the children in the community. It means that deaf children and children with mental retardation receive programs that are based on their own unique learning styles.

These requirements force us to look at our own learned racism and ableism. Since we define our programs as serving all children, then we will evaluate them according to how they serve both the minority and the majority. If we live in a community where only 1 percent of the people are Cambodian, for instance, then we will measure our success not only by how we serve the 99 percent but also the 1 percent. In addition, multiculturalism benefits not just the 1 percent, but also the 99 percent, who gain a wider lens on the world. For all children, diversity means more role models, more information, and less bigotry. This brings a safer world closer to us all.

Throughout this manual we discuss the need to practice our philosophy, to have it guide the decisions we make every day. Our philosophy keeps our goals ever clear and encourages us to the difficult achievements we must realize if all children are to be truly safe, strong, and free.

> I used one of the Safe Strong and free rules Today. this boy he said are you in kindergarten or are you a baby. I said, Im a human being, arnt I? He said yes, you're a human being. I said, I have rights don't I? He said, Yes. He said, I beter not mess with you again.
> I love you, CAP.
>
> Love Becky R.
Kindergarten
Human Being

Myths About Rape

Prior to 1970, there was a great silence about violence against women. Because of this silence, myths about rape prevailed. Many people believed that rape happened rarely, that it was primarily young women who were victims, that women who were raped "provoked" men by acting or dressing inappropriately, that rape was a function of lust, and that "oversexed" men (primarily African American men) or "crazy" men were usually the perpetrators. Women Against Rape and other feminist anti-violence groups across the country found that these common beliefs about rape were untrue.

It is estimated that one in every four American women will be raped sometime in her adult lifetime. Young women are not the only victims of rape; even babies and old women are commonly victimized. Blaming the victim rather than the perpetrator for the crime suggests that if only women would just "act right," most rapes could be eliminated. But most women are raped in or around their own homes by men whom they know. Women's reality of rape clearly illustrates the falsity of the myths. In fact, women and girls are raped by their bosses, neighbors, dates, friends, acquaintances, co-workers, husbands, and fathers, in their homes, at work, in cars, bars, dormitories, and cradles.

The mythic understanding of rape also includes a mythic understanding of the function of rape. Although many people claim to believe that men rape because they lust for a teasing woman, in fact the purpose of rape is not sexual. The purpose of rape is to *degrade, control,* and *overpower* another human being in order to feel powerful, to be in control. The penis becomes a weapon of violence. As Donna Keuck, a former Women Against Rape employee, used to say, "If I hit you over the head with a rolling pin, you wouldn't call it cooking!" When genitals are used as weapons, it is violence, not sex.

Racism complicates the problem of rape. In the United States, black men have historically been scapegoated for the crime of rape. Most white women grow up learning to be fearful of black men. Yet studies on rape suggest that white women have more to fear from their white friends, dates, and husbands than they do from African American men. In fact cross-racial rapes are relatively rare occurrences, despite the widely held belief to the contrary. When cross-racial rapes do take place, women of color are more often the targets of white men. Ableism, the belief that people without disabilities are superior to those with disabilities, has also been used to scapegoat men with mental retardation and men with a history of mental illness for sex crimes.

The Evolution of CAP and Empowerment Theory

During the mid-seventies, Women Against Rape (WAR), a nonprofit organization in Columbus, Ohio, had been working on a federal grant from the National Institute of Mental Health to develop rape prevention programs for women in Coumbus. This grant enabled WAR to begin a project called Community Action Strategies to Stop Rape (CASSR), which was funded over a four-year period and contributed much to the body of knowledge about the rape of adult women and its prevention. The women of Women Against Rape developed a theory of "reduction of vulnerability," which examined the reality of women's experiences of rape and how rape could be eliminated.[2] The facts about rape explode the myths. Women Against Rape launched a major public education campaign in their community so that real progress toward the elimination of rape could be made.

In 1978, teachers at a local elementary school requested assistance from WAR for the students at the school following the rape of a second-grade child. Some of the women employed by CASSR and the rape crisis center turned their attention to the request from the elementary school. Did the theory of vulnerability, which explained the rape of adult women, explain the rape of the second grader, or were children vulnerable for different reasons?

Ultimately the women of CASSR determined that women and children shared vulnerability for the same reasons and that second-class citizenship was the reality behind this vulnerability. It was easy to argue that adult women were worthy of equality, but it was certainly less easy to make that argument for children. What would a children's rights movement look like? What would it mean to the relationship between adults and children — between parents and offspring, between students and teachers?

Rape Prevention Strategies

Traditional Theories

CASSR began by looking at traditional rape prevention strategies to determine whether they prevented rape as it actually happens, rather than as the myths suggest. They found that traditional rape prevention strategies seek to control behavior — either the behavior of rapists or the behavior of all women. These strategies prescribe (1) control of rapist through prosecution, and (2) control of women and girls by limiting their mobility and activities (avoidance).

Prosecuting rapists in order to treat them and prevent them from harming others is a fine goal. But is prosecution a form of primary prevention? CASSR concluded that it is not. Prosecution, by definition, requires a victim or victims. Since we cannot identify rapists without a crime having taken place, prosecution accepts that some women must be raped in order to prevent other rapes.

Furthermore, prosecution rates for rape are unusually low. Few rapists are convicted since most rapes are never reported; rapists are seldom caught, and it is difficult to obtain enough evidence for a conviction. Relying on prosecution for "prevention" of rape means that rape will never be eliminated or even seriously curtailed.

Advocating avoidance strategies, the other traditional form of prevention, suggests that women can control rape by controlling their own behavior. From an early age, girls are taught never to go out alone, never to walk after dark, never to talk to strangers; women are told never to cross dark parking lots, never to open their doors to strangers, and to invest in lights and locks to deter rapists. These avoidance techniques are based on myths about how rape happens. Locks do not prevent friends whom you invite into your home from raping. Looking into the back seat of your car before you get in will not stop your date from raping you. Never hitchhiking does not protect a woman from her husband or boss. Indeed, since most women are raped by men whom they know, avoidance techniques are poor strategies against most rapes.

The women of CASSR could not in good conscience recommend these methods for prevention. Once they understood how and why rape happens, they sought to develop strategies to deal with the reality of rape.

They began by understanding that all women are vulnerable to rape. Religion, race, and socioeconomic status do not protect a woman; all women are targeted because of their gender. The fact that one woman in four will be raped in her lifetime shows that women as a class of people are vulnerable to rape. All women, therefore, need rape prevention strategies that work and are based on the reality of how rape happens.

Feminist Theory and Empowerment

When CAP started in 1978 we analyzed the similarities between the rape of women and the sexual abuse of children. As with rape, there were myths about how children are assaulted. As with rape, the only strategies called for the prosecution of child molesters and required children to avoid dangerous adults. As with women, all children are vulnerable to abuse. Pioneering author Sandra Butler points out that child sexual assault is "relentlessly democratic." In other words, children, regardless of race, religion, sex, or socioeconomic status, are vulnerable to assault. They are targeted because of their status as children, as second-class citizens. Therefore, all children have a need for abuse prevention strategies.

CASSR's theory of vulnerability for women applies equally to children's vulnerability. If we want to reduce vulnerability we must first understand why children are vulnerable.

- Children are vulnerable because they lack information about child abuse and how to prevent it.
- Children are vulnerable because they are powerless and dependent.
- Children are vulnerable because they are isolated from sources of support and assistance.

We can reduce children's vulnerability to abuse by:

- Providing children and their adult community with information that empowers them to identify and prevent abuse;
- Reducing children's powerlessness and dependency;
- Increasing children's sources of support and assistance.

Child Assault Prevention Strategies

Information

Ignorance increases vulnerability in every dangerous or potentially dangerous situation. None of us can protect ourself if we don't know what danger we're facing.

Most of us often feel vulnerable. When we try something we've never done before we feel insecure. We compensate for that vulnerability by getting information. For instance, if you are worried about your health, the best way to deal with that worry is to obtain information. Consulting a doctor and learning about the options for your care will enable you to make choices more confidently. Information lessens our feelings of vulnerability.

When it comes to lessening children's vulnerability, we use the same technique. We teach young children how to cross busy streets, how to get out of burning buildings, and what to do in case of tornadoes. We recognize that without information they would be unable to help themselves; by providing information we increase their safety.

The same is true when it comes to preventing abuse. Information given to children in age- and developmentally appropriate lessons can decrease their vulnerability to abuse. Adult survivors of child abuse often say, "If only someone had told me that what was happening to me was wrong, I could have gotten some help and stopped it!"

Of course, if we truly want to lessen children's vulnerability we must do more than just educate children. This is why every CAP model, whether for preschool, elementary, teen, or special needs children, includes parent and teacher/staff in-service programming. Adults who understand abuse and its prevention must be available to assist children.

CAP provides not only workshops to children, teachers, and parents, but also broad-based community education. This means that neighbors, doctors, rabbis, and ministers — indeed, the entire community — are more equipped to help children.

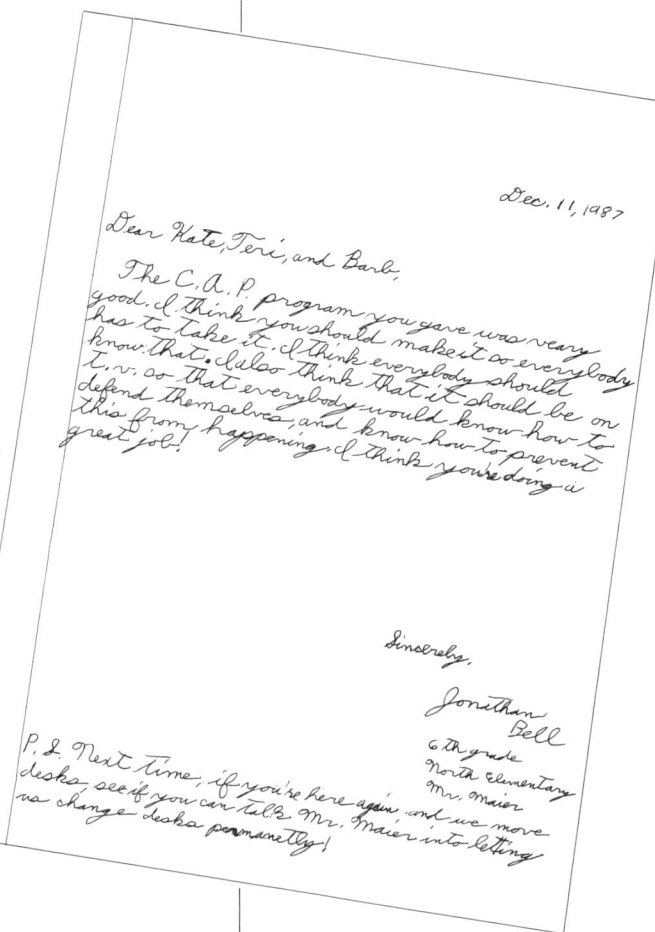

> Mrs. Morgan called our office one day after hearing a radio interview with the CAP coordinator. The interviewer asked a series of questions about reporting child abuse to the authorities. The CAP coordinator acknowledged that reporting child abuse does not always result in helping a child, but it usually does; if no report is made, there is no chance for the child to get assistance.
>
> Mrs. Morgan described her reasons for suspecting abuse of a child. She had, on a number of occasions, heard loud, angry yelling coming from the house next door. She had also observed bruises on one of the children, who appeared withdrawn and fearful. Just one week before the radio show, Mrs. Morgan had observed the child being chased across the backyard by her mother. Although she couldn't observe what happened after the child ran into the house, she did hear the child screaming. Mrs. Morgan told us that she was constantly worried about this child, but didn't know how to help. The radio program not only gave her the number to call for protective services, but also

encouraged her to think about her ethical and moral responsibilities to help a child. Because of the radio program Mrs. Morgan became aware that she didn't need proof to report child abuse; if she had good reason to suspect abuse she could and should report it.

If we are to reduce children's vulnerability to abuse, we must inform children and adults about dangerous situations and their resources to protect themselves and others.

STRATEGY: To make child abuse a public issue

OBJECTIVES:

- To provide information to children about how to identify and prevent abuse
- To provide information to parents, teachers, other professionals, and the community at large about the recognition, intervention, reporting, and prevention of child abuse

Empowerment

All vulnerable groups of people are seen as second-class citizens. American Indians, people with physical, sensory, and cognitive disabilities, gay and lesbian people, older people, and children are all victimized in huge numbers, and they also suffer from discrimination based on a theory that labels them as "less than" the dominant population.

CAP theory requires all of us to examine underlying racism, sexism, and all forms of prejudice and bias. Our society will never be safe as long as some of us are seen as less deserving of full emancipation than others. CAP theory requires us to change our conduct. When we work to prevent victimization, we are working for full citizenship for every human being.

As you can see, second-class citizenship increases vulnerability to abuse. This is particularly true for children because their vulnerability is a function of their age and development. This does not mean that we cannot increase their power and decrease their dependency, but it does mean that there are more limitations for power and independence than there are for adults. If we dissect the ways in which we *needlessly* foster children's helplessness, then we can empower children to use all their capabilities in preventing abuse.

Empower is a word much in vogue today. Unfortunately, because of its overuse, many of us don't really understand what it means, especially in terms of empowering children. The prefix "em" means "into." "Power" means "to be capable of effecting change." Simply put, empowerment means to instill or increase capability in another. That's what CAP workshops are based on: enhancing children's capabilities to resist abuse. Every CAP strategy is evaluated to determine whether it really empowers. In other words, does it make children more confident, more knowledgeable, more capable of handling potential danger?

When abuse is discussed our first impulse is often to protect children by disempowering them. Some of the abuse prevention workshops that are provided to children and parents lack a philosophy that is based on empowerment. Workshop leaders focus on dangerous situations that involve assaults by strangers. Children hear frightening stories about what strangers may do: trick them, abduct them, hurt them, or poison them. The focus of the workshop is not on the strategies children can use, but on the dangers they may encounter. All of us can be easily frightened by horror stories if we lack skills and strategies to cope. An empowerment philosophy requires us to strengthen children, not frighten them. Consequently, children leave CAP workshops feeling good about themselves and the things they have learned. (We will discuss this point further.)

Children are often judged as "good" or "bad" by how willing they are to comply with adult authority. Starting when they are very young, we reward or punish them for their obedience. "Do whatever your teacher tells you." "Listen to what your baby-sitter tells you." "Be good and do whatever your grandparents tell you." These are common rules for children, and although they may make life easier for adults, they also increase children's vulnerability. When a manipulative, abusive adult comes into contact with a child who perceives that he or she must obey adult commands without question, the results can be devastating.

CAP theory does not educate children to ignore or disrespect adults. We do, however, advocate teaching children that they can set limits for their own safety with any person, including an adult close to them. This lesson, along with the understanding that their bodies are precious and that they have a right to protect themselves, is an important one.

> Gena's mother and father came to a CAP parent program at her school when she was in first grade. Gena's parents knew that child abuse was a bigger problem than most people realize, and they wanted information about how to protect their daughter. Several years later, Gena's mother called the office to thank us. She reported that the CAP parent program gave them ways to talk to Gena about resisting abuse. Over the years since the parent program, Gena's parents had regularly reviewed with Gena her right to stop anybody who might try to hurt her and to ask her parents for help.
>
> Unfortunately, Gena had occasion to use the prevention information she had learned in the CAP workshop and from her parents when her father's college roommate visited the family. Gena's mother woke up in the middle of the night to Gena's screams. She rushed into Gena's bedroom to find the visitor, half-dressed. Gena rushed to her mother and said, "He woke me up and told me to be quiet. He didn't have any pajama bottoms on, and he scared me. I decided not to be quiet. I decided to yell!" Gena's parents were proud and grateful that Gena had been able to handle a potentially dangerous situation. Gena's mother said, "She knew she had a right to stop his behavior and to get some help. She was scared and confused, but she wasn't abused."

It may seem difficult to understand how we can decrease children's dependence on adults when we consider that children *must* depend on adults for help. CAP advocates that we lessen children's helplessness rather than foster it. This is important because children are not always with adults. In fact, independent activities are part of growing up. Riding a bike to a friend's house, walking home from school, staying alone for a few hours while adults enjoy a movie, or playing with friends on the playground are all activities that children do with other children, or alone, once they are old enough. Teaching children effective prevention skills can help children resist abuse when adult intervention is not possible.

In June 1981, an eight-year-old girl in our community was raped and murdered on her way home from school. This tragedy mobilized the community to act. Among other measures, parents began to carpool their children to and from school — an appropriate short-term remedy while the crime was investigated. Six months after the murder, though, many parents were still carpooling; it would be natural for children to infer that they were incapable of handling a dangerous situation.

All too often, adults intervene too much. An argument between siblings or friends often results in adult intervention to solve the problem. Kay Noble, principal of Douglas Elementary School in Columbus, recognizes that children need to learn how to be more independent — not just to resist abuse, but in order to develop healthy skills for adulthood. When children in her school fight, Noble requires them to talk it out. Noble reports that the children quickly learn that they can solve many of their own problems without adult help. This is empowerment at its best; such an experience of belief in oneself can be used in a potentially dangerous situation when adult help is unavailable.

A CAP children's workshop introduces abuse prevention by talking about children's rights to be "safe, strong, and free." A dangerous situation exists when a child is unable to protect these rights.

A right is an entitlement; it is not a privilege or a benefit, nor is it something that must be earned. Every child has the absolute right to grow up free from abuse. When we know our rights, we can act upon them. The concept of rights is an important one and clearly fits the issue of abuse prevention. CAP philosophy is based on a belief that everyone has the right to safety. For the purposes of the children's workshop, we define the specific rights that are taken away when safety is threatened. Teaching children that they have the absolute right to safety empowers them to protect themselves.

STRATEGY: To increase children's power and lessen their dependence

OBJECTIVES:

- To help children realize their right not to be abused
- To help children recognize actions that threaten or violate that right
- To give children information, skills, and strategies that they can use to protect their rights.

Support

Isolation is a primary cause of vulnerability. Victims of abuse often report that they had no one to turn to for assistance. In order to reduce children's vulnerability, we have to decrease their isolation by increasing their sources of support and assistance.

Adults who abuse children often increase their isolation by convincing the children they have nowhere to turn. In families where incestuous assault occurs, young people are systematically isolated from friends and outside adults.

Christine disclosed sexual and physical abuse by her father only after he was jailed for beating her mother. Christine could not remember a time when her father wasn't hurting her. She and her mother were forbidden to talk with one another unless Christine's father was present: if he caught them talking to one another, both the mother and Christine were physically beaten. Several times the beatings were so severe that Christine had to stay home from school because of bruises on her face and arms. Christine was forbidden to have friends; even in her teens, she had never gone to a friend's house to play or stayed after school for an extracurricular activity. In fact, Christine's father walked her to and from the bus stop daily, even when she was in high school. Christine and her mother were prisoners, forbidden to have relationships with anyone but him. Only her father's incarceration broke the cycle of this abuse. When he was released Christine and her mother left the state.

Children who suffer from abuse are often isolated in lesser but just as effective ways as Christine. The sexual offender may tell children that their parents don't love them and that only the offender loves them, "proving" it to the children with attention and presents. Many offenders tell children to keep the abuse a secret, enforcing that secrecy by telling the child that no one will believe him or her. Threats that the parent will go to jail if the child discloses, or that the child will be sent to a foster home, or that the parents will divorce often keep the child isolated. In fact, the offender who abuses a child over time, rather than just once, *must* isolate the child; if the child had sources of support, he or she might tell. Isolation increases vulnerability, and no one knows it better than the sexual offender.

Children are also isolated from each other. Many times, in incestuous assault, more than one sibling is abused. Unfortunately, because the children are isolated from one another, they can't see that together they might be powerful enough to get some help. Theresa Tollini's movie *Breaking Silence* features a family in which two of three daughters were sexually abused by their father. The mother did not know of the abuse until the daughters were adults. On film they describe how the assaults pitted them against one another; when dad was molesting one daughter, the other one felt relief. CAP workshops, which lessen isolation between adults and children and between children, teach children ways to help each other and gain help from parents or other adults.

Children rarely see each other as powerful sources of support and assistance. Since they see themselves as powerless, they also see other children as powerless. CAP can change this perception.

> In one classroom of third graders, more than half of the class was molested by the teacher. It never occurred to the children to go together to report the abuse. They saw themselves as utterly alone, without anyone to vouch for them or support them in their allegation. The teacher merely told each student he molested, "If you tell anyone, I'll say you are lying." It was an effective means to keep them silent, powerless, and isolated from one another.

Children must have access to adults who can help them overcome their fear of disclosure and who will make disclosure a positive experience. We incorporate this need into the curriculum's strategy and objectives.

STRATEGY: To reduce children's isolation

OBJECTIVES:

- To increase support for children among their peers
- To increase adult support for children
- To increase awareness among children and adults of existing community resources that can assist them in intervention, prevention, and treatment

These components of vulnerability are addressed in the children's classroom workshops and the parent and teacher/staff in-service programs. The foundation of effective abuse prevention programs is a philosophy that respects children's right to grow up free from abuse and empowers them to act in their own behalf.

> To whom it may consern,
>
> I think the C.A.P. program is just great it can help kids from getting RAPED, KILLED, and KIDKNAPED. I helped a friend her mothers Boyfriend would Babysit her and her little Brother Because she worked at night so the man would MALESTER her so this went on for about 2 or 2½ weeks fianilly she told me and her cosin so I told my teacher about it. I hope that the C.A.P. program can continue to go on to different schools to help other children. its helped me alot in things I didn't know about.
>
> sinserly,
> Jamie B.
> 5th grade

References

1. Webster's New World Dictionary.
2. Women Against Rape, Community Action Strategies to Stop Rape, *Freeing Our Lives: A Feminist Analysis of Rape Prevention* (Columbus, Ohio: Women Against Rape, 1978).

4
Child Abuse: An Overview

Introduction

In contemplating child abuse we have been forced to contemplate children's status in general. The facts are frightening. They cause us to conclude that children, as a class of people, are highly vulnerable to many atrocities, not just to "abuse" as we currently define it. In examining children's lives beyond the formal boundaries of abuse, we find facts that are shocking in a country as wealthy and as technologically advanced as the U.S. In 1990 children were the poorest group in the U.S. Malnutrition affects almost 500,000 American children.[1] Each day more than 100 American babies die before their first birthday.[2] Every night 100,000 children go to sleep homeless.[3] Among black children, nearly half are poor.[4]

These conditions victimize children and hamper their healthy development. It is for this reason that we consider ourselves a part of the children's rights movement. We care about children and advocate their right to grow up safe, strong, and free, not just from assault but from abuse of every kind.

Many people wonder how child abuse, which today we know claims many victims, remained invisible for so long. It is a cruel fact that in American society, as in most societies around the world, children are sexually assaulted and tortured, neglected and maimed, ignored and murdered. It is only in relatively recent history, with the coming of the civil rights, women's rights, and child protection movements, that we as a society have tried to confront rather than ignore our interpersonal sins against one another. This is surely progress, but it remains distressing that we have come so late to thinking about the welfare of vulnerable peoples, especially our children.

Secrecy

> I didn't tell, I couldn't tell. He said he would just call me a liar, and I knew he would. I knew he would, and I knew who they'd believe. Do you understand? He was successful! He was the associate pastor of the church! He visited the shut-ins, for God's sake! Now who was going to believe me?
>
> Adult survivor

Secrecy is one of the major reasons that child abuse has stayed invisible, and we are still in the process of breaking that secrecy. Although it is true that millions of people have been made aware of the extent and trauma of child abuse because of our work in the last decade, it is also true that millions more need our attention. Breaking the silence is our first task, and each and every CAP Project will devote many hours and resources to this continuing need. We simply cannot solve problems that we are not aware of; awareness is a cornerstone of prevention efforts. It requires ongoing effort.

Recognizing Diversity

Human beings are a diverse group, and so our approaches to eliminating child abuse must be diverse as well. There are great differences between rural, urban, and suburban areas in their awareness and understanding of child abuse and its prevention. Men and women often understand assault differently, as do boys and girls. Literacy plays a role, since access to information is limited without the ability to read. People from different religions, races, and income groups all see assault differently, as do people with physical, mental, or sensory handicaps. If we are to prevent abuse then we must educate everyone, and since everyone is different, the approaches that we employ will vary.

What we all have in common is the need for accurate information about how child abuse happens, to whom it happens, why it happens, and how to intervene to help children escape from their individual silences. This chapter incorporates up-to-date information about what we know so far. CAP Project staff must undertake a constant search for new information, since the body of knowledge in this field is growing rapidly.

Children's Status

Historically children have not fared well in many cultures. From earliest recorded history people have treated children — indeed, defined them — as property, undeserving of any inherent rights. Given this history it is not hard to understand why so many children in the U.S. and around the world are victims of abuse. It is our task to move children further along the continuum from the hostility and apathy with which adults have treated them toward the true empowerment that each human being, regardless of age, intellect, race, sexual preference, gender, or ethnic origin, should enjoy as an inalienable right.

We have so far to go. In the U.S alone, more than two million children are victimized every year.[5] They are victimized by family, friends, strangers, caretakers, and even each other. Neglect, physical abuse, emotional maltreatment, and sexual abuse are common realities in many children's lives.

Defining Child Abuse

We begin with definitions of abuse, since this is where the confusion begins. There are many different definitions of child abuse, which have been created by groups and individuals to serve specific purposes. For instance, legal definitions in criminal statutes tend to be very specific regarding actual illegal acts against a child. Child protective caseworkers also use specific definitions to decide whether intervention into a family is necessary. For instance, if a child has been beaten, the case worker wants to know what was used in the beating: A belt buckle is different from a belt, an open hand from a fist. CAP Projects tend to find inclusive definitions most helpful, since our primary mission is prevention and identification, rather than prosecution and intervention. Definitions that encompass a wide range of behaviors that threaten or hurt a child are the ones we find most beneficial when providing teacher, parent, and community education.

Child abuse is defined in the Federal Child Abuse Prevention and Treatment Act as the "physical or mental injury, sexual abuse, negligent treatment or maltreatment of a child under the age of 18 by a person who is responsible for the child's welfare under circumstances which indicate that the child's health or welfare is harmed or threatened."[6] For our purposes in our work with CAP, we define child abuse as "acting or failing to act in a way that harms a child physically, sexually, and/or emotionally." In much of the literature, child abuse is then subdivided into four distinct types, which we also use to help illustrate exactly what happens to children when they are victimized. These four types of abuse are *physical abuse, sexual abuse, neglect,* and *emotional maltreatment.*

Physical Abuse

> She beat me for no reason at all with whatever she found lying nearby. One time she jammed a fork into my stomach and I had to go to the hospital. The whole way over in the car she told me over and over again to tell the doctor that I fell on the fork. That's what I told him, and that's what he believed.
>
> Adolescent victim

Any act that results in a nonaccidental injury to a child is *physical child abuse*. It often happens when a parent or other caretaker is stressed to the point of lashing out against a child. It also happens because parents and other caretakers believe that children need harsh punishments to learn obedience. Physical punishment can involve slapping, biting, beating, burning, shaking, throwing, punching, or kicking a child — any action, in fact, that harms the child's body. Approximately 35 percent of all abuse and neglect cases involve physical abuse; of those, 85 percent involve mild to moderate abuse. Fifteen percent of cases are severe or extreme.[7]

In 1962 Dr. C. Henry Kempe published an article in the *Journal of the American Medical Association* describing battered child syndrome, or BCS.[8] BCS is a condition resulting in injury to a child's nervous or skeletal system or skin. Children who are victims of BCS usually have multiple injuries at various stages of healing, and X-rays may reveal evidence of repeated fractures.[9] Dr. Kempe's work and subsequent article are now seen as important landmarks in our history of recognizing child abuse. The article received widespread publicity, and the general public and lawmakers were outraged that innocent children could be intentionally injured. As a result all 50 states have passed mandatory reporting laws requiring doctors and other health professionals to report suspected abuse.

According to former Surgeon General C. Everett Koop, homicide is the fifth leading cause of fatalities for children under the age of 18 in the U.S. Approximately 13,000 children under the age of one year are killed annually. Three-quarters of these children are victimized by their own parents.[10] According to the National Center on Child Abuse Research, in 1986, '87, '88, and '89 a minimum of three children per day were fatally injured by child abuse.[11] Since 1985 the number of reported child abuse fatalities has increased by more than 38 percent.[12]

Nonaccidental injuries to children that do not result in their death often cause handicapping conditions. Shaking an infant can result in cranial and ocular bleeding that causes brain damage and consequent mental retardation in infants.[13]

Parents who physically abuse their children often hesitate to seek medical help, have a distorted belief in the need to use physical force, and set unrealistic expectations for the age and maturity of the child. Some parents abuse their children because they were abused and don't know how to parent differently. Men are 1.2 times more likely than women to physically abuse a child with both minor and severe actions.[14]

Sexual Abuse

> He was my Boy Scout troop leader, and I really liked him. But looking back now, I think he took advantage of me because my dad was dead and I wanted a man to do stuff with me. I think he knew that I wouldn't leave scouting. Even though he was abusing me, scouting was the best thing in my life. He knew that. He counted on it.
>
> Adult survivor

Sexual abuse includes many behaviors directed at a child: molestation; forced oral, anal, or vaginal penetration; forced participation in pornography; forced prostitution; voyeurism, wherein a child is forced to dress or bathe without privacy; and exhibitionism, wherein a child is forced to look at a naked person or at another person's genitals. Sexually abusive language directed at a child, or behaviors that sexualize the relationship, such as sexual slaps on the behind or sexual kissing on the lips, are also forms of sexual abuse.

Offenders can be family members, adults known to the child, strangers, and even other children. Although violence is used in some cases of child sexual abuse, coercion and routine adult authority are more typical.

Sexual abuse of children is all too common in the United States, and it is not a new phenomenon. In a study conducted in 1953, nearly 25 percent of 4000 women interviewed said that as a child they had had sex with an adult man or had been approached by a man seeking sex.[15]

In 1979 Diana Russell interviewed 930 women and found that 38 percent had been sexually abused by an adult before the age of 18.[16] In a national poll conducted by the *Los Angeles Times* in July 1985, 2627 men and women were interviewed. Twenty-two percent said they had been sexually victimized as children. One-third had never told anyone, and only 3 percent of the incidents were reported to the police. One in three questioned was over the age of 45, and one in ten was over 65 years of age, indicating, again, that child sexual abuse is not a new phenomenon.[17] Gail Wyant of UCLA also conducted a random sample of 248 adult women in Los Angeles County. Half of the participants were white and half were African American; 59 percent reported at least one unwanted sexual experience with an adult when they were children.[18]

It is clear from the studies in the field that most children do not report abuse to anyone. Children fear they will not be believed and so they are reluctant to talk about sexual abuse. They are also easily manipulated into secrecy by the offender. For this reason, every CAP model, preschool through teen, teaches children their right to seek adult help when they feel threatened.

Children are sexually abused regardless of their sex, age, ethnicity, area of residence, and family income. However, studies indicate that some children are more at risk than others. For instance, children aged 8–12 are more vulnerable than either younger or older children.[19] The California Department of Developmental Services, Office of Human Rights, estimates that 50–90 percent of people with developmental disabilities will be sexually abused at some time during their lives.[20]

David Finkelhor notes that virtually every study performed to date has found that girls are more at risk for sexual abuse than are boys.[21] It is now estimated that one of every three female children will be sexually victimized before the age of 18.[22] Recent studies suggest that from 3–16 percent of boys will experience sexual abuse during their childhood.[23] Boys are also more likely than girls to be assaulted by a man rather than a woman, by several men, and by men outside the family.[24]

Although it is difficult for any child to report sexual abuse, it may be particularly difficult for boys. Many boys continue to believe that sexual abuse happens only to girls. Boys who have been assaulted feel "feminized" by the experience. They intuitively believe that sexual abuse has "reduced" them to female status: second-class citizenship. Ashamed and feeling that their manhood is at stake, they stay silent in order to conceal their shame and weakness. Compounding the problem are societal attitudes that identify any sexual experience for young men as positive. This results in minimization or even denial of boys' experience as victims.

Children are most often sexually abused by people they know. This includes family members, family friends, and the vast array of adults on whom children rely for education, caretaking, and extracurricular activities. Although parents commonly instruct their children about the danger presented by strangers, these warnings fail to help children cope with assaults by people they know. Research suggests that only 15 percent of child assault cases involve strangers.[25]

Finkelhor found higher rates of father-daughter sexual abuse among fathers who held patriarchal family values and believed in women's submissiveness.[26] Finkelhor also found that stepfathers were significantly more likely to sexually assault their stepdaughters than were natural fathers, and that sexually punitive mothers (that is, mothers who punished their daughters for sexual inquisitiveness and repressed healthy sexual development in girls) were more likely to have daughters who had been sexually abused by their fathers.[27]

Studies suggest that men constitute 95 percent of all perpetrators in sexual abuse cases against girls, and 80 percent in cases against boys.[28]

The reasons for high male perpetrator rates are complex and not completely understood. Male socialization plays a role; boys are more likely to be taught that sex is conquest and that force and aggression are acceptable behavior. Finkelhor hypothesizes that male nurturing and bonding with young children may be an important deterrent. Since men have only recently been encouraged to take responsibility for child rearing, this may be a factor in why men have been more likely to abuse children sexually.

Although adults report widespread sexual abuse when they were children, there is reason to believe that it is still underreported in the studies. Time and trauma have suppressed or erased abuse from the memories of many survivors; others have not labeled even severe and harmful treatment as abusive. Finally, abuse is difficult for many people to reveal even in an anonymous poll. Current studies of children suggest that sexual abuse is even more frequent than originally thought.

Incest

Incest is defined as "sexual intercourse or marriage between close blood relatives."[29] CAP Projects recognize a broader definition referring to any sexual contact against a child by an older member of his or her family. Live-in caretakers who are not related to the child, such as a mother's boyfriend, often develop a parentlike relationship with a child and are vested with parental authority. Such people are often therefore also considered by CAP to be family members.

Incest often involves a slow conditioning process in which the level and type of sexual abuse increases over time.[30] The child is manipulated into compliance and secrecy. Physical violence is rarely used; the child is coerced into escalating sexual abuse by bribes, threats, and mere adult authority.[31] Common threats to a child include: "If you tell, I'll go to jail," "You'll go to a foster home," "Your mother will divorce me," or "No one will believe you."

Knowing the three types of force used against a child can be helpful in understanding sexual abuse of all types, but incest in particular. *Physical force* means that a child is hurt physically or threatened with a weapon or physical harm. *Emotional force* is employed when an adult uses tricks and manipulation or threatens the child with undesirable outcomes so that the child's feelings compel him or her to comply and to maintain secrecy, as in the examples just cited. *Force of authority* happens when an adult uses the status of adulthood, parenthood, or caretaking to force the child into compliance. "I'm your father, and you'll do what I say" is an example of force of authority. Sometimes force of authority does not even need to be spoken; the child knows that privileges will be denied or punishments will follow if he or she fails to comply.

Offenders also manipulate children by providing for their emotional needs. Spending time with children in fun activities and expressing love and appreciation for them draws children to the offender so that their needs for love, attention, and approval can be met.

Child Blame/Mother Blame

The professional literature throughout this century has tended to put the blame for child sexual abuse on the victim or on the mother of the victim, rather than on the perpetrator, particularly in incest cases.[32] Children have been described as "provocative," "appealing," "cooperative," "promiscuous," "charming," and "seductive"; offenders have been labeled "harmless," "passive," and "helpless." Although this is no longer the dominant position in the field, there is still a noticeable hesitancy to hold the offender responsible and a tendency to blame the mother.

It is true that some mothers are aware that incest is being perpetrated but fail to protect the child. But some authors have still suggested that mothers are to blame even when mothers do take steps to protect the child.

Unfortunately, CAP staff across the nation and internationally have found this view prevalent among parents, educators, and professionals. The health and welfare of children is seen as a woman's domain, and if a child is hurt it is seen as a mother's failure. But research reveals that incest is more likely to take place in a home where the husband/father is "king of the castle," and where the mother is powerless either because of his rule, or because of physical illness, mental illness, or hospitalization.

Neglect

Whereas abuse is often defined as the commission of acts that harm a child, *neglect* is defined as the omission of acts that protect a child. Because neglect often results in lack of adequate food, clothing, and shelter for a child, it is often confused with poverty. In neglect, more than any other type of child abuse, the children of the poor represent most of the reported cases.[33] Although poor people may also be negligent with their children, too often poverty, not child neglect, is the cause. Neglect occurs when a parent or caretaker *willfully causes* or *permits* the health of a child to be placed in jeopardy.

In order for children to grow into healthy adults they need not only the necessities of life such as adequate nutrition, clothing appropriate for the climate, and safe shelter, but also appropriate supervision, an education, and medical assistance.

According to Howard Dubowitz, MD, Assistant Professor of Pediatrics at the University of Maryland School of Medicine, neglect has been neglected — we have, in the U.S., "largely ignored neglect in favor of abuse."³⁴ Since neglect is a complicated matter that concerns values, upon which a diverse community does not always agree, more investigation and definition of neglect would benefit us all. Dubowitz raises crucial questions. If a child lives in an unsafe home and the parents are too poor to fix broken appliances or keep gas and electric services connected, are the parents neglectful, or is society? What is the responsibility of the utility companies and the landlord?

As the number of children living in poverty grows each year, it becomes more and more crucial for citizens and elected officials to talk about the implications of poverty. One implication is that poor families are more likely to be accused of deliberate failure to care for their children and have their children taken away.

Emotional Maltreatment

"Sticks and stones may break my bones, but words will never hurt me." Research suggests otherwise: In fact, words can and do hurt. Verbal abuse is one major component of emotional abuse.

Emotional abuse is treatment of a child that assaults his or her emotional development and sense of self-worth. Statistics concerning the incidence of emotional abuse are not yet available. Emotional abuse is something we are just now beginning to understand and take seriously. Paying attention to the emotional self of a child is new behavior. Compounding the problem of obtaining realistic data on incidence is the fact that definitions of emotional abuse vary greatly from state to state. Finally, researchers believe that emotional abuse is vastly underreported. According to the National Committee for the Prevention of Child Abuse, approximately 80,000 cases of serious emotional abuse were reported nationally in 1986.³⁵

Emotional abuse is defined by the National Assault Prevention Center in two categories.³⁶ First is the consistent *presence* of denigrating actions and/or language directed at a child, resulting in harm to the child. These actions can include belittling, criticizing, and/or rejecting the child. The second category involves the consistent *absence* of actions and/or language that indicate pride, love, and acceptance for the child. These actions can include consistent failure to hold a child who needs comfort, to share time with a child, and to tell a child that he or she is important and loved.

In order to deter false identification and reporting of emotional maltreatment cases, it is important to remember that emotional maltreatment is characterized by *consistent* and *repeated* behaviors. Each of us, unfortunately, is at times emotionally abusive to those whom we love. Stress, frustration, anger, and other normal human reactions cause all of us to say and do things that we regret. Every parent lacks the patience a child demands from time to time. The important thing to educate parents about is the fact that consistent emotional maltreatment actually harms the child; it attacks and can arrest the child's emotional development.

Researchers Garbarino, Guttman, and Seeley (1986) have outlined a system for identifying acts that constitute emotional abuse. They have identified five types of emotional maltreatment.³⁷

1. Rejecting: Actively avoiding, belittling, or refusing to acknowledge a child's needs.

2. Terrorizing: Threatening extreme punishments or setting impossible expectations.

3. Ignoring: Being psychologically unavailable or failing to protect a child from threats or maltreatment from others

4. Isolating: Prohibiting a child from developing normal social relationships with others

5. Corrupting: Exposing a child to maladaptive or harmful influences

At this point in our history it is fair to say that only the most severe cases of emotional abuse will be identified as such and will allow investigation by protective services. This means that many children will fall through the cracks of the system that is designed to protect them. It is our belief, however, that over the next decade we will make real headway in our willingness and ability to intervene on behalf of children who are emotionally maltreated.

Ritualized Abuse

Ritualized abuse is a form of emotional, physical, and sexual abuse that involves the systematic use of symbols or group activities. These symbols or activities are usually repeated over time and are used to frighten and intimidate victims into compliance and silence. Ritualistic abuse often involves multiple offenders and multiple victims. It is often so violent and so despicable that it challenges our willingness to see atrocity.

Ritualistic abuse is not a new phenomenon, although only recently have we come to recognize and study it. Ritualized abuse practices recorded by an Egyptian priest as early as 355 AD are similar to accounts that therapists, police, and prevention professionals are currently hearing in the U.S. What *is* new is the number of disclosures.

Recent disclosures by adult and child victims have enabled professionals to develop an ever-growing list of common characteristics. Whether the abuse is perpetrated by family members or those outside the home, the accounts tend to have some common elements.

- Most accounts involve multiple offenders, with a higher representation of female perpetrators than in other forms of child physical and sexual abuse.

- The accounts usually involve multiple young children, often between the ages of two and six.

- Pornography is often used, with victims being forced to look at materials or forced to participate in sexual activity that is photographed or videotaped.

- Many cases involve victims being tied, gagged, chained, or taped and then isolated in dark places.

- Accounts often involve the use of urine, blood, and feces. Children are forced to ingest these substances or have them smeared on their bodies.

- Victims are often drugged.

- Sexual abuse is common in these cases, and it is often sadistic in nature.

- Vaginal and anal penetration with objects is common, as is oral copulation.

- Often child victims are forced to sexually or physically abuse other children.

- Cruelty to animals, including dismemberment, mutilation, and killing, is common, as are threats to harm animals.
- Victims are often told that their parents know of and encourage the abuse.
- Extreme physical abuse is common, as is withholding of food or water and sleep deprivation.
- Perpetrators often disguise themselves as heroes or authority figures.
- Symbols, robes, candles, and other props are used, and children report being taken to cemeteries and churches for mock ceremonies.
- Children describe the killing of adults, children, and infants, and sometimes describe being forced to participate in these killings.

Ritualized abuse cases do not always involve Satan or cults. Ritualized abuse takes place in preschools, daycare settings, summer camps, churches, and within families.

Incidence of Ritualized Abuse

It is difficult to determine how common ritualized abuse of children is. Research is in its preliminary stages, and accounts of ritualized abuse are often so bizarre that a child's disclosure may be viewed as imaginary.

However, some data do exist. In a nationwide study of 270 cases of sexual abuse in daycare settings, for example, at least 36 were identified as having ritualistic elements.[38] Another study by S. J. Kelley (1989) compared reports of children who had been ritualistically abused with those of nonritualistically abused children.[39] She found that ritualistically abused children experienced more types and greater amounts of abuse at the hands of a greater number of abusers, as shown in Table 1.

Table 1
Comparison of ritual and nonritual child abuse

	Ritual	Nonritual
Ingestion of drugs	74%	28%
Use of physical restraint	71%	37%
Consumption of excrement	51%	25%
Sexual activity with other children	94%	43%
Threats of death	85%	56%
Threats of dismemberment	37%	15%
Threats to kill parents	94%	75%

Ritualistic abuse is destructive to young children especially, since many victims are born into a situation in which they are raised to believe in and perform certain roles in the abuse. Thus, young victims literally have no safe place and lack a support system beyond the circle of those involved in the abuse.

Our understanding of ritualistic abuse is only beginning to come into focus. Additional research and identification of ritualized abuse cases will one day help us to understand the scope of the problem.

Munchausen Syndrome by Proxy

A little-known form of child abuse by parents is called *Munchausen Syndrome by proxy*. Parents falsely claim medical problems affect their children, falsify blood or stool samples, or intentionally hurt children in order to have them hospitalized. This results in unnecessary medical tests and treatments for the children. Little is known about this form of child abuse but researchers believe it is largely unidentified and unreported.

Child-on-Child Violence

Unfortunately, adults are not the only ones who victimize children. There is a growing body of research that is beginning to investigate violent children and their assaults against other children.

When we think about children being victimized by other children, we often think of a schoolyard bully who threatens, robs, taunts, or otherwise bothers a younger or smaller child. Adults in general tend to minimize this type of assault, believing that the child bully is merely an inevitable part of childhood and that child victims are not seriously harmed.

But information now coming to light suggests that adults should take child violence against other children very seriously indeed. Physical, sexual, and emotional abuse by children against other children may be more common and more serious than we have previously thought.

The National School Safety Center (NSSC) produced a paper in 1987 that explores the problem of child bullies.[40] The NSSC defines a bully as a child who is "overly aggressive, destructive, and enjoys dominating other children." Bullying includes a vast array of aggressive behaviors: name calling; petty theft; extortion; ethnic, racist, sexist, or anti-gay harassment; sexual abuse; battering; and injuries and death resulting from the use of weapons. Boys are more likely to be bullies than are girls; boys outnumbered girl bullies by four to one.

According to the NSSC, 15 percent of all school-age children are involved in bully problems, and 10 percent are regularly harassed. The NSSC further found that the schoolyard bully has a 25 percent chance of having a criminal record by the age of 30. Forty percent of bullied students in the primary grades reported that teachers tried to stop the bullying "only once in a while." Other evidence indicates that a high percentage of bullies drop out of school or do poorly, and grow up to commit abusive crimes against their spouses and parents.[41]

Of course, bullies may also be the siblings of their victims. In a national study of family violence, Strauss, Gelles, and Steinmetz found that sibling violence happens more often than either parent/child or husband/wife violence. Their survey suggests that 53 percent of children commit a violent act against a sibling at some time during childhood.[42]

Sibling abuse runs the gamut from relatively minor forms to serious and life-threatening abuse. Vernon Wiehe's study of sibling abuse reports:

> The most common forms of physical abuse reported were hitting, slapping, pushing, punching, biting, hair pulling, scratching, and pinching. Respondents reported having been hit by a sibling with objects such as broom handles, rubber hoses, coat hangers, hairbrushes, belts, and sticks, and being threatened and stabbed with broken glass, knives, razor blades, and sissors.[43]

Interestingly, many of the victims in Wiehe's study reported the violence to their parents, who usually offered little help. Wiehe reports that parents often blamed the victim for provoking the attack or punished both children physically.

Wiehe also investigated sexual abuse by siblings; 67 percent of the respondents in his survey reported sexual abuse by a sibling when they were growing up.[44]

There is a danger in writing about the long-term effects of childhood victimization. That danger is that the reader will conclude that adults victimized as children are nonproductive, or violent, or pathologically ill. This would be the wrong assumption to draw. Although childhood abuse is certainly traumatic and does cause, for many, a variety of adult problems that must be addressed, it is important to note that many adult survivors turn that victimization into positive life achievements. Oprah Winfrey, Rod McKuen, Maya Angelou, former Senator Paula Hawkins, Michael Reagan, and others are examples of adult survivors who have achieved a great deal despite childhood victimization.

But the trauma of childhood victimization frequently remains in adulthood. Case studies reveal that many adult survivors experience difficulty in trusting others, feel extremely fearful, and suffer from poor self-esteem. Many survivors of child sexual assault are sexually dysfunctional, and some who were severely physically or sexually abused suffer from a variety of mental health problems including depression, suicidal ideation, dissociative disorder, and multiple personality disorder. A study conducted by the National Assault Prevention Center in 1986 found that men and women receiving mental health services were more likely to have a history of abuse than people in the general population. Sixty percent of women residents of a psychiatric facility reported rape, compared to 32 percent in the control group. Thirty-six percent of the male residents reported rape, compared to 2 percent of men in the control group.[45]

Drug and alcohol abuse and prostitution are also cited in case studies and in the research, as are eating disorders, insomnia, withdrawal, and intense feelings of guilt and shame. Adult female survivors regularly report tremendous feelings of powerlessness and self-hatred, and female survivors are more likely to turn their anger inward in self-destructive and self-mutilating behavior. Adult male survivors tend, on the other hand, to turn their anger outward, sometimes hurting family members and others.

Diana Russell's study of 930 women found that childhood incest victims were twice as likely to marry a batterer, and three times as likely to have been raped by their husbands, suggesting that childhood sexual abuse in females can be an early training ground in victimization.[46] Similarly, many adult male offenders have histories of childhood victimization, suggesting that for men, childhood victimization can be training for adult aggression.

A number of studies have found that some women who were victimized as children have clinical mental illness. One study found that women who had been sexually abused were at twice the risk for depression and psychiatric hospitalization as women who had not been abused.[47]

One of the most common characteristics in children who have been victimized is anger and hostility. It is no surprise that juvenile delinquency is correlated with childhood abuse. David Sandberg writes in *The Child Abuse-Delinquency Connection:*

> In fact, I am convinced that if we could prevent child abuse, we would eliminate much crime and delinquency, not to mention an assortment of other societal ills and personal afflictions encountered in adolescence and adulthood. This is not to suggest that all

Implications of Abuse

or most victims of child abuse grow up to be destructive members of society. However, based on mounting research evidence, it is increasingly clear that a disproportionate number of highly destructive and self-destructive members of adult society share a common experience of severe maltreatment as a child.[48]

Jose Alfaro conducted a study that examined the relationship between child abuse and delinquency when he was director of the New York State Assembly Select Committee on Child Abuse between 1973 and 1978. He found that 21 percent of the boys and 29 percent of the girls reported as delinquent in the early 1970s had been previously reported as abused or neglected. He also found that 50 percent of the families reported for child abuse and neglect had at least one child who was later taken to court for delinquency.[49]

The Need for Prevention

It becomes clear when we listen to survivors' experiences and when we look at the research that there is a great need for prevention. Our efforts will not just stop the immediate pain of the abuse itself but will, in fact, unalterably change the course of life for many.

> A woman who lives in Columbus has spent the last seven years, since she first remembered childhood abuse, in therapy. Her memories continue to emerge, and she has reexperienced a great deal of despair in looking back at her early family life, when a child needs love and guidance to develop trust and self-esteem. She has gone through periods of endless bathing in her futile effort to feel clean. She has believed for years that she was not merely dirty on the surface, but that her soul was permanently smeared with the ugliness of the abuse she suffered. She is a loving, giving, talented, dedicated, and fearless advocate for the children she works with as a therapist. No one knows better than she how dangerous it is to "forget" the abuse, to have no one to talk to and nowhere to turn for help.

Even those who must struggle every day with the trauma of their childhood abuse can contribute to a better and safer world for us all.

References

1. National Commission on Children, *Interim Report*, "Opening Doors for America's Children" (Washington, DC: National Commission on Children, March 1990), 3.

2. "Opening Doors," 3.

3. "Opening Doors," 3.

4. Children's Defense Fund, "A Vision for America's Future: An Agenda for the 1990s" (Washington, DC: Children's Defense Fund, 1989), 17.

5. National Center on Child Abuse and Neglect, *Child Abuse and Developmental Disabilities: Essays* (Washington, DC: National Center on Child Abuse and Neglect, Department of Health and Human Services publication no. 79-30226, 1980).

6. Public Law 93-247, as amended: *Child Abuse Prevention and Treatment Act of 1984* (42USC 5101).

7. R. W. ten Bensel et al., *Child Abuse and Neglect* (Reno, NV: National Council of Juvenile and Family Court Judges, 1985), 27.

8. C. Kempe et al., "The Battered Child Syndrome," *Journal of the American Medical Association,* 181 (1962):17–24.

9. "Opening Doors," 29.

10. C. Everett Koop, "Family Violence: A Chronic Public Health Issue" (paper read before the Western Pennsylvania Psychiatric Institute, Pittsburgh, 1982).
11. National Center on Child Abuse Research: The National Committee for Prevention of Child Abuse, *Current Trends in Child Abuse Reporting and Fatalities: The Results of the 1989 Annual Fifty State Survey,* Working paper 808.
12. National Center on Child Abuse Research.
13. J. Caffey, "The Whiplash Shaken Infant Syndrome: Manual Shaking by the Extremities with Whiplash Induced Intercranial and Intraocular Bleedings," *Pediatrics* 54 (1974): 396–403.
14. D. A. Wolfe, "Child Abuse Implications for Child Development and Psychopathology," *Developmental Clinical Psychology and Psychiatry* 10 (1989): 20.
15. Judith Herman, *Father-Daughter Incest* (Cambridge, MA: Harvard University Press, 1981), 12–13.
16. Diana Russell, *The Secret Trauma: Incest in the Lives of Girls and Women* (New York: Basic Books, 1986).
17. L. Tinnick, *Los Angeles Times* Poll, Aug. 25, 1985.
18. G. Wyant, "The Sexual Abuse of Afro-American and White American Women in Childhood," *Child Abuse and Neglect* 9 (1985): 507–19.
19. David Finkelhor et al., *Sourcebook: On Child Sexual Abuse* (Beverly Hills: Sage Publications, 1986).
20. Association for Retarded Citizens, "State to Improve Prosecution of Sexual Abuse Cases," *The ARC* 34, no. 5 (1985): 4.
21. Finkelhor, *Sourcebook.*
22. V. Van Hasselt et al., *Handbook of Family Violence* (New York: Plenum, 1988).
23. Finkelhor, *Sourcebook.*
24. Finkelhor, *Sourcebook,* 166.
25. Van Hasselt, *Handbook of Family Violence.*
26. David Finkelhor, *Child Sexual Abuse: New Theory and Research* (New York: Free Press, 1984), 26.
27. Finkelhor, *Sourcebook,* 27.
28. Finkelhor, *Sourcebook.*
29. *Webster's New World Dictionary.*
30. Suzanne Sgroi, *Handbook of Clinical Intervention in Child Sexual Abuse* (Lexington, MA: Lexington Books, 1982), 71.
31. Sgroi, 15.
32. Anna Salter, *Treating Child Sex Offenders and Victims* (Newbury Park, CA: Sage Publications, 1988), 25.
33. Howard Dubowitz, "Some Thoughts on Child Neglect," *The Advisor* 3, no. 4 (Fall 1990): 4.
34. Dubowitz, 4.
35. J. Grayson, P. Printz, and D. Gresham, "Emotional Abuse," *FLEducator* (Summer 1988): 5.
36. "But Words Can Hurt," *Technical Assistance Bulletin* 7 (Columbus, Ohio: National Assault Prevention Center, n.d.): 3.

37. J. Garbarino, E. Guttman, and J. Seeley, *The Psychologically Battered Child: Strategies for Identification, Assessment, and Intervention* (San Francisco: Jossey-Bass, 1988), 8.
38. D. Finkelhor and L. M. Williams, *Nursery Crimes: Sexual Abuse in Daycare* (Newbury Park, CA: Sage Publications, 1988).
39. S. J. Kelley, "Stress Responses of Children to Sexual Abuse and Ritualistic Abuse in Day Care Centers," *Journal of Interpersonal Violence* 4, no. 4 (1989): 505–13.
40. Stuart Greenbaum, "What Can We Do About Schoolyard Bullying?" *Principal* (November 1987): 21.
41. Stuart Greenbaum, "Schoolyard Bullying: A Fighting Chance Students Don't Deserve," *News Service: A Service of School Board News* (October 7, 1988).
42. M. Strauss, R. Gelles, and S. Steinmetz, *Behind Closed Doors* (Garden City, NY: Anchor Books, 1980).
43. Vernon Wiehe, *Sibling Abuse, Hidden Physical, Emotional and Sexual Trauma* (Lexington, MA: Lexington Books, 1990), 10.
44. Wiehe.
45. D. Nibert and M. Crossmaker, "Patient Assault Prevention Training in a State Psychiatric Institution" (Columbus, Ohio: National Assault Prevention Center, March 1986).
46. Russell, *The Secret Trauma*, 160.
47. David Finkelhor, "The Sexual Abuse of Children: Current Research Reviewed," *Psychiatric Annals: The Journal of Continuing Psychiatric Education* 17, no. 4 (April 1987): 235.
48. David Sandberg, *The Child Abuse-Delinquency Connection* (Lexington, MA: Lexington Books, 1989), 123.
49. Sandberg, 109–10.

5
Presenting the Children's Workshops

Introduction

The children's workshops are fun for the children and exhausting for the facilitators. One facilitator said, "I feel like I've just spent one hour with 25 dry sponges, and I was the only source of liquid!"

When we enter a classroom of students, we must put everything else out of our minds. We focus entirely on the students. We must attend to every word and every body movement (even mind-read a little) while we present the workshop and watch the clock at the same time. A facilitator from New Jersey said, after a particularly busy week of workshops, "You have to keep an eye on 25 individual kids, your watch, the teacher, and your co-facilitators. You need 29 eyes just to do one workshop!" This underscores the importance of teamwork; since three people conduct the workshops, three people share the many and varied responsibilities.

Still, the children's workshops are great fun for us, too. This is where we put all our theory into practice and discover who kids really are. We learn new ways of relating, of disciplining, of listening, and of teaching. The lessons are not just for the students; they are just as important to us.

Someone once said, "You teach best what you have most to learn," conveying the idea of learning as a shared activity: You learn while you teach. This is certainly true when it comes to teaching assault prevention, for each of us knows that we must learn assault prevention for ourselves. We know that just as we believe in the capabilities of children to prevent abuse, we must learn to believe in our own capacities to prevent abuse. This circle is nourishing because every time we conduct a workshop for children, we conduct it for ourselves.

In this violence-ridden world of ours, no one has all the answers. One important thing to remember is that you are not just a teacher in the classroom; you are also a student. If you stay open and listen, children teach you new things and you will grow as well.

Developmental Levels

The study of human development tries to explain the phases we go through from birth to death, the issues we are confronted with during certain times of our lives, and the needs we must meet in order to be healthy. In order to conduct effective workshops for the elementary school-aged population, it is helpful to understand the developmental period of which they are a part.

From infancy through preschool is a time of dramatic human development, characterized by quantum leaps in learning. We learn to move our muscles, first to reach out, then to roll, crawl, and walk. We learn to communicate, first by crying and smiling, then by babbling; then we speak our first words. We grow teeth so that we can eat solid foods, first with fingers, then with utensils. We learn control of our bladders and bowels. We learn simple rules — the word "no" at first, and then we can follow simple directions and rules. From birth to age five we grow and develop more, physically and mentally, than we ever will again in such a short space of time.

When we enter kindergarten at five or six years of age, we begin a period of development called the *middle years*. These middle years are characterized by "doing." We are driven to master skills, both physical and mental. We see everyone around us doing things, and we want to join them, to learn to do things on our own and with others. The CAP children's workshop capitalizes on this desire to *do*. Children have an opportunity in the workshop to practice the strategies needed to prevent abuse. When we ask for volunteers to help us, most of the hands in the room go up: They want to "do."

Although the middle years are not nearly so dramatic to the onlooker as the preschool years, we are still learning rapidly. We refine our physical skills, form our first friendships, and find acceptance outside our families. We refine lessons we learned in our preschool years. These new lessons are also incorporated into the design of the children's workshop.

We are a diverse group of people during our middle years, not simply because the span from five to twelve years is so great, but also because our life experiences are so different. We may come to the classroom from abject poverty and homelessness or from great wealth and privilege. We may live in a single-parent household, or one where our grandparents live with us, or a gay household where we have two moms or two dads. We may live in a household where alcohol is rarely seen or one where alcohol is frequently abused. We may celebrate Christmas, Chanukah, or Kwanza, or we may celebrate no religious holidays at all. We may feel like cherished members of our families or we may feel utterly unloved and unwanted.

CAP Project facilitators will meet some children who, unfortunately, were not provided with prevention information in time to avert abuse. Their behavior often gives clues to this abuse (see Chapter 4, "Child Abuse: An Overview," and Chapter 7, "Responding to Children"). The middle years rest on the foundation of the preschool years; the preschool years rest on infancy. If these foundations of our human development include abuse, the elementary years can be a difficult struggle, with which children deserve our help. When abuse begins or continues during the elementary years it interrupts the tasks that children would normally achieve. Children then must use their energies to cope, rather than to develop and grow.

Choosing Workshop Facilitators

Self-Selection

Workshop facilitators come from all walks of life. We are women and men, young and old, low-income and upper-middle-class, gay and straight, of varied ethnic, racial, and religious heritages. Some of us are survivors of assault. But we have all chosen to look the beast of violence in the eyes. This decision to empower ourselves and others to prevent assault binds us together.

Workshop facilitators are not required to have a college education or initials after their names, although many do. They need not be parents, although many are. What *is* required is that we care about children, that we respect them and their capabilities, and that we support their empowerment (see Chapter 8, "Creating, Implementing, and Running a CAP Project"). If we approach the workshops from this perspective we will be the teachers and advocates that children need.

Diversity

> A Puerto Rican facilitator was approached by two white, male children after the classroom workshops. They told her that they were afraid of Puerto Rican children because "they carry knives." The facilitator affirmed the children's fears about knives and discussed strategies for staying safe. Then she asked them how they knew that boys who carry knives are Puerto Rican. The boys indicated that one of their fathers had told them so. The facilitator gently told the boys that she was Puerto Rican and that she didn't carry a knife, nor did her brother. The boys were shocked. The conversation continued with the boys acknowledging that they had never spoken with a Puerto Rican person before. The boys left with a different understanding of Puerto Rican people, and with strategies for keeping themselves safe.

The pool of workshop facilitators should represent the community in which you live. For all but the most culturally diverse communities, this gives each child a member of his or her own community to talk with and confide in. In our first year of doing workshops, the team was composed of three white women who did all the workshops. In the second year the task force was enlarged. An African American team member started hearing stories from children about being called "nigger" and other racial slurs. The original group, which hadn't heard any such stories during the first year, had to conclude that children evaluate with whom they can talk, and about what. In our racist society children need to have members of their own community as role models and trusted adults, or we end up denying them support and assistance.

A diverse task force also sends another message to children: "We can work together with respect for one another. We value each other." We model cooperation and trust. Last, having a diverse task force permits children and communities to have advocates who are knowledgeable and respectful of cultural practices. With knowledgeable and understanding people in place communities find safety in discussing violence.

A Decade of Experience

The original CAP curriculum has stood up well over the years. First created in 1978, the curriculum went through many revisions in the first few years as we refined our techniques and increased our knowledge base. Very few changes were made after 1981. The CAP elementary curriculum is well-respected nationally and internationally, which is why it has been adopted by so many communities around the world. But we've learned a few things over the years that will affect the way you do the children's workshops. We know it will improve the outcomes.

Some of these changes were developed by our national office in Columbus. Others were tried and shared by Montreal CAP, New Jersey CAP, and CAP Projects in Ohio, West Virginia, California, and Massachusetts. Only after careful review and testing have we revised or added to the curriculum. We intend to keep revising our work, ever careful to give kids the best we know, as soon as we know it.

Researchers have also aided and greatly enhanced our work. David Finkelhor, Jon Conte, Jon Briere, and many others have worked with our own researcher, David Nibert, to help us scientifically evaluate the outcomes for children. This research also added to the new, improved CAP curriculum (see Chapter 9, "CAP Program Evaluation").

Women and Men Working Together

In the 1990s there are more men who share the work load and the spirit of CAP efforts. Because our work began in the women's movement we spent years working as women together to prevent the abuse of children.

But as our knowledge has grown, so has our desire to place men in the classroom. It has become clear to us that boys need men as role models, as confidants, and as teachers.

Thus, you will find throughout this manual the inclusion of men both in and out of the children's classroom. Although it is still difficult to find men who have the time, the personal philosophy, and comfort level required, a growing number of male leaders are positively affecting the quality and quantity of abuse prevention services to kids.

Some of our original thoughts still hold true, however. We believe that the team of three facilitators who conduct the actual classroom workshops should remain "woman heavy." When two women are on the team of three, we convey the understanding that women are capable and strong even in the face of danger. If two men and one woman make up the team, we risk conveying that women, and by association children, need men to protect them.

We continue to believe that gender-based stereotypes must be dealt with in the children's workshops, so it is always a woman who demonstrates the self-defense component.

With younger children we always have a woman play the part of "Uncle Harry," reinforcing the fact that role-plays are "pretend." We found that some young children were more frightened when Uncle Harry was played by a man. It is not necessary to frighten children to teach prevention, nor is it effective. We empower instead.

Finally, primary facilitation responsibilities must either be performed by a woman or shared among the team members. When we work with men we want to convey, once again, a sense of cooperation between men and women, rather than protectionism. When we show women as competent, smart, and strong in the face of abuse, we counteract myths, and we believe that we teach children that they, too, are powerful.

The Curriculum

- The actual children's workshops are one hour long (give or take ten minutes), and we spend approximately one-half hour after the workshop talking with children individually.
- Three adults conduct the workshop, either with two people providing the role-playing and the third person acting as primary facilitator, or with primary facilitation shared equally among all three facilitators.
- The basic workshop format is the same for all elementary school grades. However, the vocabulary and style of facilitation are different across the grades (see Modifications for Young Children later in this chapter).
- Follow-up materials for the teacher to use in the classroom are available from our office and should be provided to the school so that children have the prevention strategies reinforced.
- It is most effective to conduct workshops for all the classes in a school at the same time. In this way, the entire school spends concentrated time on prevention, and all the teachers attend in-service training. Since the school is a community, it is important that all members of the community participate.
- Classrooms should not be combined; in fact, the workshop was designed for a *maximum* of 25 children. Fewer children allow for greater participation.

Observers in the Classroom

Journalists should never attend a children's workshop with a tape recorder or camera. Mock workshops can be scheduled for media interested in featuring children's workshops. In this way we protect the children who have been victimized from inadvertently disclosing abuse to a journalist, and we don't divert children's attention from us to the camera. We often set up mock workshops for reporters, being careful to obtain school and parental permission. A classroom of children who have already participated in a workshop are asked to help us, and they understand in advance that a reporter is in the room.

It is not unusual for school principals, guidance counselors, or other staff members to ask whether they may watch a children's workshop. Although we welcome them into the classroom, there are some guidelines we recommend.

First, no more than two observers should attend any classroom workshop. We have found that if the observer group is larger than two, the children are distracted from the workshop itself. Second, all workshop observers must sit behind the semicircle of children, so that children are not facing the observers. When these two requests are met, observers pose little distraction to students in the classroom.

On rare occasions parents ask to watch a workshop. We respond affirmatively, but ask that they not observe their own child's classroom. When parents are in a classroom, children often change their behavior. They may try to impress their parent or they may withdraw from participating, afraid of failing in their parent's eyes. Since we want the children's workshops to be as comfortable and as positive as possible for every child, we ask parents to help us secure it by choosing another classroom. We have never had an objection to this request.

Modifications for Young Children

Conducting a workshop for a kindergarten class is different from conducting a workshop for older children because young children's vocabularies, experiences, and understandings are limited. When we conduct workshops for younger children we have to be more concerned about frightening them. This means that we change the role-plays so that the bully is less intimidating, and the stranger less forceful. We lighten the role-playing for younger children so that they always feel safe during the workshop.

Since younger children think so concretely, we are careful to clearly mark the beginning and end of every role-play. Clapping at the end of a role-play signifies that we were pretending, and now it is over. We carefully point out, and repeat several times, the role each facilitator is playing, so that young children are certain of who is who during the role-plays.

We do not use complex, open-ended questions with younger children. Instead of "What happened?" we ask, "Did the stranger trick Tom?" "What was the trick?"

We keep the workshop moving by increasing our own animation and energy, all to keep shorter attention spans focused on our workshop. Finally, we repeat and repeat important concepts and strategies. We repeat and repeat important concepts and strategies!

Curriculum Adaptations

In general, we urge you not to make adaptations to the CAP curriculum. One of the benefits you gain from using a national model is that you know the materials have been tried in many diverse communities and evaluated for their effectiveness (see Chapter 9, "CAP Program Evaluation"). When you change basic aspects of the curriculum, you can no longer be sure that the changes you have made will have the same impact as does the tested model. This means that you can no longer directly benefit from the research on the CAP model.

CAP has come to be synonymous with high-quality, comprehensive programming for children. That reputation must be protected. Therefore, if your intention is to "borrow" from the CAP materials, adding your own materials and perhaps materials from other prevention programs, do not call yourself a CAP Project (see "Working Together: NAPC and You," Chapter 10).

The name *Child Assault Prevention (CAP) Project* is protected by registration. We give permission to each CAP Project to use the name. But in order to protect that name, and the work of thousands of us across the country, we require anyone using the name to use the curriculum *as it is written,* with only limited exceptions.

These exceptions include multicultural adaptations that enhance cultural competence. For instance, American Indian projects have adapted the curriculum to reflect the language and style of American Indian culture. All the key elements of the workshop are retained, but the workshop content has been changed to a storytelling format. This not only enhances the workshop for those children, but also communicates pride in their heritage.

Any multicultural changes to the CAP program must be carefully evaluated to determine whether workshop effectiveness remains intact. Workshop adaptations should be made only if they enhance children's understanding of the information, skills, and strategies that are taught. For instance, eliminating the "Uncle Harry" role-play because some members of a community fear a discussion of family violence is not appropriate.

Without doubt, some communities will put pressure on a CAP Project to change various parts of the curriculum. Sometimes a principal wants only the school counselor to provide the individual review time, or wants this component eliminated altogether. Projects that have succumbed to such pressure have often lived to regret it. Their intentions were noble; they told themselves that if they didn't provide services as the school mandated, then children wouldn't have any prevention information at all. It is easy to understand why projects faced with this type of ultimatum feel forced into changing the curriculum. But making changes in the curriculum based on what schools or individuals find acceptable sometimes means that the children who need us the most are denied access to help.

> In a rural Ohio community the CAP coordinator was told during a teacher/staff in-service workshop that the principal alone would conduct the "talk time" component in her office. The coordinator tried to argue diplomatically against this change, but the principal seemed unwilling to budge. After children's workshops in 25 classrooms, not one child had gone to talk with the principal. Yet, in another school in the same district, four cases of child abuse were reported to protective services, and more than half of each classroom came to talk with the facilitators after the workshops.

The CAP model involves the parent program, the teacher/staff in-service training, the actual children's classroom workshops, and talk time. All these components meet different needs, none of which can be overlooked. Any time that a CAP Project is asked to omit all or part of a component, we diminish our effectiveness and, in the end, fail to help children. You may be asked to make sacrifices that cause you to feel uncomfortable. When you are asked to amend the program in a way that you know diminishes your ability to reach children, then we hope that you will defend the model. We believe that in defending the model, you defend children's rights to be safe, strong, and free.

Curriculum Goals by Grade Level

Table 2 reflects the competencies for the elementary classroom workshops. It demonstrates that the concepts taught in a CAP Project will be *introduced* to younger children, *developed* for middle-grade children, and *reinforced* for upper-grade elementary school students. In practice, this means that older children will have a more sophisticated understanding of the workshop content, and will be able to generalize it to more situations than will younger children.

For instance, young children will have only a cursory understanding of the concept of rights, whereas older children will have a more sophisticated view of rights. Our goal with first-grade students is for them to understand that rights are important, especially the rights to be safe, strong, and free. Our goals with older children are to enable them to discriminate between rights they currently have, such as the right to eat; rights that they do not have, such as deciding what time they will go to bed; and rights they will obtain later in life, like the right to vote.

It becomes clear that child abuse prevention information must be regularly taught to children, affording them the opportunity to increase their level of understanding. We believe that an appropriate goal for program instruction is for workshops to be offered to children at least every other year: once in kindergarten or first grade, once again in second or third grade, and again in fourth or fifth grade. Sixth graders would receive workshops if they had not received training in their fifth-grade classrooms. Although this is an ideal goal to set, very few CAP Projects achieve such regularity, due to funding limitations.

See Table 2 on next page

Preparing for the Children's Workshops

Materials Needed for Each Children's Workshop

- Three magic markers and three pens
- Name tags for each child and facilitator
- Three "Evaluation of Children's Workshops" forms (see Appendix B)
- Optional: Sign that says "Safe, Strong, and Free

The script that follows covers a one-hour children's workshop. Included are the primary facilitation narrative, the role-plays, and staging instructions. The names used in the workshop — Juan, Barb, and Frayda — are examples only; during a CAP workshop each facilitator will use his or her own name. In the script, Frayda is performing the role of primary facilitator; Juan and Barb are the role-players.

Curriculum Goals by Grade Level
Table 2
Skill Levels: Introduce (I)   Develop (D)   Reinforce (R)

		Grade Level	K	1	2	3	4	5	6
GOAL I:	**Students will define personal safety rights**								
Objective 1:	Students will define the concept of rights and give examples of rights they have.		I	I	D	D	D	R	R
Objective 2:	Students will define their personal safety rights: • The right to be safe • The right to be strong • The right to be free.		I	I	D	D	D	R	R
Objective 3:	Students will identify when these rights are being threatened or violated.		I	I	D	D	D	R	R
GOAL II:	**Students will identify potentially dangerous situations**								
Objective 1:	Students will recognize abuse situations involving peers.		I	I	D	D	D	R	R
Objective 2:	Students will identify potential assault situations involving an unknown adult.		I	I	D	D	D	R	R
Objective 3:	Students will identify abuse situations involving a known adult.		I	I	D	D	D	R	R
GOAL III:	**Students will be aware of effective prevention strategies**								
Objective 1:	Students will demonstrate the ability to say "No" and be assertive in potentially dangerous situations.		I	I	D	D	D	R	R
Objective 2:	Students will demonstrate giving and receiving peer support in a potentially dangerous situation.		I	I	D	D	D	R	R
Objective 3:	Students will demonstrate a safety yell.		I	I	D	D	D	R	R
Objective 4:	Students will demonstrate basic physical self-defense behaviors.		I	I	D	D	D	R	R
GOAL IV:	**Students will be aware of support networks available to them.**								
Objective 1:	Students will identify trusted adults in their community setting.		I	I	D	D	D	R	R
Objective 2:	Students will recognize teachers and other school personnel as trusted adults.		I	I	D	D	D	R	R

The children's workshop involves guided group discussions and role-plays. Each role-play is performed by the facilitators twice. The first time a role-play is performed, it demonstrates a potentially dangerous situation. After group discussion, wherein prevention strategies are determined, the facilitators reperform the role-play as a success story, incorporating the prevention strategies. In the "bully" and "stranger" role-plays, children are then invited to participate, giving them an opportunity to practice the strategies and to model abuse prevention behaviors for the watching children.

When the team of facilitators includes a man, he plays the victim in the first and third role-plays, and the stranger in the second. This balances the roles of aggressor and victim. The role-plays break down in the following way:

Male victim vs. Female bully

Female victim vs. Male stranger

Male victim vs. Male offender

As you can see, we have male and female victims and offenders. If all three members of the team are female, however, it breaks down like this:

Female victim vs. Female bully

Male victim vs. Male stranger

Female victim vs. Male offender

Female facilitators sometimes play the part of men when a man is not on the team. As you will see in the script, the primary facilitator is careful to point out several times that both boys and girls can be victimized.

A great deal of practice is required to provide a high-quality children's workshop. The primary facilitator and role-players should not read from the written script in an actual workshop. By the time you enter a classroom of children, the material should be so familiar to the team that the script — even the use of note cards — is unnecessary.

The following script, when delivered in combination with the children's comments, questions, and suggestions, takes approximately one hour to perform. It is not uncommon for new facilitators to rush this presentation. If the workshop is taking you either less than 50 minutes or more than 65 minutes from the time you first enter the classroom, you'll need to determine the reason(s) for this and rectify the timing. The workshop succeeds best when delivered in a brisk and animated fashion. This holds the children's attention and keeps them involved in learning the prevention strategies, which they might have to use some day.

We have provided a script as it would be performed for Ms. North's second-grade class and have noted script changes for older children. When you perform the workshop, substitute the children's grade level and their own teacher's name.

Good luck. This is the fun part; enjoy it with the children.

Workshop Script

Introduction

The team enters the classroom quietly and waits for the teacher to finish whatever activity has preceded the workshop. Then the primary facilitator approaches the teacher to remind him or her that desks and chairs are to be moved so that children can sit on the floor. The primary facilitator also asks the teacher whether there are any children in the class about whom the teacher is concerned or who need special attention.

During this conversation the two role-players move furniture and then get the children seated in a semicircle on the floor. The primary facilitator then rejoins the team and begins the workshop.

PRIMARY FACILITATOR ■ ■ ■ "Good morning! My name is Frayda. This is Barb and Juan. Does anyone know why we are here? We are here to talk with you about how kids can get hurt by other people and what we can do about it. This means we may be talking about some scary things adults may not talk to kids about."

(Younger children often hug each other and giggle, or put their hands over their eyes.

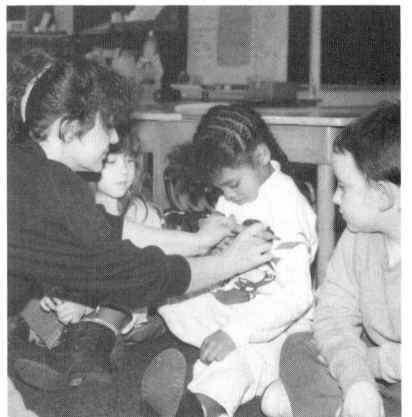

■ ■ ■ "The first thing we want to do is give you name tags, just like the ones we're wearing. This way, we can learn your names and we can call on you during the time we are together. Barb and Juan and I will spend a few minutes giving you name tags, then we will get started. Can you sit quietly while we do this?"

Leaders should give out name tags and have brief individual conversations with each child. These conversations help to relax both the leaders and the children before the actual workshop begins. They set a tone of informality and trust. Ask, for example, "Is that Snoopy on your shirt?" or "How do you spell 'Aisha'?"

Occasionally teachers prepare name tags for all the children in an effort to be helpful. If you share the reason we prefer to give out name tags during the teacher/staff in-service training, you will avoid this problem. However, if name tags are provided prior to your arrival, you will still want to "warm up" the classroom. Each facilitator should personally introduce himself or herself to each student, taking a moment to notice Snoopy on a shirt.

■ ■ ■ "Does everyone have a name tag? Great! Could you all agree to leave your name tags on the front of your shirts until we're finished today? Thank you!"

For younger children: "Since we may be talking about some things that could be scary, we want you to know that there are a couple of things you can do if you feel uncomfortable. You may go sit beside Barb or Juan or your teacher. You also have the right to leave your classroom if you get uncomfortable, or just decide that you don't want to be here. If you want to leave, just tell your teacher. We will come to get you when we are done. But I don't think you'll want to leave. I think we're going to have fun together."

For older children: "We are from the Child Assault Prevention Project. Can someone tell me what the definition of *assault* is?"

The primary facilitator writes Child Assault Prevention on the board. Children define assault as hitting, punching, or hurting someone.

■ ■ ■ "Right, assault means to hurt someone. How about *prevention*? Can you define *prevention*?"

Children will say "Keeping something from happening," or "To stop something."

■ ■ ■ "Right. Prevention means to stop something from happening. So, child assault prevention means to stop a child from being hurt. Talking about children being hurt can be scary and upsetting. But I don't think you'll be scared because we are going to have fun.

"Since there are so many of you, and only three of us, we need to make an agreement with you. When you speak in class, what do you usually do? Why do we need to raise our hands before we speak?"

Children will nod, say "Yes," or acknowledge the agreement. With rowdy classes, it will be necessary to remind the children of this agreement.

Children's Rights

PRIMARY FACILITATOR ■ ■ ■ "In order to talk about staying safe, we need to talk about rights. Who can give me a definition of *rights*? What does it mean when I say I have rights or you have rights? Can you give me an example of a right you have as second-graders?"

Older children can be asked for examples of rights they don't have (e.g., driving and voting).

The CAP workshop approaches the question of rights within the framework of basic human rights. An assault is a violation of one or more of our rights to be respected and to be safe. A child's right to say "No," or the right not to be touched in a way he or she doesn't like, are concepts central to the workshop.

Young children with limited vocabularies and/or with rigid rules at home often speak in terms of "right to obey your parents" or "right to rake the leaves." Children with more options speak of the right to "play" or the right to "be heard." Help the children realize that rights include the right to eat and to go to the bathroom. If our rights are taken away, we have problems.

■ ■ ■ "Do you have the right to eat? What would happen if you went home tonight and your parents said, 'No one is going to eat tonight'? Would you be hungry? Sure you would. You'd have problems. What problems would you have? What about the right to go to the bathroom? What would happen if your teacher said, 'Today, no one is allowed to go to the bathroom'? Would you have problems? Of course!"

(Children understand the problems losing these rights would cause.)

■ ■ ■ "That's my point! When someone takes away one of your rights you begin to have problems. But today we are not going to talk about the right to play, eat, or go to the bathroom. We are going to talk about three special rights that everyone in this room has. I want you to remember them: The first is the right to be *safe,* the second is the right to be *strong,* and the third is the right to be *free.* Safe, strong, and free! These are rights that may get taken away when someone tries to frighten us or hurt us."

> The primary facilitator should ask younger children to repeat the rights in unison several times. For second grade and older, write "Safe, Strong, and Free" on the board, or prepare a sign that says "Safe, Strong, and Free" and take it to each classroom workshop.

■ ■ ■ "Who can give me a definition of *safe*? Where do you feel safe?"

> Younger children may talk about feeling safe when they are in their beds during a thunderstorm, or holding an adult's hand. Older children define safe in more sophisticated ways: "Not doing drugs," or "Going to the basement during a storm."

■ ■ ■ "What about *strong*? What does it mean to be strong?"

> Children start out by defining physical strength: muscles, eating good food, running fast.

■ ■ ■ "Right! One kind of strong is body strong. There is also mind strength, or inside strong. When you have confidence in yourself, when you feel good about yourself and what you can do, you feel strong inside.
"What about *free*? Can someone tell me what 'free' means?"

> Some children will say, "Free is not being in jail." African American children often say, "Free isn't being a slave." We talk about freedom with older children by saying, "Free is when you have choices."

■ ■ ■ **For younger children:** "The three rights we've talked about today are the ones that get taken away when someone tries to hurt or frighten us. I brought Barb and Juan with me today to act out stories for you. How many of you have been to the theatre and have seen people pretend to be other people? Well, that's what Barb and Juan are going to do. They might pretend to be mad at each other, but remember, they're just pretending! They really are friends."

> (Children understand the concept of pretending and will nod affirmatively.)

■ ■ ■ **For older children:** "The three rights we've talked about today are the ones that get taken away when someone tries to hurt or frighten us. Barb and Juan came with me today to do some role-plays."

Introduce the "BULLY" Role-Play

PRIMARY FACILITATOR ■ ■ ■ "Let's begin our first role-play. Juan will pretend to be a boy in your class. How old are you?"

Children will typically call out two ages. Second graders will call out "seven" and "eight." One role-player always plays a child the same age as the children in the classroom.

If three women are facilitating the workshop, then both the victim and the bully are girls.

■ ■ ■ "Let's make Juan 7½ years old. He's in Ms. North's second-grade class. Let's pretend he sits beside you, and goes to art and music when you do.

"It's Monday morning and Juan is walking to school. This is the sidewalk where Juan walks to school every morning. Barb will pretend to be an older, bigger, stronger child. Barb will come up to Juan and they'll have a conversation. Let's watch and listen, and then we'll talk about it."

Role-players now assume their positions and act out the "child against child" role-play.

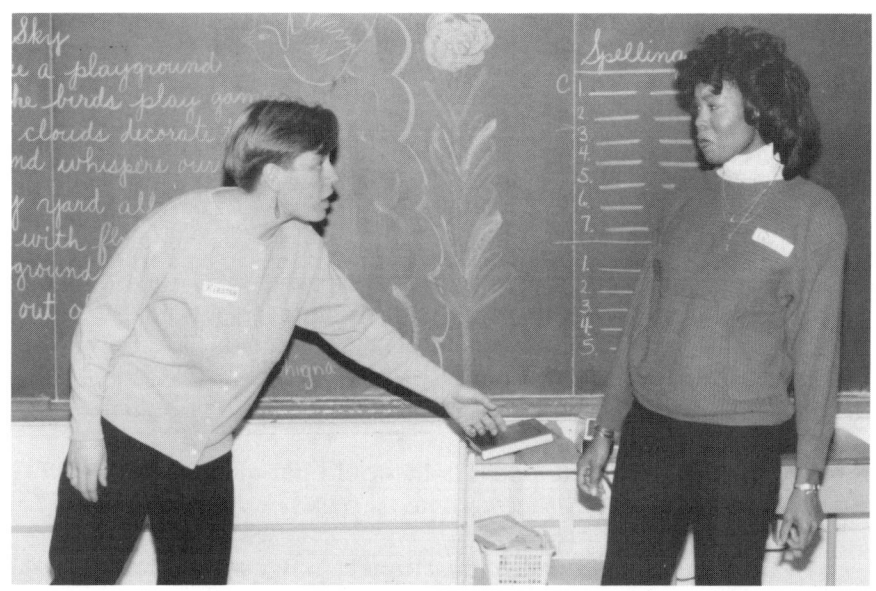

Child Against Child Role-Play

(Juan is walking to school by himself when Barb spots him.)

Barb (aggressively): "Hey, Juan, where are you going?"

Juan (a little frightened): "I'm going to school."

Barb: "Come over here, Juan! Come here!"

(Reluctantly, eyes downcast, Juan walks over to Barb.)

Barb: "What do you have in your pocket?"

Juan (afraid): "I don't have anything in my pocket."

Barb: "Yes, you do, Juan! You have lunch money in your pocket. I want it. Give it to me!"

Juan (quietly protesting): "I don't have —"

Barb (more aggressively): "I said, give me your lunch money! Right now!"

(Juan fumbles with his pocket. Barb looks at and takes the money.)

Barb: "Wait a minute! There's only a quarter here. You can't buy lunch with a quarter. I want the rest of your money!"

(Looking sad, Juan gives Barb the rest of his lunch money.)

Barb: "Now listen, Juan. We've got a deal. You meet me here every day, and I'm going to get your lunch money. Do you understand me?"

Juan (hanging his head sadly): "Yes."

Barb: "Good! Now go on and get out of here, stupid!"

(Barb walks away.)

The role-play ends and the role-players rejoin the circle of children on the floor.

Role-players must change their demeanor based on the age of the children. Older children who are bullied will act more defiant. Younger children will act more frightened.

If children do not carry lunch money to school, then Barb can take Juan's lunch. However, children can and do relate to this role-play even if they don't carry lunch money or walk to school. Children understand how it feels to lose something that belongs to them.

■ ■ ■ "Thank you (to the role-players). Let me ask you a question. How did Juan feel? Did he feel safe, strong, and free? Did Barb feel strong? Is that a good way to feel strong? Why not?"

Children readily identify with this role-play. They recognize that Barb took away Juan's rights to be safe, strong, and free. Juan felt "scared," "hurt," "frightened," and the like. Sometimes a child will say that Barb was "mad." This response leads right into a discussion on fighting and the rights of bullies.

■ ■ ■ "What do you suppose Juan would like to do to the bully? How many of you would secretly like to punch Barb in the nose?"

With younger children, it is important to acknowledge fantasy. Without the safety of "laser guns" or "bionic strength," a child may be left feeling small and vulnerable. Most children will enthusiastically endorse punching Barb in the nose, only reluctantly granting Barb the same rights as anyone else.

■ ■ ■ "Does Barb have a right to eat? How about the right to go to the bathroom? Barb also has the right to be safe, strong, and free like everyone else. And if we punch her, we're taking away her rights! Remember *everyone* has the right to feel safe, strong, and free. We all have the right to feel strong, but who can tell me why Barb *doesn't* have the right to be strong in this way?"

Children respond by saying, "Because Barb hurt Juan." A child in Montreal CAP said, "Because she is taking away someone else's strength."

■ ■ ■ "We want to keep our rights, not take away Barb's! We can protect our own rights without taking away someone else's, or we'll be doing just what the bully did. What could Juan do to keep his rights?"

> Usually, children respond with avoidance techniques: "Pack his lunch," "Walk a different way," or "Get his mom or a policeman to walk to school with him."

■ ■ ■ "Doesn't Juan have the right to carry his money and buy his lunch at school? What if the bully stole his lunch when he packed it? If he walked a different way, would he still be scared that he might run into the bully, or the bully might figure out that he was trying to hide? Doesn't Juan have the right to walk to school?

"What could he do to feel safe, strong, and free? What words could he say to the bully so that he could keep his lunch money? 'No!' is a safe, strong, and free word."

> With young children, it is helpful to have them shout "No!" Write the word *"No!"* on the blackboard, or take a sign with the word *"No"* on it to the classroom.

■ ■ ■ "What if Juan feels scared to say 'No!' all by himself? Could he ask a friend to walk to school with him? Sure, two people can stand up for each other. What else could Juan do? Who could he tell? If he told his parents or the teacher, would he be a tattletale?"

> Tattling is a big issue for children. The class will usually be divided on the question of whether Juan is a tattler. Since it is important to get adult help when you need it, we are careful to define tattling.

■ ■ ■ "Some people say yes, some people say no. Let's make a definition. If Juan goes to his teacher or the principal just to get Barb in trouble, he's tattling. But if he goes to get himself some help, he isn't. He's a safe, strong, and free person. You always have the right to ask for help. Do you agree with that definition?

"Okay. Let's do this role-play again and this time, we will use your suggestions. We'll ask Juan to stand up for his rights and say, 'No! No, you don't have the right to take my lunch money!' I'll pretend to play the part of Juan's friend. He'll ask me to walk to school with him and help him say 'No!' to the bully. Together we can tell Barb that we will tell an adult to get help."

> Role-players and the primary facilitator assume their positions and act out the "successful child against child" role-play.

Successful Child Against Child Role-Play

Juan (walking up to Frayda): "Hi, Frayda. Do you know that older girl, Barb?"

Frayda: "Yes I know her."

Juan: "Well, she's been taking my lunch money each morning on the way to school. Will you walk to school with me today and help me say 'No' to Barb?"

Frayda: "Sure, Juan. She doesn't have the right to take your lunch money. She doesn't have the right to do that to anyone."

(Juan and Frayda begin walking to school. If they are playing the part of young children, they may hold hands.)

Barb (spotting Juan, she calls out confidently): "Hey, Juan, come on over here! I've been waiting for you. You're right on time. Give me your lunch money."

Juan (assertively): "NO!"

Barb (surprised): "What do you mean, 'No'? We have a deal!"

Juan: "The deal is off, Barb."

Barb: "What do you mean, the deal is off?"

Frayda: "Yes, Barb, the deal is off. You don't have the right to take Juan's money."

Barb (pointing to Frayda): "Who is this?"

Juan: "This is Frayda. She's my friend."

Barb: "Well, I don't want your money, Fradya. Why don't you just go on to school? This is between Juan and me."

Frayda: "No. We're together. I'm staying with Juan." (Juan nods his head in agreement. They link arms — or hold hands, for younger children.)

Barb (incredulously): "Juan, are you going to give me your lunch money?"

Juan: "No, and if you don't stop, we're going to tell our moms and the teacher about you!"

Barb (embarrassed and upset): "Oh, forget it! I don't want your dumb lunch money anyway! You're both babies!"

(Juan and Frayda look at each other and smile as Barb turns to leave.)

The primary facilitator claps her hands to signify the end of the role-play. The other role-players rejoin the circle of children on the floor.

■ ■ ■ "Did you like this one better? How did Juan feel this time? Did he keep his rights to be safe, strong, and free? I have a question. Why did Barb say, 'I don't want your dumb lunch money, you're both babies'? Why did she call them names?"

> Even young children will recognize that Barb was just pretending she didn't want the money because she was afraid Juan would tell an adult or because she was embarrassed.

■ ■ ■ "We need a volunteer. Who would like to be a friend to Juan and walk to school with him and help him stand up to Barb? Who can use their words to help him stand up to the bully?"

> A particularly quiet child may simply stand next to the role-player and nod. The role-player can encourage the child to speak by saying, "You don't have the right to take my money, does she, Kip?" All leaders applaud any performance and thank each child.
>
> If a child becomes too aggressive, the primary facilitator might choose to stop a scene to have a frank discussion about the bully's rights. Children never play a bully, for that reinforces undesirable behavior.
>
> The primary facilitator should assess the interest of the class and redo this role-play three or four times, if time permits.

Introduce the "Stranger" Role-Play

PRIMARY FACILITATOR ■ ■ ■ "It's hard to stand up for a friend, but you helped Juan keep his rights! I'm sure Juan felt safer with a friend.

"That was great! I think you can be good friends who stand up for the rights of others. Now we want to move on to another role-play. This one may be a little scary. We want to talk about strangers. Strangers can take our rights away, too. What is a stranger?"

Young children will often say, "A stranger is someone who gives you poison candy," or some other negative illustration. Stress that not all strangers are bad; a stranger is just someone you don't know. Repeat this definition several times for younger children.

■ ■ ■ "What have your parents told you to do or not to do about strangers?"

The primary facilitator should go around the circle and elicit one comment from each child who raises his or her hand, repeating their comments: "That's right, don't take candy from strangers," or "Good job, don't talk to strangers."
Sometimes, children talk about assault. If possible, let them make a statement. Validate their feelings, and tell them you'd like to talk to them after the workshop.

■ ■ ■ "Those are all good things to remember. But we need to know what to do if a stranger *does* come up to us. In the next role-play, I want you to pretend that Barb is a girl in your classroom."

Be sure there are no children named "Barb" in the class; if there are, choose another name. Remember, if three women present the workshop, Barb plays a boy whose name is not duplicated in the class. Children do not have a problem pretending Barb is a boy.

■ ■ ■ "Can you pretend that Barb is 7½ years old? She's a friend of yours, perhaps she sits beside you and plays with you at recess. This is still the sidewalk on which Barb walks home from school." (Indicate the sidewalk.)
"This time, it is after school. She stayed after school to help her teacher, so there are not many people around. Barb is walking home, and she is thinking about helping her older sister with her paper route. Barb meets Juan. Juan will pretend to be an adult stranger, someone that Barb doesn't know. The stranger will walk up to Barb and they will have a conversation. Listen carefully; the stranger uses a trick and I want you to remember it so we can talk about it."

Role-players now assume positions and act out the "stranger against child" role-play.

Stranger Against Child Role-Play

Stranger: "Hi, little girl, I've seen you around here. You have a paper route, don't you?"

Barb: "Yes."

Stranger: "Yeah, and you live in that green house over there, don't you?"

Barb: "No, I live in the white house next door."

Stranger (friendly): "Oh, yeah. What did you say your name was?"

Barb (shyly and passively): "Barb."

Stranger: "Barb, huh? Barb what?"

Barb: "Barb Jones."

Stranger: "Barb Jones! Isn't your mother Mrs. Jones?"

Barb (looks stranger in the eyes): "Yes, that's my mom."

Stranger: "Listen, your mother is sick, she's in the hospital. She asked me to pick you up from school. I'll take you to her."

Barb (confused, scared): "My mom's in the hospital?"

Stranger (reassuringly): "Yes, yes. She's okay, but I'm supposed to take you to her."

Barb (passively): "But I'm not supposed to go with strangers —" (She begins to back away.)

Stranger (angrily): "Look, kid, you're coming with me!"

(The stranger reaches out, grabs Barb, and pulls her to the exit door of the classroom.)
   The role-play ends. Barb joins the circle of children on the floor. Juan, who portrayed the stranger, leaves the room and waits in the hall for the second part of this role-play, where children describe the stranger.

■ ■ ■ "Our stranger left the room, but he will be back in a few minutes. Who can tell me how Barb felt?"

Children acknowledge that Barb felt scared, sad, and confused.

■ ■ ■ "Yes, Barb lost her rights to be safe, strong, and free.
   "What was the trick? You don't believe Barb's mom was really in the hospital? You're right. That was a trick. But if you don't go with the stranger, does that mean you don't love your mom? How could you find out if your mom was okay *without* going with the stranger?"

Children will suggest that Barb go home or back to school to check out the stranger's story.

■ ■ ■ "Right, you never have to go with a stranger to find out if your mom is all right. Barb gave her name to the stranger because she was tricked."

Children are quick to recognize that Barb should not have given her name to the stranger.

■ ■ ■ "Should you ever give your name to a stranger? How about your address? Your telephone number? Or where your parents work?"

Children will call out "No" to each question.

■ ■ ■ "No, you should never give a stranger any information about yourself. Also, Barb got too close to the stranger. It's a good idea to keep a safe distance from the stranger. This way, if the stranger reached out to grab you, you would have time to run away."

This will be easier for the children to grasp if you demonstrate the concept. The role-player and the primary facilitator stand up, with outstretched arms, to demonstrate the distance between them. Frayda moves to grab Barb, who turns and runs. Frayda demonstrates by quickly grabbing Barb's arms and putting her arms around Barb's waist.

■ ■ ■ "But Barb didn't know to keep her distance and she got grabbed by the stranger. What could you do in this situation?"

Listen to the children's suggestions and *demonstrate* their good ideas, discussing them in the order they are given.

■ ■ ■ "Kicking is a good idea. If you are facing the stranger, you can kick him in the shin. Aim low. If you aim too high, the stranger could grab your leg and pull you off balance. If you are being held from behind, then you can kick backward.

"Scraping down the shin and stomping on the stranger's foot are also good ideas. Use the heel of your shoe to scrape down the stranger's shin. The part of your foot called the instep, or the arch, is very sensitive. There are a lot of little bones there, so that when you stomp on the stranger's instep, it really hurts him."

Illustrate the difference between toes and instep. Ask children to place their hands on their own insteps.

■ ■ ■ "Your elbow is a good weapon because it's sharp. If you're being held from behind, jab your elbow really hard into the stranger's stomach. If you're tall enough, you can aim for the throat. If you're small enough, you can elbow him between the legs."

Point to all of these vulnerable parts on the role-player's body and illustrate all techniques.

■ ■ ■ "What could you do if the stranger puts a hand over your mouth?"

> Young children often suggest that licking the stranger's hand would make him pull his hand away. Redirect the giggles at this response by reminding the children that the idea is to get away.

■ ■ ■ "You can bite! But sometimes the stranger cups his hand and it's hard to bite. You could also grab hold of his little finger. Brace your other fingers against the back of the stranger's hand and pull his finger back as far as you can. Try it on yourselves. It doesn't take much strength to pull a hand away from your mouth.

"All of these ideas are good ones, but what very important thing should Barb be doing the whole time she is trying to get away?"

> Children respond with "yell" or "scream." If children have mentioned "yell" earlier, emphasize that yelling is a great idea and that we'll come back to it. Saving the yell for the end of the self-defense section keeps chaos from breaking out and puts closure on this "active" portion of the workshop.

■ ■ ■ "That's right, yelling! And I'm going to teach you a new yell. I think I learned how to yell, and kids learn how to yell, from TV and movie stars. They have a high-pitched scream that comes from the top of the throat and sounds like this: (a high-pitched shriek). Sometimes, children do that on the playground, or playing hide and seek, or on a roller coaster. Do adults always come when they hear that yell? No, they don't. So we need a yell that says, 'Hey, pay attention to me, I need help!' It also says, 'Leave me alone, I'm a safe, strong, and free person!' This is a safety yell, so you should only use it when you're in danger. Do not play with this yell. The yell doesn't come from the top of your throat; it comes from a small place between your ribs called your diaphragm. With your fingers, walk up the inside of your ribs and find the soft spot."

> The primary facilitator should walk her fingers up her ribs and show the spot, her diaphragm. She should point it out on a few children who have trouble finding their own.

■ ■ ■ "This is the spot the yell comes from. This is not a high-pitched scream, it is a low yell. It tightens up all your stomach muscles and makes you feel strong. I am going to do the yell. I am going to be the only one who does it right now, on the count of three. It's pretty loud, so you may want to cover your ears. You want to do this yell from the moment you feel in danger until you are someplace safe or with someone safe."

> The primary facilitator demonstrates the safety yell (a low, loud, guttural yell). This may be done while running across the room, pretending to run to a house, or pretending to fight back.

■ ■ ■ "Now we are all going to do this yell. Everyone stand up. Get your body straight and strong. Put your hand in the air. Make a safe, strong, and free fist. Now put your fist on your stomach so you remember where the yell comes from.

"There is one agreement we have to make before we start. When my hand is up, everyone can yell, but when my hand comes down, everyone must stop yelling. Does everyone agree? Now, whom will everyone be watching?"

The class will nod affirmatively and state "You!"

■ ■ ■ "Ready? One, two, three —"

Children yell. Practice the yell at least twice. The first time, young children often resort to high-pitched screams. Remind them to push the sound out from their stomachs. They need to yell "loud enough to wake up the neighbors" or "so that someone who is watching TV will hear."

■ ■ ■ "Okay, that was great! Give yourselves a hand. Everyone please sit down and take a deep breath. Now, let it out slowly."

With young children, the facilitator may do a single focusing exercise to center the class's attention back to the discussion.

■ ■ ■ "Point to the ceiling, point to the floor, point to the friend next to you, point to your nose. Now point to me. Thank you. Okay. Let's go on!

"Now, is everybody listening? We have already decided that Barb shouldn't give her name to the stranger, that she should keep far away so she doesn't get grabbed, and that she should yell as soon as she feels she's in danger. Pretend you're in your backyard with some friends, playing basketball, and you hear Barb do her yell. What could you do?"

Children often say they would run to help Barb, get a parent, or call the police.

■ ■ ■ "These are good ideas! Another thing you can do is yell with Barb, because two or three voices are louder than one. So if we do our yell, too, someone else might hear us and come out to help. Together, you could yell and watch Barb to find out if she's all right. Strangers are like bullies. They're not looking for a fair fight. They're looking for kids who are scared, quiet, and confused, just like Barb. Do you think a stranger is going to stand around when Barb and her friends begin to yell? Of course not!"

Children are often pleased and excited at the turn of events. It is important to remind them that it is not their job to catch the stranger.

■ ■ ■ "Do we ever want to chase the stranger? No, we leave that up to the police. We never even want to get close to the stranger. We are just concerned about our friend, Barb. Once you've found out that Barb is all right, what information do you need about the stranger to tell to adults or the police?"

Children answer: "What the stranger looks like, what kind of car the stranger is driving, the license plate number on the car," and the like.

■ ■ ■ "Right! We need a description of the person and, if he had a car, information on the car. Remember Juan was our stranger? He left the room because we wanted to see how well you could describe someone whom you had seen for only a few minutes. Who can tell me what Juan looked like? I'll take one answer from each person who remembers something."

Children will raise their hands to describe Juan's "short hair," "brown eyes," "yellow shirt," "brown shoes," and so on. Role-players should be forewarned that this can be a humbling experience. "Kind of chubby," "he had pimples," or "he had a sleepy face" are all comments we've received. Whereas most responses should be repeated by the primary facilitator, she should *not* vocalize comments that are derogatory to the role-player. Simply acknowledge them by saying "Okay" and move on.

When asked how tall the stranger was, children often have a distorted perception of height. A young child might respond "six feet tall." By drawing comparisons with the primary facilitator's own height, however, guesses can be made surprisingly accurate.

Following this discussion, the "stranger" should return to the classroom and stand in front of the class so that the children have an opportunity to confirm or alter their observations. Again, derogatory remarks should be met without comment. Focus on things the kids may have missed.

■ ■ ■ "Okay, now we will redo this role-play using your suggestions. This time, Barb will refuse to give her name to the stranger. Barb will keep her distance from the stranger. When Barb feels she's in danger, she will yell. I will pretend to be a friend across the street. When I hear Barb's yell, I will do my yell, too, and run to find out if Barb is okay. Together, we'll get a description of the stranger to report to an adult or the police.

"Listen carefully. Strangers use lots of tricks and this trick will be different."

Role-players assume their positions in front of the children and act out the "successful child against stranger" role-play.

Successful Child Against Stranger Role-Play

(Barb is walking down the sidewalk alone. A friend — the primary facilitator — is playing basketball in the distance, at the side of the classroom.)

Stranger (friendly): "Hi! Hey, little girl, what's your name?"

Barb (assertively, looking the stranger in the eyes and keeping distance): "I don't give my name to strangers."

Stranger: "Oh, come on, kid. I'm just trying to be friendly. What's your name?"

Barb: "No. I told you, 'No'!"

Stranger: "Listen, I have some puppies in my car. Come with me and I'll show them to you." (Stranger reaches out to grab Barb's arm.)

Barb: "No!" (She backs away. Staying out of the stranger's reach, Barb does her yell. The friend who was playing nearby yells, too, and comes running toward Barb but doesn't get close to the stranger. The stranger sees this and runs away to the other side of the room.)

Barb (relieved): "Thanks for coming."

Friend (concerned): "Barb, are you all right?"

Barb: "Yes, a stranger tried to grab me. He said he had puppies to show me."

Friend: "What did the stranger look like?"

Barb: "Well, I saw a blue shirt. Did you see anything? What did you see?" (Friend describes the stranger in detail. The friend should create details about the stranger, such as the color of his car and license plate number.)

Barb: "Hey, thanks for coming. Are your parents at home?"

Friends: "My parents are home, let's go call someone to help."

The role-play ends and the role-players rejoin the circle of children.

Children applaud this role-play, clearly appreciative of the fact that Barb got away from the stranger and glad that Frayda was there to help.

■ ■ ■ "Did you like this one better? How did Barb feel this time? Did she keep her rights to be safe, strong, and free? What was the trick the stranger used this time? Who wants to be a friend to Barb and practice their yell?"

Usually, the whole class will raise their hands. In order to accommodate as many children as possible, it is necessary to choose three or four children at a time. Have them pretend to play basketball, four-square, or a similar game down the street. The primary facilitator will stay with the group. Remind them to listen for Barb's yell. When they hear her yell, they should: (1) yell; (2) run toward Barb; (3) find out if she's okay; (4) describe the stranger; and (5) determine whose house they should go to in order to call an adult or the police.

■ ■ ■ "If you have already had a chance in the first role-play, put your hand down. We'll try to give everyone a chance to participate.

"The rest of you should watch Barb and the stranger. Make sure Barb uses your suggestions. Also, listen closely to the stranger to see if you can pick out the trick he uses."

Each time the role-play is repeated, the stranger changes the trick. "Help me get groceries out of my car," "A storm is coming; I should drive you home," or "I lost my cat, can you help me find it?" are examples.

The role-player playing the part of the victim needs to elicit the appropriate responses: "Oh, I'm so glad you heard me yell! Did you see that stranger? He tried to get me to go with him. Does anyone remember what he looked like? Did anyone see the license plate number? I can write it on the sidewalk with a stone. Whose mom is home now? Kadisha, is there an adult home at your house? Can we call the police from there? Thanks a lot, everyone."

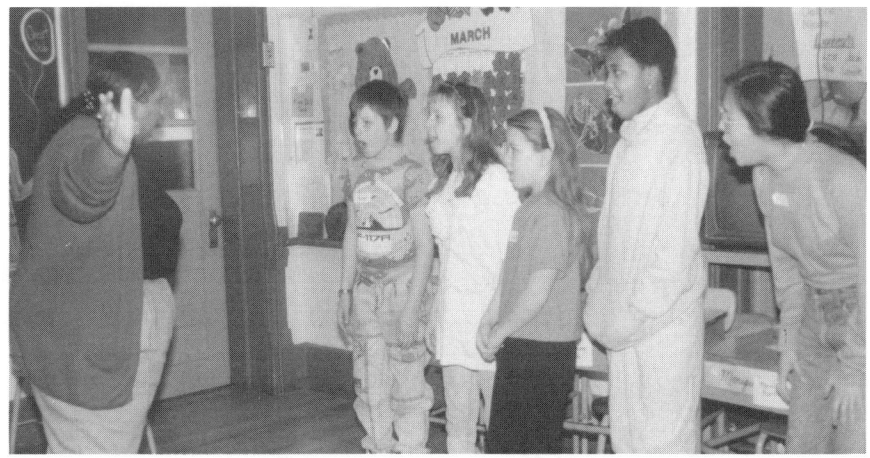

It helps focus children if the primary facilitator initiates a round of applause between practice role-plays.

Introduce the "Known Adult" Role-Play

PRIMARY FACILITATOR ■ ■ ■ "You were great friends! Now, please remember that special yell. Remember, it is a yell we never play with. I want you to go home and teach it to your parents. Be sure to explain that you will use this yell only if you are in trouble.

"Now it's time for our last role-play. This one is a lot different from our first two, so I really need you to watch and listen very closely. We've talked about bullies and strangers who try to take our rights away. This time, we are going to talk about someone that you know who may frighten you.

"Now, we know that most of the time moms, dads, uncles, neighbors, babysitters, grandmothers, grandfathers, and all the people we know love kids, care about kids, and would never want to hurt or frighten them. But sometimes, someone that you know — a friend of your family, a neighbor, a cousin or uncle, might try to touch you or have you touch them in a way that frightens you or confuses you.

"When this happens, we need to know what we can do about it. The next story might be a little embarrassing to watch. If your face gets hot, or you want to giggle or look at the ground, that's okay. I know you can handle it. And it's important to watch and listen carefully. Sometimes boys think that this only happens to girls, but this happens to both girls and boys, and we need to get help if it does.

"Juan will again pretend to be a boy in this class. But this time, it is a Saturday morning and Juan's parents had to go out of town for the day, so they dropped him off to spend the day at his aunt's and uncle's house.

"Let's say Juan is watching cartoons and his Aunt Mary comes into the room and says, 'Honey, I have to go out to the grocery store for 15 or 20 minutes. Do you want anything?' Juan says, 'No, I don't want anything. I think I'll just watch cartoons.' 'Well, if you need anything, Uncle Harry is upstairs.' Juan says, 'I won't need anything. I'll just watch TV.' Aunt Mary leaves, and Juan is watching TV. Barb is going to pretend to be Juan's Uncle Harry, who comes into the room and starts a conversation. I want you to watch and then we'll talk about it."

The primary facilitator can play the part of Aunt Mary and the previous description can actually become part of the role-play.

Role-players assume their positions and act the "known adult against child" role-play. You'll need two chairs for this one.

Known Adult Against Child Role-Play

(Juan is sitting in one of two chairs facing the children. The chairs are about 12 inches apart. Juan is watching TV when Uncle Harry walks into the room and sits down in the other chair.)

Uncle Harry: "Hi, Juan. How's my favorite nephew?"

Juan (giving Uncle Harry a quick nod without taking his eyes off the TV): "Oh, hi, Uncle Harry."

Uncle Harry: "Hey, what are you doing?"

Juan: "Oh, watching cartoons."

Uncle Harry: "Well, let's just turn that TV off for now."
(He leans forward and turns the TV off.)
(Juan begins to pout.)

Uncle Harry: "Juan, why don't you come and sit closer to your Uncle Harry?" (Uncle Harry pats his own thigh.)
(Shyly, Juan scoots his chair about two inches closer.)

Uncle Harry (sternly): "I said, over here, young man!" (He grabs Juan and his chair and pulls them very close to his own chair.)

(Juan begins to look very sad and scared and tries to shift his body away from Uncle Harry.)

Uncle Harry (beginning to stroke Juan's hair, to hold his hand, and to pat his knee, now very friendly): "Now, that's better. Juan, you're getting to be such a big boy! How old are you now?"

Juan (eyes downcast): "I'm seven and a half years old." (Age should correspond to the age of the children in the class.)

Uncle Harry: "You are sure growing up fast."

(Juan avoids his eyes, looking sadly down at the floor.)

Uncle Harry: "Do you like to eat at restaurants?"

Juan (quietly): "Yes, I like to…"

Uncle Harry: "How would you like your Uncle Harry to take you out for a pizza?"

Juan (brightening): "I'd like that!"

Uncle Harry: "Well, if you give your Uncle Harry a great big kiss, he'll make sure you get pizza."

(Juan, hesitant and uncomfortable again, tries to move away.)

Uncle Harry (sternly, grabbing Juan's arm): "I said, a big kiss, young man!"

Juan (quickly kisses Uncle Harry on the cheek, then looks away): "I think I hear Aunt Mary coming."

Uncle Harry (firmly grabbing Juan's shoulders and turning Juan toward him, sternly): "Now listen, Juan. I don't want anyone to know about this. This is our little secret. Do you understand?"

(He lightly shakes Juan by the shoulders to make his point clear. Juan nods his head yes, looking at the floor.)

Role-play ends and the role-players return to the circle of children.

NOTE: The role-play bribe can be changed. Pizza need not be used, but whatever is used should appeal to all the children. Bikes and roller skates are good bribes.

Children are usually very quiet following this role-play. Older children sense that Uncle Harry was being "weird"; younger children usually need to talk about this role-play point by point to understand exactly what happened.

Begin the discussion with Juan's feelings, then focus on the violation of his rights.

■ ■ ■ "How did Juan feel? Did he feel safe, strong, and free? Did he want to sit close to Uncle Harry? Did Uncle Harry force him to sit close? Did Juan want to kiss Uncle Harry? Did Uncle Harry force that kiss? Did Juan like the way Uncle Harry was touching him?"

Children are quick to ascertain that Juan was uncomfortable, that he didn't feel safe, strong, or free.

■ ■ ■ "What was the last thing Uncle Harry said?"

> Children respond by saying that Uncle Harry told Juan to keep it a secret. The key to the children's understanding of this role-play is understanding this secret. Ask for clarification of the secret. Children may recognize that pizza was a bribe. Explore why Uncle Harry wanted to take Juan out for a pizza. Even if the children lack the vocabulary to define *bribe,* they know it was a trick to get Juan to kiss him.

■ ■ ■ "Right, he said: 'Don't tell anyone about this, it is our little secret!' Let me ask you a question. When you were small, and you fell down and hurt your knee, if your mom or dad kissed your knee to make it feel better, did they say, 'Don't tell anyone, this is our little secret'? Of course not! Kisses and touches that we like don't have to be kept a secret. Did Juan like this kiss or touch? Is this a good secret? Can someone give me an example of a good secret?"

> Children may suggest a surprise party, or when your dad gets your mom a present for her birthday and asks you not to tell her.

■ ■ ■ "Yes, that's a safe secret. But should Juan keep this secret? Who could he tell?"

> Children are adamant that Juan should get help. They are well aware, however, of their lack of credibility, and know that adults often dismiss children's stories as make-believe.

■ ■ ■ "What if Juan's mom and Aunt Mary don't believe him? Do adults always believe children? Who else could Juan tell? (Suggest a friend, teacher, rabbi, minister, or grandparent.) The most important thing is that Juan keep telling people that he trusts until he finds someone who will listen to him, believe him, and help him. What could Juan do to keep his rights to be safe, strong, and free? What words could he use?"

> Children are often reluctant to say "No" to an adult they know. The primary facilitator may have to discuss "risk" if children think Uncle Harry might be angry with or punish Juan.

■ ■ ■ "Yes, he could tell Uncle Harry that he does not want to kiss him. But Uncle Harry might get mad, so Juan might decide to go ahead and kiss him this time, but be sure to tell someone later on. If Juan kisses Uncle Harry because he's afraid Uncle Harry might get mad, is he wrong? No, Uncle Harry is wrong for wanting secret touching that makes Juan feel unsafe. Juan could also get up and move away from Uncle Harry. Maybe he could go to a neighbor's house or sit on the front porch steps until Aunt Mary gets home. The most important thing to remember, though, is that Juan can tell someone about what happened. Let's do this one again and see if Juan can keep his rights this time. Remember, Juan will tell Uncle Harry 'No,' move away from him, and tell someone."

Role-players assume their positions and act out the "successful child against known adult" role-play.

Successful Child Against Known Adult Role-Play

Uncle Harry: "Hi, Juan, how's my favorite nephew? What are you doing?"

Juan: "Oh, watching cartoons."

Uncle Harry: "Well, let's just turn that TV off for now." (He leans forward and turns the television off.)

Juan (assertively): "Uncle Harry! I was watching that!"

Uncle Harry: "You can watch television any time. Besides, I want you to give me one of those big kisses of yours."

Juan (standing up, assertively): "No, Uncle Harry, I don't want to."

Uncle Harry (incredulously): "What do you mean, you don't want to? You always used to like it."

Juan (firmly): "No, Uncle Harry, I never liked it! *You* liked it!"

Uncle Harry: "Are you getting smart with me, young man?"

Juan (positively): "No, Uncle Harry, I'm not getting smart. But I'm going to tell my mom and Aunt Mary and I'm going outside." (Juan backs away and leaves the room.)

End of role-play. The role-players rejoin the circle of children. The primary facilitator returns to front of the class.

Introduce the Teacher Role-Play

PRIMARY FACILITATOR ■ ■ ■ "Juan felt better this time. He told Uncle Harry 'No' and left the room to get away from him. He kept himself safe. He told Uncle Harry that he was going to tell his mom and Aunt Mary.

"Now we're going to get your teacher involved. We want to see what it would look like if you had to go to an adult with a problem. Let's pretend that Juan is a boy in your class and he has a problem with Uncle Harry. He goes to your teacher for some help. Let's see what Ms. North would say. Who would like to be a friend to Juan and go with him when he tells his teacher?"

One child is selected to go with Juan. The role-players assume their positions and act out the "telling a trusted adult" role-play. (When the teacher comes to the front of the room the children often clap.)

Telling a Trusted Adult Role-Play

(The teacher sits in one of three chairs in front of the children. She pretends to be at her desk, working.)

Juan: "Hi, (child's name). I want to tell Ms. North about my problem with my Uncle Harry. Will you come with me? It would help me."

Child: "Sure."

Juan: "Let's go!" (They approach Ms. North.)

Juan: "Hello, Ms. North. Can I talk with you for a moment?"

Teacher: "Hello, Juan; hello, _____. Sure, we can talk. Have a seat."

Juan (sitting down in the other chair): "Ms. North, do you remember those people who came to talk with us about ways to be safe?"

Teacher: "Yes, I remember them. I'm glad they came to our classroom."

Juan: "Well, my Uncle Harry touches me in ways I don't like and I don't know what to do about it. _____ came with me to tell you, she's my friend."

Teacher (sincerely concerned): "Juan, I'm glad you and _____ came to talk with me. Why don't you and I have lunch together today? Then we can talk in private. I'd like to help you. Would you like that?"

Juan: "Oh, yes, I'd like that very much!"

Teacher: "Good. I'll see you at lunchtime, then."

Juan: "Thanks, _____, for coming with me. You are a good friend."

NOTE: The role-play ends and the teacher returns to the rear of the classroom. Children clap as the role-players rejoin the circle of children.

■ ■ ■ "How did Juan feel going to his teacher? Did Ms. North say, 'Oh, Juan, I don't believe that!' No, of course not! Ms. North said, 'Juan, I'm glad you came to talk; let's spend some private time together and I'll try to get you some help.' Do you think Juan felt good about talking to an adult he trusts? Do you think you could find an adult to talk with if you had a problem? Great!

"Well, we're finished now. We want to thank you for having us. Remember to stand up for your rights and for the rights of others. Remember the safe, strong, and free word? What was it?"

The class will resound with "NO!"

■ ■ ■ "Remember your special yell. Be sure to teach your parents. And remember to talk with an adult you trust when you have a question or problem. What are your three rights? Yell them out loud! 1—2—3—"

The children will say, "Safe, strong, and free!"

■ ■ ■ "We are going to be in the library (or other safe space) for about 15 or 20 minutes, and if you have a question, an idea, a problem, or just want to talk with us about anything at all, you can come and talk with us. Just ask your teacher and she will send you, three at a time. You can have a private conversation with me, Barb, or Juan. Okay? Thanks again for having us! Bye!"

> The primary facilitator and the role-players gather up all belongings, name tags, markers, and the folder of evaluation forms, and retreat to the "review space" to talk with children individually.

(END OF WORKSHOP)

The following role-plays can be used in place of the standard role-plays in the curriculum if you are returning to a school to serve children who have previously participated in a children's workshop. Be aware that there will be new students in the class; therefore, the workshops cannot be treated as a review. Every concept must be thoroughly discussed.

As in the standard curriculum, the discussion after the "unsuccessful" role-plays always focuses on how the child felt. Strategies are discussed and the role-plays are reperformed as successful.

Each scenario's discussion should also focus on preventing abuse through:

- Assertive communication
- Peer support
- Trusted adult help

However, the alternative role-plays do include some new concepts that build children's understanding of resistance. These new concepts are discussed after each role-play.

> NOTE: The new role-plays have not been formally evaluated.

Alternative Child Against Child Role-Play
Stolen Ball

(Barb is playing alone on the edge of the playground at recess. She got a big, red ball for her birthday, which she brought to school. Juan, a bigger, older boy, approaches Barb.)

Juan (friendly): "Hi, Barb, what are you doing?"

Barb (smiling, bouncing ball, proudly): "I'm playing with my new ball."

Juan: "I want to play, too. Want to play catch with me?"

Barb: "Well, okay. I'll throw you the ball and then you throw it back."

Juan (slyly): "Sure, Barb."

(Barb throws the ball to Juan. Juan grabs it and starts bouncing it to himself.)

Barb: "Throw it back, Juan, throw it back."

Juan: "Get out of here, you brat. I want to play with this ball. Scram!"

(Barb moves to the side of the classroom and watches Juan play with her ball.)

> The role-play ends and role-players return to the circle of children.
>
> NOTE: The primary facilitator uses the same script that follows the standard bully role-playing.

Alternative Successful Child Against Child Role-Play Stolen Ball

(Barb is playing with her new ball when Juan approaches. Frayda is playing off to the side.)

Juan: "Hi, Barb, that looks like fun, can I play?"

Barb (bouncing ball): "I got this ball for my birthday. Sure, you can play. Want to play catch?"

Juan: "Sure, sounds like fun."

Barb: "I'll throw you the ball, and you throw it back."

Juan: "I'm ready, throw it here!"

(Barb throws the ball to Juan. Juan catches it and then begins to bounce the ball, playing with it himself.)

Barb: "Throw it back, Juan, throw it back!"

Juan: "No way. Get out of here, you brat!"

(Barb looks around and sees Frayda and approaches her to ask for help.)

Barb: "Frayda, Juan stole my new ball. Will you help me get it back?"

Frayda: "Sure, Barb, let's go. He doesn't have the right to take your ball."

(The two children approach Juan.)

Barb (aggressively): "Juan, give me back my ball."

Juan: "No way, get lost!"

Barb (assertively): "The ball is my ball, and I want it back."

Frayda: "That's right, Juan. You don't have the right to take her ball."

Juan: "Get out of here, Frayda. This is none of your business."

Frayda: "I won't leave until you give the ball back to Barb. Give it back to her!"

Barb: "Give it back to me, Juan. If you don't, I'll talk to the teacher or the principal and ask for help, too."

Juan (bouncing the ball back to Barb): "Here! Take it! I was done with it anyway."

Frayda: "Great."

The role-play ends and the role-players return to the circle of children.

Alternative Stranger Against Child Role-Play
Newspaper Photographer

(Child is playing on playground jungle gym after school. Stranger with camera approaches.)

Stranger (friendly): "Hi, there. I'm taking pictures for the newspaper. Would you like to have your picture taken? Your parents would love it. You could surprise them."

Juan: "My picture would be in the newspaper? Wow! That would be great. Let me climb up to the top and then you can take it." (Turns to climb up.)

Stranger: "Wait! I need your name first, so your name will be in the paper, too."

Juan (hesitant): "My name is Juan."

Stranger: "Great, Juan. But I want a picture of you in the park across the street; let's go over there."

Juan: "I'm not allowed to go to the park. I told my mom I'd stay here."

Stranger: "Come on, I'm going to put your picture in the paper! It will be a great surprise for your parents. They'll never know, you'll only be gone 20 minutes.

(For younger children, say "a few minutes" rather than 20 minutes.)

Juan (intimidated): "I'd better not."

Stranger: "Look, Juan, I said we're going to the park!"

Stranger takes Juan's arm and forces him to go. Stranger and Juan go to the exit door. The stranger leaves.
    The role-play ends and Juan returns to the circle of children.

Alternative Successful Child Against Stranger Role-Play
Newspaper Photographer

(Juan is playing on the jungle gym after school. Stranger with camera approaches.)

Stranger: "Hi, there. I'm taking pictures for the newspaper. I'd like to take your picture."

Juan (keeping distance): "No way, I don't talk with strangers."

Stranger: "I'm not a stranger! I work for the newspaper. Why don't you come with me to the park across the street and we'll get some neat pictures. Your parents will love it!"

Juan: "No, I'm staying here."

Stranger: "Look, kid, I said you're coming to the park with me."

Juan: "No, No!" (Stranger gets closer. Juan gives his self-defense yell.)

> Role-play continues, the same as the standard successful stranger role-play.

Here is an alternative role-play for older children.

Alternative Stranger Against Child Role-Play
Video Arcade (Grades 4-6)

(Juan is playing on video game [using back of chair] when a stranger [an adult he's seen before but doesn't know] comes up to Juan and watches him play.)

Stranger (approaches and watches for a moment): "Wow, are you ever good. What's your name?"

Juan (unsure): "Juan."

Stranger (friendly and insistent): "Yeah, Juan, you're really good. Hey, did I make you lose your game? Here, take a quarter, go ahead, it was my fault you lost."

Juan (takes quarter hesitantly): "Thanks!"

Stranger: "Listen, I've got an idea. You know that new arcade that just opened up down the road?"

Juan: "You mean on the other side of the street, by the high school?"

Stranger: "Yeah, that's the one. Well, my friend owns that arcade."

Juan: "Really?"

Stranger: "Yeah and he is looking for kids who are really good like you. I mean, you've got to be one of the best. And this guy would let you play for free just to have someone good playing there — you know, serious players. So what do you say? My car's just outside, and I can drive you there."

Juan: "Well, I don't know. My mom knows I'm here, so I really can't leave."

Stranger: "Come on, Juan, you're not a baby. Besides, your mom will never know. We can be back in 20 minutes."

Juan: "Well, I don't think —"

Stranger (grabs Juan): "Come on, kid, I said you're coming with me." (Stranger moves Juan to the door of the classroom; the stranger leaves the room. Juan returns to circle of children.)

Discussion

Discussion should follow the same script as the standard stranger role-play. Discussion should include these points, however:

PRIMARY FACILITATOR ■ ■ ■ "What did Juan do that made it easier for the stranger to take him away?"

> - Took quarter; stood close
> - Stayed and talked
> - Gave name

■ ■ ■ "What did the stranger do that made Juan feel happy?"

- Flattered him
- Boosted his ego

■ ■ ■ "What could Juan have done to be safe?"

- Stand away — keep distance
- Don't give name
- Don't accept money
- Self-defense

Alternative Successful Child Against Stranger Role-Play Video Arcade

(Juan is playing video game. Becoming aware of a man approaching, he stops game and backs up when stranger gets too close.)

Stranger: "Hey, you're a good player! Did I make you lose your game? Here, take this quarter."

Juan: "No — it's okay." (He moves away from stranger.)

Stranger: "I've seen you play here before — you're one of the best. What's your name?"

Juan: "I don't want to tell you my name."

Stranger: "Well, I'm just trying to be friendly. Listen, I have a friend who owns that new arcade down the street. He'd let you play for free because you're so good. What do you say?"

Juan (friendly): "No, I'm gonna stay here."

Stranger: "Oh, come on, just check it out." (Stranger reaches for Juan, who is out of reach.)

Juan: "No! (louder) No!" (Yells.)

(Children yell and run to Juan; stranger runs away.)

Juan: "Thanks for coming! Did you see the stranger? The stranger tried to grab me. What did the stranger look like? Is your mom home? Thanks for coming!"

Alternative Known Adult Against Child Role-Plays

1. Same as standard role-play, except that known adult is a baby-sitter.

2. Same as standard role-play, except that child is at home, grandfather is visiting.

3. Same as standard role-play, except that child visits neighbor.

Primary Facilitator's Outline

Primary Facilitator — PF
Role-Player — RP
Victim — V

This outline is meant to be a guide as you facilitate the standard children's workshop. You should already be familiar with the role of primary facilitator and with the role-plays of the children's workshops.

I. Introduction: Who we are

A. Grades K–3: "We will discuss ways to keep children safe by acting out stories that are pretend."

B. Grades 4–6: Define child assault prevention (CAP). Introduce the role-players and observers to the children.

II. Classroom agreements: Rules of the workshop

A. Children have the right to leave the workshop if they are scared or uncomfortable. They can go to another location for the next hour.

B. Children have the right to sit close to their teacher or the role-players if they are uncomfortable (younger children).

C. Children have the right to be heard; make agreement that one person talks at a time.

III. Rights

A. What does it mean to say a person has *rights*? What rights do you have as fourth graders?

   1. Children give definitions and examples of rights they have. Older children can discuss rights they don't have.

B. When someone takes away your rights, you have problems.

C. PF focuses on three rights: "Safe, strong, and free!"

   1. Children give examples of being safe, strong, and free.

IV. Introduce the first role-play: Child Against Child Assault, or "The Bully" role-play

A. Describe what is going to happen.

B. "Pretend RP is a child in your class who eats lunch with you, plays at recess with you, or walks to school with you."

C. After the role-play:

   1. How does V feel? Did she or he feel safe, strong, and free?

   2. Did the bully feel strong? Is that a good way to be strong? Why not?

   3. Did V have the right to walk to school in safety?

   4. What could V do to keep himself or herself safe and keep his or her rights?

D. Focus on options: Sort out "avoidance" or fantasy strategies.

   1. Assertive response: Use your words to say "No!"

   2. Peer support: Walk to school with a friend (use your words to ask a friend).

   3. Talk with a trusted adult, teacher, or parent.

E. Children will offer suggestions:

   1. What words could V use to keep his or her rights?

   2. Can V ask a friend to walk to school with him or her? Are two people stronger than one?

3. Who can he or she tell? Would he or she be a tattler?
4. Define tattling.
5. How many of you would secretly like to punch the bully?
6. Does the bully have the right to eat, sleep, and go to the bathroom?
   a. The bully has the right to be safe, strong, and free. We want to keep our rights, not take away the bully's rights. Punching him or her would take away rights. Why is this way of feeling strong not so good?

F. Other issues children may raise:
   1. Gangs. Acknowledge their fear of danger; discuss staying safe and getting adult help.
   2. Weapons. Acknowledge their fear of danger; discuss talking to an adult.
   3. Fighting/Name-calling. Remind the children of the bully's rights.

G. Model the Successful Child Against Child role-play.

H. Practice the successful role-play three or four times.
   1. Get volunteers from the class to participate so the children can practice saying "No!" to the bully.
   2. After each success story, congratulate the participating child. Ask:
      a. How did V feel this time?
      b. Did V keep his/her rights this time?
      c. Ask children if they like this role-play better.
      d. Ask children if they think this strategy will work.

V. Introduce the Stranger Against Child role-play

A. "What have your parents told you to do or not to do about strangers?"
   1. Children give "shoulds" and "shouldn'ts" they have heard from adults.

B. Describe what is going to happen in this role-play.

C. RP is a child in your class who goes to art or music when you do.
   1. How did V feel? Did V feel safe, strong, and free?
   2. Did V have the right to walk home safely?
   3. Did you believe the stranger? What was the trick?
   4. How could you find out if your mom was okay without going with the stranger?
      a. Children give examples
   5. Discuss problems. What were they?
      a. Don't give your name to a stranger. Don't give a stranger your address or telephone number.
      b. Don't get too close to strangers. Keep distance from a stranger so you'll have time to run away (demonstrate).

D. Self-Defense.
   1. What could you do in a situation like V's? (PF and RP demonstrate)
      a. Children call out suggestions to V to get away from the stranger. Demonstrate self-defense.
      b. End with the PF teaching children the self-defense yell.
      c. Agreement from the children: PF is the only person who does the yell first.
      d. This is a safety yell; it's never used for playing.
      e. Everyone practices the yell.
      f. Friends running to rescue V do the yell.
   2. What else could you do to help V in this situation?
      a. Tell an adult you trust.
      b. What do you need to know about the stranger?
E. Other issues children may raise:
   1. Gangs. Acknowledge their fear. Get adult help.
   2. Tricking the stranger. Emphasize that they shouldn't even talk with the stranger, so they can't trick him.
   3. Catching the stranger. "That's the police's job!" Never get too close to a stranger.
   4. Answer their "what if's" by saying, "There are no guarantees for success, but children are strong and able to protect themselves most of the time."
F. Model the Successful Child Against Stranger role-play.
G. Practice the successful role-play four or five times.
   1. Use volunteer children to give everyone a chance to practice his or her yell.
   2. Afterward, congratulate the volunteers for their help.
      a. How did V feel this time?
      b. Did V keep rights to be safe, strong, and free?
      c. Ask children if they would feel good if their friends came to help them.
      d. Ask children if they think this strategy would work.

VI. Introduce the Known Adult Against Child role-play
   A. Describe what is going to happen and the need to pay attention.
      1. "Most of the time, people we know love kids. But sometimes, someone we know may try to frighten us, or ask us to touch them or touch ourselves in a way that is confusing to us and we don't like."
      2. Children need to protect themselves in these situations, too.
      3. Set the scene; tell the children that this happens to boys as well as girls.
      4. Acknowledge that they may find this embarrassing to watch.

B. After the role-play, ask "What happened?"
   1. How did V feel?
   2. Did V feel safe, strong, and free?
   3. Did V want to sit close to Uncle Harry?
   4. Did Uncle Harry force V to sit close to him?
   5. Did V want to kiss Uncle Harry?
   6. Did Uncle Harry force that kiss on V?
C. What was the last thing that Uncle Harry said to V?
   1. What was the secret?
   2. What are good secrets? Bad secrets?
   3. What is safe touching? Unsafe touching?
   4. Does Uncle Harry's secret make V feel safe, strong, and free?
   5. Does V have to keep this secret?
   6. Who could V tell?
   7. Do adults always believe children when children tell them something?
   8. Is there someone here at school V could tell?
D. What could V do to keep rights?
   1. Assertive response: say "No!" to Uncle Harry.
   2. Move away from Uncle Harry.
   3. Tell Uncle Harry what action V will take if he makes V kiss him.
   4. Tell an adult V trusts.
E. Model the Successful Child Against Known Adult role-play.
   1. Review strategies. How did V feel this time?
   2. Discuss what to do if Aunt Mary doesn't believe V.
   3. Did V feel safe, strong, and free?
   4. Was V still a little bit scared? Acknowledge that it's scary to assert yourself with an adult.
F. Other issues children may raise:
   1. Will V hurt Uncle Harry's feelings? Did Uncle Harry respect V's feelings? V has a right to be safe.
   2. What if Uncle Harry gets mad? Evaluate the risk.
   3. Will V lose the present Uncle Harry promised? Teach the children what bribery is, and how to recognize it.

VII. Introduce the Telling a Trusted Adult role-play
A. Describe what is going to happen.
   1. What would happen if you went to talk with a trusted adult about something scary that happened to you?
   2. Ask child to be a friend.

3. After the role-play, ask the children, "What happened?"

   a. How did V feel talking to his or her teacher?

   b. Did teacher believe V?

   c. Do you think teacher will help V?

   d. You can go to your teacher for help, just like V did.

VIII. Summary and Closing

   A. The three rights: Safe, Strong, and Free. Children yell them out.

   B. Be assertive; stand up for your rights.

   C. Support your peers; stand up for the rights of your friends and classmates.

   D. Use the safety yell if you're in trouble, and teach it to your parents. Don't use it or self-defense techniques for play.

   E. Talk to an adult you trust when you have a scary problem.

   F. "We will be around for a little while in the 'review space' if any of you want to talk with us. If you have a question, come talk to the PF or the RPs. Your teacher will send you to us, three at a time, and we can talk privately."

   G. "Thanks again! We had a great time!"

6
Presenting the Adult Workshops

Introduction

It is crucial for parents and educators, who are children's inner support circle, to be fully educated about child abuse and its prevention. For this reason CAP always provides a parent program and a teacher/staff in-service program at each school.

The presentation for both adult workshops varies in length. At new schools — those where CAP has never before been offered — we need at least an hour and a half. This is easier said than done.

Parent Participation

In the early years of CAP, it was not unusual to have more than 50 parents at a parent program, but over the years our ability to attract parents has decreased significantly. The reasons for this decrease in parent participation are diverse. For some parents, child care in the evening may be a problem. In-school prevention programming is now readily accepted by parents. Since skepticism brought many parents to in-service programs in the early years, the decline reflects parental awareness and acceptance. For working parents (especially single working parents) energy to attend a presentation may be limited. We also sense that parents feel overwhelmed by the burgeoning problems that children face. Each day they are confronted with news reports about drugs, gangs, alcoholism, teen pregnancy, and juvenile delinquency. We believe that some parents feel unable, even helpless, to face this litany of problems.

David Finkelhor's Boston study of parent knowledge suggests that parents have accumulated a body of knowledge about child abuse, perhaps leading them to the conclusion that they would not learn anything new by attendance at our program.[1] But although Finkelhor's study offers good news in the knowledge category, it also indicates that parents are still uncomfortable and unskilled at talking with their children about anything other than stranger-danger.

One way to confront this problem is to advertise the parent program by focusing on this area of parent involvement. Since parents indicate a lack of knowledge about how to talk with their children, and since we discuss this in the parent program, communities advertising this component may draw additional participants.

Offering child care during the parent program has been successful for some CAP Projects, and we have offered the parent program during regularly scheduled PTA meetings and gained access to additional parents.

We have often held two parent programs, one during the day and one during the evening, so that we could reach parents with differing schedules. The daytime parent programs draw more mothers than fathers; the evening programs draw more couples. Because of this, the tone of the parent programs is usually different. The daytime group is more informal, and mothers often venture into talking about rape and the threat of violence that they, too, must face. The evening programs are more formal and involve less personal sharing among the group. It is not unusual, following the parents programs, to provide crisis intervention to adults who have recently been victimized or who were abused as kids and to those whose children have been victimized. We offer support and provide referrals to parents who are living with the trauma of abuse and seeking recovery.

Parents tend to express many fears during the program. They read the newspaper and listen to the news, and they understand that their own children are vulnerable to abuse. They are looking for help with their fears, wanting information that will allow them to confirm that their own children have not been victimized, and to help prevent it from occurring in the future. Teachers' needs are somewhat different. They concentrate more on understanding their rights and responsibilities under the law, and they often vent their frustrations about cases in which they have been involved in the past. Although the information presented to both groups may be similar, the tone and specific interests of the groups are different.

Teacher/Staff In-Services

Teachers lack enough hours in the day even to get the basics done. Regularly scheduled staff meetings include a host of other issues that need to be addressed by school staff. Since staff meetings are usually limited to an hour, asking staff to spend an hour and a half at the end of a busy day is increasingly difficult.

In one community, the CAP Project has effectively dealt with the problem by scheduling teacher/staff in-service programs up to a year in advance and by seeking grant monies that pay teachers for their time out of the classroom. This is a good solution, but not possible for many CAP Projects, since many of us don't know that far in advance which schools will actually receive services in a given year. Money is another problem; our data from CAP Projects around the country indicate that many CAP Projects' operating budget is less than $10,000 per year.

For those reasons, we are careful to use everyone's time wisely. If we are returning to a school where most of the teachers and staff have already been to one of our in-service programs, we agree to a tight 45-minute review. Then we meet with new teachers and staff on an individual or small group basis in order to provide additional information.

Both the parent program and the teacher/staff in-service program should take place no more than a week before the children's workshops begin. The teacher/staff in-service program can be held during a regularly scheduled staff meeting or in-service training day, or a special meeting can be set up. Some CAP Projects have had success in combining teachers and staff from several different schools that are scheduled to have CAP. This is a bit difficult because of the timing. We do not want much time to pass between the adult in-service programs and the children's workshops. But some projects have then sent CAP teams into several schools during the same week (see Chapter 8, "Creating, Implementing, and Running a CAP Project").

We want as many school staff in attendance as possible. School secretaries, counselors, cafeteria workers, janitors, and bus drivers should all be invited. These personnel are often "trusted adults" to the children they come in contact with, and their participation further broadens children's support systems. If it is not possible for them to attend the teacher/staff in-service program, we encourage the school administration to invite them to the parent program. If teachers must miss the staff meeting, they should also be encouraged to attend the parent program.

> At one school the principal was so committed to his staff and to prevention programming that he personally supervised an assembly for the children while staff attended the teacher/staff in-service training. At another school the principal showed a movie for students so that all teachers would be free to participate. These actions sent a message to the entire school community that prevention was important.

Community Education

Since we believe that educating adults is so important, we also conduct adult presentations outside the school community whenever asked. Speaking engagements at churches, settlement houses, parent support groups, volunteer organizations, and business brown-bag luncheons, as well as radio and television interviews, provide many opportunities to reach parents and teachers. We also send information about child abuse and its prevention to hundreds of adults annually in our local community. In these ways we try to reach not only the greater community, but also the parents we've missed at parent presentations.

But less time with teachers and parents has negative implications for our work. Our empowerment model is based on increasing information to the adult community, which lessens children's isolation. Children, particularly those who suffer abuse, need supportive adults to help them safeguard their rights to feel safe, strong, and free. When we fail at educating the adult community, we can't help but undermine the effectiveness of our project's work. We urge you not to settle for reduced adult participation.

We hope you will find your own creative ways to ensure that adults are educated about abuse and its prevention, and can therefore assist children in this endeavor.

The goals of both the parent and the teacher/staff workshops are to:

- Educate adults about the problem of child abuse
- Educate adults about the importance of empowering children in many areas of their lives
- Develop an effective support system for children
- Provide skills and resources to adults that will assist them in helping children
- Enhance both parents' and teachers' roles in abuse prevention
- Provide information about child abuse reporting laws

Logistics and Program Content

Take care of scheduling the children's workshops in the teacher/staff in-service program unless the principal wants to handle this independently. We want teachers to schedule workshops at their convenience, but not in place of art, gym, or music. At the same time we have a need to set up workshops back-to-back each day until we have completed all classrooms in the school. We balance both needs, and allow teachers to select times within certain boundaries for their individual classroom workshop. (See "Children's Workshop Sign-Up Sheet" in Appendix B.)

Since teachers also participate in the last role-play, illustrating the part of a trusted adult, we also enlist their support during the teacher/staff in-service program. We carefully review their role and the script and ask them to decide whether they can participate. No classroom teacher who feels that he or she cannot provide support to a child in crisis should participate in this role-play. It has been our experience that most teachers want to participate, both in the role-play and in helping children. However, on rare occasions and for a variety of reasons, a teacher may not want to take an active role. In this case, we enlist the help of the school counselor, homeroom mother, or other familiar adult in the school.

Materials Needed for Adult Presentations

Children's Workshop Sign-Up Sheet (see Appendix B)

Handouts (see Appendix A)

Defining Abuse and Neglect

Myths and Facts About Child Abuse

Prevention of Abuse: Theory of Vulnerability

Research on the CAP Elementary Model

Clues to Possible Victimization

Talking with a Child

Responding to Abuse or Neglect

Reporting: Rights and Responsibilities (specific to your area)

Optional: Parenting to Prevent Abuse (for parent program), available from our office.

Adult Questionnaire (see Appendix B)

Blackboard or flip chart

Optional: Agenda for your presentation

Shared Components of the Adult Workshops

1. **Introductions, History, and Goals:** In the opening few minutes, introduce yourself and the Child Assault Prevention Project. You should provide information about CAP Projects' shared history and then discuss your project's individual history in your community. Provide an agenda and outline the goals of your presentation.

2. **Overview of Child Abuse:** Share general definitions of the different types of child abuse, provide statistics about the scope of the problem, and examine the common myths associated with child abuse. Special emphasis is placed on child sexual assault, since the very nature of the problem encourages secrecy and misinformation.

3. **Empowerment, Feminism, and Community:** The theory we use is based on an empowerment model with feminist roots and community involvement. Carefully describe the traditional forms of prevention and the CAP analysis that is the foundation of the children's workshop.

4. **Description of the Children's Workshop:** Adults should leave your presentation with a clear understanding of what we actually do with children, the language we use, and the strategies that are

taught. You can either provide a verbal overview or use the CAP videotape *Safe, Strong, and Free,* available from our office. Using the handout titled "Research on the CAP Elementary Model" you can also briefly describe CAP's effectiveness with elementary students as documented in this research summary.

5. **Identifying Children Who May Have Been Abused:** Using the handout that lists common indicators of abuse, review characteristics of children in crisis.

6. **Crisis Intervention:** During this part of the presentation, provide information to both parents and teachers about how to help a child who has been abused or who may have other problems that need intervention.

7. **Legal Rights, Responsibilities, and Resources:** In order to help children obtain intervention every parent and school staff member must have accurate information about reporting abuse. You will also want to provide community resources that can assist families and school staff.

When you are conducting the parent program, your next topic should be "talking to your child about prevention." Talk with parents about the need for open and honest communication and techniques for parent/child discussions about safety. During this discussion you can pass out copies of the booklet *Parenting to Prevent Abuse,* available from our office. This will give parents additional information about how to discuss prevention with children.

In the teacher/staff in-service program, your next topic should be scheduling the children's workshops. At the end of each presentation, make yourself available for personal discussions.

The adult presentations can be conducted by one or two facilitators. Using two facilitators allows the audience to hear from two individuals and allows you to demonstrate actual role-plays for the group, if you choose not to show the video. It also helps when answering questions from the audience, since a cofacilitator can help you if you stumble. Our recent experience, however, forces us to conclude that sending two facilitators is not only more expensive, it is sometimes just plain impossible. Therefore, the adult in-service program sample script is written as though only one presenter is available. When you facilitate the adult workshop alone, we heartily recommend that you use the videotape *Safe, Strong, and Free* (available from our office), rather than verbally describe the children's workshop. Demonstrating a role-play is difficult (but possible!) if you are alone.

Conducting the Adult Workshops

Introduction

Good afternoon. I'd like to welcome you to our Child Assault Prevention, or CAP, Project (teacher/staff or parent) workshop. My name is _____, and I'm (describe your role, e.g., coordinator) for the Child Assault Prevention Project of _____ County. This workshop today is one of three components of the CAP Project. We will also be conducting a (teacher/staff or parent) workshop and classroom-by-classroom workshops for grades K–6.

We will be describing the CAP Project, as well as providing you with some basic information on the issue of child abuse — how often it happens, to whom, who the offenders are, how to recognize an abused child, how to report abuse, how to talk to a child who discloses abuse, and finally, some local resources you might want to have on hand if the need to refer someone ever arises. We welcome you and encourage you to ask questions, to increase your knowledge about protecting children, and to join with us in the belief that prevention education is the most effective way to combat child abuse.

Before we look at the issues I just mentioned, let me take a moment to explain the CAP Project to you. CAP has been implemented here in _____ since (founding year) and has been offered to more than _____ children and _____ parents and teachers.

The original CAP Project began in Columbus, Ohio, in 1978. In that community a second grader was raped. The parents of other children in that school began to notice their children exhibiting behaviors that children typically demonstrate when they are fearful — bed-wetting, nightmares, fear of being alone. In an effort to help the children feel less vulnerable and more empowered, parents asked the local Women Against Rape organization in Columbus to help. Since that time, the curriculum has been used in 36 states, as well as in eight other countries. It has been translated into seven languages, including American Sign Language (ASL). It has been described as "one of the most comprehensive and innovative prevention programs in the world today."

The key to success lies in its foundation — its basic philosophy of empowerment and positive reinforcement for children.

Child abuse is a very difficult subject to discuss. As people who care about children, we have a lot of fears. For women in the audience, these fears are linked to our own fear of being attacked, a fear we live with every day. No matter who we are, the thought of a child being abused, molested, or raped ties a knot in our stomach.

We know, just by the statistics on rape, that there are probably a number of women here today who have been raped as adults. We also know that there are probably men and women in the audience who were assaulted as children. For each of you, this conversation may be particularly difficult. We want to be sensitive to survivors of assault, but at the same time we need to discuss this subject matter with some candor. We want to let you know that if the discussion here today raises some feelings that you would like to talk about, we'll be available after our presentation to talk with you privately. Or, you may want to contact (provide resource/crisis line number) and talk to someone over the phone when you get home.

Sexual Assault and Prevention

When the CAP program was in its developmental stages, the originators asked themselves what would constitute a successful approach to the issue. They saw that in order to do effective prevention work in any area, the first thing that we have to understand is how something happens. If you don't clearly understand how something takes place, you are less able to prevent it.

They decided to look at their own efforts to prevent the rape of adult women. One of the main goals of their program was to provide the community with accurate information about rape, to dispel the myths. Let me explain what I mean.

It used to be believed (and maybe in some places it still is) that women who were raped were young women, assaulted in dark alleys at 3:00 in the morning, wearing a halter top and short skirt. It was widely believed that the victims provoked the rape by their actions and dress. The rapists were thought to be men of color who had just gotten out of jail and were overcome by lust.

For years, most of us believed all or parts of these kinds of stories. For years, it was situations like these that women prepared themselves to avoid. But the reality of the sexual assault of women is far different from this scene. Organizations such as the Columbus-based Women Against Rape tried to prepare women for the reality of assault.

They taught community women the truth — that all women of all ages are vulnerable to rape. Women dressed in construction clothes, waitress uniforms, and prom gowns have been victims. Statistics show that when black men rape, they tend to rape black women, whereas Hispanic men rape Hispanic women, and white men rape white women. Most important, we learned that in 50–60 percent of cases, women are assaulted by someone they know, often in their own home or another familiar setting. Finally, Women Against Rape showed that sexual assault has nothing to do with lust but is an issue of power: The assaulter wants control over another person.

You may be wondering how all this relates to us here today. Simply put, the folks doing rape prevention work discovered early that teaching women the realities of assault — not the myths — was one effective way to decrease their vulnerability to assault.

Child Assault and Prevention

In designing the program we are presenting to you today, the same philosophies were put into effect. We should teach children the reality of how assaults happen; only then can they be prepared and comfortable in dealing with them. In 1978 that kind of thinking was revolutionary. Today it has become the foundation of any effective prevention program.

Let's talk now about assaults on children, and you will see how we have established the same myths and inaccurate pictures of how children are assaulted.

Most people have believed for years that a typical molestation scene looks like this: a pig-tailed eight-year-old girl is skipping home from school one day when she is approached by a stranger — a dirty old man in a raincoat, with a beat-up old car. He offers the little girl candy, or money, or a puppy, whisks her away behind the school, and assaults her.

In reality, boys are assaulted as well as girls. Conservatively, national studies suggest that at least one in four girls and one in six to nine boys will be sexually assaulted before they reach the age of 18. The offender is a stranger only 15 percent of the time. Most studies suggest that the child knows the offender in 85 percent of cases.

The similarities between adult and child sexual assault are alarming. But these very similarities formed the cornerstone of the CAP Project. CAP is based on teaching children the realities of assault so that they can be better prepared to recognize and deal with potentially dangerous situations. Whether those situations are sexual assaults, physical abuse, or bully situations on the playground, the philosophy of CAP is to help children be less vulnerable.

Child Abuse

Let's define child abuse so we all know what we're talking about. Child abuse is any nonaccidental injury to a child. There are four different types of abuse.

First, there is *physical abuse,* or causing physical harm to a child's body by hitting, burning, punching, striking with objects, kicking, throwing, or otherwise injuring a child. More than _____ children are physically abused in the United States annually. Here in _____ County there were _____ cases reported last year. (Provide some local statistics, which you can obtain from your children's protective services office.)

The second type of abuse is *neglect,* which is the intentional failure to provide adequate food, appropriate clothing, and safe housing to children, as well as failing to obtain medical assistance, failing to supervise a child adequately, or failing to provide an education. Neglect is often confused with poverty, a family's financial inability to provide for a child. However, poor families are usually not *intentionally* neglecting their child or children. (Provide local statistics on neglect cases.)

Emotional maltreatment is the third type of abuse. Emotional maltreatment is the presence (or absence) of behaviors and languages, the result of which interferes with a child's emotional development. Constant belittling, criticizing, or threatening a child are forms of emotional abuse if they happen consistently. The absence of praise, love, and affection is also harmful to a child and constitutes emotional maltreatment.

All of us lose our tempers from time to time; we are impatient or irritable, and snap at our family members, including our children. Emotional maltreatment is different from the occasional outburst that we later regret. Emotional maltreatment is consistent denigration of the child or consistent absence of expressions of love and concern. Self-esteem is established early in life by feeling valued and cared for. The absence of these feelings prohibits a child from developing normally and becoming emotionally healthy. Only 80,000 cases of emotional abuse were reported nationwide in 1986, but experts in the field agree there are significantly more cases that go unreported.

Sexual abuse is the fourth type of abuse. Reports have increased as we have made this subject more public over the last decade. More than _____ children are sexually abused annually. In this county there were _____ reports of sexual abuse in 19___ (latest year for which statistics are available).

Traditional Prevention Strategies

Now let's talk about prevention. Traditionally we have used two different strategies to prevent assault.

Each traditional method tried to control someone's behavior. The first, prosecution, tried to control the behavior of the offender. It operates on the assumption that if we take all the rapists and child molesters in the world, lock them up, and throw away the key, that's the end of the problem. Now, please don't misunderstand what I am saying here. Prosecution certainly has its place, but it is not a primary prevention method. Why not? For a number of reasons: First of all, it is an after-the-fact process. It occurs only *after* a child (or many children) has been assaulted and the offender has been caught and successfully prosecuted. It does not make children feel secure if you send them out the door, saying, "Don't worry, honey, if anyone bothers you on the way home from school, we'll prosecute him."

The second traditional approach is to control the behavior of potential victims. We call this *avoidance,* and those of us who are women have been raised on this one. Typical advice to adults is: "Don't take your garbage out after 9:00 at night. Always look in the back seat before you get in your car. Always have your key out as you approach your front door. Don't ever answer your door after a certain hour." But the list goes on and on. There are hundreds of reasons why, if you are assaulted, it is your fault, because you have failed to avoid the situation.

If you are a child, avoidance sounds like this: "Don't ever ride your bike in the park. Never give a stranger directions. Always travel with a friend."

Although we might have given advice like this at some point to our friends or our children, it should not constitute the primary prevention information that we as parents and teachers give to children. Not only is avoidance not effective or positive for children, it may even be dangerous. Children who have been raised with avoidance, and who then find themselves in a dangerous situation, have no strategies, resources, or skills to deal with what is happening. This kind of thinking prevents us from having healthy, mobile, independent children. It attaches blame not to the offender, but to the child.

One of our CAP Projects tells the story of a small boy who was assaulted in a local park. He had refused to tell anyone because, as he said, "I shouldn't have been in the park. I'm not allowed to go there."

In addition to placing blame on the child, avoidance also carries with it another major drawback: It creates fear. One child in a CAP workshop described a stranger as "someone who cuts you up and puts you in the trunk of his car." Avoidance creates paranoia. Children need positive, encouraging, and empowering information that can make them feel confident in themselves, their families, and those around them.

Another problem with avoidance techniques is that they fail to address the disquieting fact that most children know their assailants. Avoidance techniques address stranger-danger, not abuse by an adult the child knows and trusts.

Factors in Children's Vulnerability

The originators of CAP decided that neither prosecution nor avoidance had been effective methods of prevention. They decided to look at the problem from another perspective: vulnerability. Why is it that children are vulnerable to abuse? How can we, as teachers, parents, and others who care for and about children, help reduce their vulnerability? What they discovered in 1978 is still the primary foundation of CAP in the 1990s. Children are vulnerable because they lack information and empowerment, and because they are isolated from sources of help. (Write on the board or flip chart:)

1. Lack of information
2. Powerlessness and dependency
3. Isolation

Let's look at this approach as it applies to prevention.

Lack of Information

Sometimes, as teachers and parents, we are afraid we might frighten or confuse children, and so we limit the information we give to them. We need to remember that information about anything makes us less vulnerable and less fearful of that issue or object.

In order to teach children to protect themselves it is not necessary to frighten them. For instance, when we teach children to cross the street, we don't do it by taking them to a street corner, pointing at an oncoming truck, and saying, "If you cross now, that truck will hit you. You will have all your bones broken, there will be blood everywhere, and your head will be cracked open." Rather, we focus on what the child can do to stay safe. We explain what traffic lights do and how cars respond to them. Then we explain the importance of looking around to make sure the cars have stopped. With that positive and empowering information, even a small child can face a potentially dangerous, life-threatening situation with little or no stress or fear. That's what we encourage in our children's workshops — positive strategies that encourage strength and the power to prevent victimization.

Many people are concerned that children will be unduly frightened if we talk with them about abuse. It is very important, in order to avoid frightening children, to focus on what they *can* do. When we teach children to cross the street we focus on the knowledge and skills they need to do it safely. The same is true in abuse prevention. We focus on what a child can do, not on the danger itself.

Furthermore, CAP has been extensively evaluated to determine whether children feel more fearful after our presentations. The results of those evaluations reveal that both children and parents feel less anxious following CAP and that children do not become afraid of legitimately concerned adults. In many cases, parents report other positive outcomes, such as increased parent/child communication. (Pass out "Research on the CAP Elementary Model" handout; see Appendix A.)

Powerlessness and Dependency

In addition to providing more information for our children, we must also empower them to use that information. I'm not talking here about the right to stay up after 11:00 or the right to refuse to eat their green beans. I'm talking about the right to be *safe*. Children need to know that adult authority must never be unqualified — that there are times when children's rights supersede adult authority. They need to recognize those times and have the strategies to deal with them. We often say, "Do whatever the baby-sitter (or teacher or neighbor) tells you." Then if a baby-sitter says, "We are going to play a secret game," the child may believe that he or she must obey. Children need to know that they have the right to say "no" to an adult who tries to hurt them, confuse them, or frighten them.

Another way in which children are vulnerable is their dependence on adults. Parents are acutely aware of children's dependence for food, shelter, clothing, education, moral development, and protection. Ironically, children are dependent on the same group of people who might abuse them. Prevention must seek strategies that empower children. We use the concept of rights (to be safe, strong, and free) to explain how assault happens. If children understand that they have the right to say "no," to determine how their bodies can be touched, and to get assistance in keeping these rights, we are empowering them to stop assault. Once children understand the notion of rights, CAP teaches assertive skills so that they can defend these rights and protect themselves in a dangerous situation.

Isolation

The last way that children are vulnerable to assault is their isolation from each other and from support in the community. Although we don't often think of children as being isolated from each other, in fact, children see each other only as playmates, and not as allies who might be able to help them when they need it. Recognizing their own powerlessness, children rarely seek help from other children. CAP emphasizes peer support, offering children opportunities to practice being friends to other children who need assistance.

Children are also isolated within the community. Their access to resources is through adults within the family. A child does not often call the rape crisis center for help, nor do children go to the police station to press charges. If the adults in a child's life are uninvolved or abusive, the child is left without support.

CAP helps children identify adults within the community to whom they could go if they needed help. To reduce children's isolation within the family, the community must share responsibility for the safety of all children.

For this reason the CAP program consists of both adult and children's workshops. As members of the community, you must be prepared to help a child in crisis.

The prevention strategies that we teach children are designed to reduce their vulnerability to abuse. CAP focuses on three main strategies to help children protect their rights: self-assertion (standing up for yourself); peer support (standing up for the rights of others); and telling a trusted adult.

The Children's Workshop

Every classroom in grades K–6 will participate in a one-hour student workshop. The workshop I'm about to describe for you is geared to younger children, grades K–2, since this is the age group parents are most concerned about. Although the material is the same for all children, the language used and the sophistication of the role-plays changes to accommodate older children's experience.

Three facilitators will conduct each workshop. One assumes primary responsibility for leading the discussion, and the other two demonstrate role-plays. Before the workshop begins, leaders spend a few minutes giving children name tags. Then the primary facilitator introduces the leaders, saying, "We're here to talk about things that scare us, and how we can protect ourselves."

Parental permission is required for all children who attend. In addition, all children are given the option of participating in the workshop or attending another class. They are also told they have a right to leave the class at any time if they become uncomfortable. In our experience, children rarely choose to leave the workshop. Indeed, the workshop is a lot of fun for children; after all, how often do three visiting adults come into a class to talk about real-life feelings and experiences children have?

Use the language of the workshop itself, illustrating children's responses by actual examples. To clarify the roles, use your own name as a classroom workshop facilitator.

We open with a discussion of rights. "What does it mean when I say, 'I have rights' or 'You have rights'? What examples can you give me of rights that you have?" Children volunteer examples: "I have the right to ride my bike," "to sleep in my own bed," "to play with my friends."

The leader asks whether children have the right to eat or the right to go to the bathroom. These are two rights that children can easily see are important, the loss of which would cause problems. After pointing out that you have problems when someone takes away one or more of your important rights, we focus on three basic rights that get taken away when someone tries to hurt us: the rights to be safe, strong, and free. We have children define and describe these three rights.

For "safe," some children talk about how safe they feel when they are sleeping in their own bed or sitting on a parent's lap. One little girl described "safe" as "not talking to strange snakes you don't know." Feeling strong is "being able to jump off high buildings," as well as an inner strength — confidence or bravery, like "going to school even when your puppy is sick." Free is "a butterfly," or "the last day of school." One African American third grader told a facilitator that free was "not having to ride in the back of the bus any more." Children give us their own examples based on how they think about these concepts.

The leader then has the other two facilitators act out a story for the class in which a girl loses her rights to be safe, strong, and free.

The "Bully" Role-Play

> Describe the child against child role-play in which Anne has her lunch money stolen by an older girl, or the alternative role-play included in the curriculum.

"Let's pretend that Anne is a girl in your classroom," the leader says. She meets Barb on the way to school. Barb is a bully who takes Anne's lunch money." Following the role-play, the primary facilitator asks the children how Anne must have felt. After the class describes Anne's feelings of being sad, mad, confused, and alone, we conclude that Anne had her rights to feel safe, strong, and free taken away. The class thinks about what Anne could have done. They often fantasize using bionic muscles or laser guns to protect themselves. Unfortunately, they also focus on avoidance techniques. "Pack her lunch" is one common suggestion. But if Anne packs her lunch, she still doesn't feel safe, strong, or free. Her behavior is still controlled by the bully.

Discussion then centers on three prevention strategies: saying "no" and standing up to the bully, asking a friend to walk to school with her, and telling an adult that she trusts. Children agree that going to an adult when they need help is not tattling. Tattling is telling on someone to get him or her in trouble.

We ask the role-players to do this role-play again, using these strategies. Children are eager to play the part of Anne's friends. Frequently, we do this scene several times to give three or four children a chance to practice being assertive and helping each other out.

The "Stranger" Role-Play

> Describe the stranger against child role-play where Tom meets a stranger on the way home from school, or the alternative role-play included in the curriculum.

In the next role-play, children pretend that Barb is a boy in their class named Tom. He's on his way home after school to help his sister with her paper route. Anne pretends that she's an adult stranger Tom has never seen before.

The stranger approaches Tom and asks his name. Tom becomes confused when the stranger says that Tom's mother is in the hospital and has asked him to pick up Tom after school. As Tom protests, the stranger grabs him by the arm and pulls him toward the classroom door.

This scene represents every parent's nightmare. When we ask children what their parents have told them about strangers, we hear all those "don't" messages. They know they must not take candy from a stranger or give out any personal information. What children don't know, however, is what they should do if they are approached.

Following this role-play, we go through the same process of identifying the victim's feelings and the violation of his rights. Then we ask children what Tom could have done differently. They are quick to point out that he shouldn't have given his name nor allowed the stranger to get so close.

We conduct a brief self-defense demonstration that teaches children to run away, to keep distance from a stranger, how to kick to get away, and a special yell to be used as a call for help. Of course, the children can't quite believe that they're going to be allowed to yell in school! We're going to teach you that yell, too, in hopes that you will practice with the children (at home or in the class).

Kids know that when they play outside and make a lot of noise, no one pays attention. We are taught to scream from watching movies: a high-pitched scream that sounds like this: (a shriek).

We say, "The yell we are going to learn today is a self-defense yell that comes from your diaphragm. It sounds like this: (a low, deep, guttural yell)."

Demonstrate the yell. Have the audience practice yelling. The yell is a nice break for the audience and increases their involvement in the presentation.

We say, "Please stand up. On the count of three, I want you to yell as loud as you can. When my hand comes down, I want everyone to stop." After the yell, we may do some quiet focusing exercises, such as deep breathing, to settle children down for discussion.

Once quiet, we ask children what they might do if they were outside and heard Tom yell. Yelling and running to see if Tom's okay or getting help from a neighbor are both good ideas. Getting a description of the stranger for the police is the next step. The role-player who played the stranger left the room following the skit. Children are then asked to describe him or her. For workshop leaders, this can be a very humbling experience, since children are quick to point out the extra pounds and wrinkles!

Then we redo this role-play. Now Tom knows not to give his name to the stranger and to keep his distance, and when approached, he yells. Meanwhile, we ask a few children from the class to pretend they are playing nearby. When they hear Tom yell, they start yelling and run over to see if Tom's all right. Together, they ask Tom to describe the stranger and go with Tom to his house to talk to his mom and to call the police.

The "Uncle Harry" Role-Play

The third role-play is about safe and unsafe touching. We introduce this scene by saying: "Most of the time when Mom and Dad, or our teacher, or a friend or neighbor touches us, it's a safe touch. Touching is good when it makes us feel relaxed and safe. But sometimes, someone that we know and like might try to touch us in a way that does *not* make us feel safe. In the next story, let's pretend Anne is a girl in your class who is at her Aunt Mary's and Uncle Harry's house because her folks had to go out of town. It's a Saturday, and Anne is watching TV when her aunt comes into the room and says she's going to the grocery for a few minutes. Barb is going to pretend that she's Uncle Harry, who comes downstairs to talk to Anne when Aunt Mary leaves."

Demonstrate the known adult against child role-play. This gives parents and teachers an opportunity to see firsthand the tone and follow-through of role-play.

Children are often very quiet following this role-play. Older children may feel embarrassed. We assure them that it's okay to feel embarrassed, but that we still need to talk about what happened.

Younger children need to have everything clarified so that we are sure that everyone in the class understood exactly what happened. We ask children how Anne felt. After concluding that Anne was scared, we ask whether she wanted to sit close to Uncle Harry or kiss him. We talk about how kisses and hugs need to be mutual, not forced. Children identify with Anne's discomfort.

We then ask children about the secret. We lead children to differentiate between good and bad secrets, such as a surprise birthday party or "when your mom buys your brother a present and you don't tell him what it is." Through this process, children understand that Uncle Harry's secret was a bad secret. We have a right to talk about any secret that frightens us or confuses us, even if we told Uncle Harry we would keep it.

Children know the limits of their credibility. They are well aware that Aunt Mary, or even Mom, may not believe them. We encourage children to keep talking until they find an adult who will believe them, perhaps a teacher. That is why Anne turns to the classroom and asks children what she should do. All the children agree she needs to tell someone else.

The threat of physical violence against their child is a common fear of parents. If Anne stands up to Uncle Harry, will he retaliate by force? Most cases of child sexual abuse do not entail physical force. Other forms of coercion are used. Often the advantages of age, size, and adult authority are enough to gain a child's compliance. The risk is real, however, and we warn children that if Anne is afraid to say "no," she may choose to kiss Uncle Harry now, but she should be sure to tell someone later.

We redo the role-play, asking Anne to stand up for herself, saying, "No, I don't like it." She also leaves the room in order to get away from Uncle Harry. Most important, she must tell an adult she trusts, or more than one, if necessary.

Demonstrate the "successful" Uncle Harry role-play.

This final role-play involves the classroom teacher. Anne approaches the teacher with a friend and asks to speak with her. She says, "Ms. North, do you remember when those people came and talked about our rights to be safe? Well, my Uncle Harry touches me in a way I don't like." We ask the teacher to respond supportively: "Anne, I'm really glad you told me, it must be hard to talk about it. Will you come and talk with me when the class is at recess? I'd like to help."

At this point, children usually applaud their teacher's performance. It is important to make a visual link for children of someone in their community responding to a child's request for help.

The workshop ends with a reiteration of our rights to be safe, strong, and free. We tell children that we are going to the library or other predesignated review location, and anyone who wants to talk about a question or problem can talk to one of us there and we'll try to help him or her find an answer.

The classroom activity following the workshop may determine how many children come to talk with us. If it's recess, we don't get as many children. If the workshop is followed by math, we may get the entire class. Their concerns are about TV programs that they didn't understand, bullies that they can't figure out how to handle, and an occasional abusive situation. When a child tells us about abuse, we work with the child to establish a link with the school to resolve the problem.

A great deal of research has been conducted on the elementary CAP model, and more research is being done every year. We revise our materials when research suggests we can make our workshops more effective.

Briefly, the research so far suggests the following:

- Children have more information and strategies to protect themselves following a CAP workshop than before.
- CAP does not promote emotional or behavioral problems.
- CAP increases communication between adults and children.

At the conclusion of this section, ask for questions.

Recognizing Child Abuse

As parents (or teachers) in this community, you may be someone a child could come to for help. Or you may already be concerned about a particular child.

Pass out "Clues to Possible Victimization" handout (see Appendix A).

This handout is a list of characteristics that may be clues that a child is being abused. Much of the information on this sheet comes from research conducted over the years. These behaviors are recognized as common indicators.

Key Points

- Qualify use of indicators.
- Emphasize that suspect behaviors are extreme, pervasive, and of long duration.
- Elaborate on selected items on handout:
  1. personality extremes
  2. physical symptoms
  3. lying
  4. age-inappropriate behaviors
  5. learning disabilities
  6. acting-out behaviors

By themselves, these characteristics may be perfectly normal. However, when extreme and combined, they may indicate abuse. A child exhibiting new or strange behaviors at home or at school, and over a period of time, is clearly in trouble. You should ask questions to determine the problem. Abuse must be considered as one possible cause of this behavior.

One other word of caution: Although abuse occurs in families of all incomes, poor families, whose lives are open to public scrutiny through social services, are more likely to be discovered in abuse cases than well-to-do families who can afford private physicians, therapists, and other services. Also, educated, middle- and upper-class parents are more likely to be believed if they lie about abuse and the causes of injury.

Let's look at some of the behaviors listed on the handout. Some abused children are extremely withdrawn and fearful. Others may be very outgoing, sometimes to the point of being inappropriately affectionate with strangers. This behavior is often misperceived as "seductive." Remember that children are taught these behaviors and learn to use them to meet their needs for love, affection, and security.

Physical Symptoms

Sexual abuse may be difficult to detect, because the wounds are not always obvious. A venereal disease in a child is always a clue to sexual contact and thus, perhaps, abuse. Urinary infections are rare in children, and can be an indication of sexual abuse. Sometimes children manifest their pain by complaining of stomachaches, hurting "down there," or by vomiting. Such symptoms, after physical ailments have been ruled out, could indicate that a child is under great stress, and they may be clues to abuse.

Activity and Habit Clues

Far too often, abused children become "problem children." Delinquent behavior, stealing, lying, running away, and taking drugs are identified as the problem; CAP believes that these behaviors are symptoms of something troubling a child. If we want to help, punishment is inappropriate. We need to ask, "Why are you doing this?"

Children who lie are sometimes victims of sexual or physical abuse. They need to lie in order to hide the truth. The truth may be so horrible that children fear no one will believe them, and the consequences of telling may be too costly. They may have been told that they will be sent to a foster home or Dad will be put in jail if they reveal the truth.

Children may lie in order to protect themselves. Anne may tell her mother that she doesn't want to go to Uncle Harry's any more because he has rats in his basement. Certain that Mom would not want her to be in this type of danger, Anne anticipates a positive response from her mother. But Mom may know that Uncle Harry doesn't have rats in his basement, so she accuses Anne of lying.

Finally, a child who is being assaulted may have to lie to protect the offender. If a child is told that his or her father will go to jail or that Mom will get a divorce if she finds out, the child may lie to protect the parent. Children need adults to question beyond the obvious when assault is involved.

Responding to Children

When a child tells us that abuse has happened, we need to be able to respond in the best way possible for the child. We may have feelings of grief, guilt, and rage, but our feelings need to be put aside for a while so that we can find out what the child needs. Many of us are unsure of how to handle a delicate situation like this. We want to do what is best for the child, but figuring out what that is may not always be easy.

Pass out "Responding to Abuse or Neglect" (see Appendix A).

This handout explains basic ways to respond to crisis with a child who has been traumatized. We will go over each of the items in the list and talk about why we need to respond the way we do.

Children need a safe, quiet place to discuss the problems they are having. If a child tells you about an assault situation (or another traumatic experience) in a hallway where others are present, or over dinner, find a way to take the child someplace quiet, where others cannot overhear the conversation. If the child wants a friend or sibling to go along for moral support, you will have to determine how this discussion will affect the other child and suggest an alternative, if necessary. In school, find a location where children won't be coming in and out, since distractions or the fear of being overheard might stifle what needs to be said.

Always remain calm when a child is telling you his or her problems. An emotional outburst on your part may discourage the child from telling you everything. Children don't like to upset adults, especially those they care about.

No matter what, believe the child. The child's story may not be chronologically correct, and you may hear parts of the story that don't seem to fit together. The child may not remember everything just as it happened, or he or she may be telling you the least embarrassing parts to see how you deal with them. You may hear more and more details as the child trusts you to hear even more serious aspects of the assault.

Always assess the child's immediate safety needs. If a child is facing danger at home, or on the way home from school, or at the piano teacher's house that afternoon, you may need to find specific options to ensure the safety of the child. Later on, in the reporting section of this discussion, we talk about what to do if the child can't go home because of explicit danger.

When discussing the assault with a child, use the vocabulary the child uses. His or her words may be family terms for private parts, or they may be street language. If you step in with words you feel more comfortable with, the child may not be able to understand the conversation. Your primary concern must be the child's comfort, not your own. If a child doesn't have words for what he or she is trying to describe, and is pointing or making faces to help you understand, you can supply words for the child. But try to keep them simple.

Do not avoid certain areas of the conversation. The child may perceive this and feel that you don't want to hear what he or she has to say. Don't sidestep the issues involved; just be honest and calm in your reactions.

Make sure to validate the child's feelings. We have been through situations where we wondered whether we were crazy for feeling what we felt. Children share this experience, and you need to say that you understand that feelings of anger, fear, sadness, or loneliness are normal.

When children come to us with this type of problem they are trying to keep their rights from being violated. However, children may feel that they are doing something wrong, particularly if the adult told them to keep it a secret. Let the child know that he or she has a right to be safe and that getting help is a good and a brave thing to do.

Find out, specifically, what the child wants you to do. By asking exactly what the child wants, the caring adult has an opportunity to clarify what he or she can do and to show the child what options are available. Be careful not to promise anything you can't deliver. It is possible that a child with difficulties may be sent temporarily (or even permanently) to a foster home. If you promise that the child will never have to leave his or her mom or dad, you may be setting the child up for disappointment later.

Always let the child know what action you will take. If you are going to call the child's parent or protective services, tell the child. This gives him or her the opportunity to tell you problems that may arise if this happens, and it gives you the opportunity to prepare the child for the next series of events. There are certain areas of confidentiality that need to be handled sensitively. For instance, the child may not want to do anything. If this is the case, you need to help the child get to the point emotionally where he or she can accept assistance. If you break the trust and tell someone without letting the child know, then the child may "forget" what he or she told you when interviewed by a caseworker and may believe that adults are not trustworthy.

Rights and Responsibilities

In the United States teachers, principals, school nurses, and other professionals are legally mandated to report suspected child abuse, and they are immune from prosecution.

> Describe how a report is made in your area, provide the telephone number, and discuss the procedure for reporting. Hand out a list of community resources. This list should include places where families can get immediate crisis services, medical assistance, and long-term counseling in your community. Always try to call attention to low-cost services. We list community mental health facilities that operate on a sliding-fee basis. Law enforcement officials should be included on the handout as well, because in most states only the police can remove a child or an offender from the home temporarily without a court order. Present the procedures involved clearly, so that the participants understand the options available to them. Usually, they will discuss the effectiveness of the system. Acknowledge the limitations of the available services and stress the need to advocate for more effective support. Hold a question and answer session at the end of the presentation. Workshop leaders should make themselves available afterward to talk privately with parents or teachers about problems or feelings that may have been generated by the program.

Following are some notes and experiences we've had with parents and teachers in CAP workshops, and in-home and at-school activities parents and teachers can do with children to reinforce our assault prevention strategies.

Classroom teachers are in an excellent position to reinforce the children's workshop through follow-up activities. At the end of the teacher/staff in-service workshop, discuss possible classroom follow-up activities.

Tips for Adult Workshops

Parents' Role in Prevention

The three most important things to tell parents at the workshop are:

- Be available to talk with your children about scary subjects,
- Believe them, and
- Work with them to build confidence and positive self-image.

Honest communication between children and adults is perhaps the most important assault prevention strategy. Unconsciously, parents often convey messages to their children about topics that they do not feel comfortable talking about. Subjects such as sex and violence are particularly hard for parents to discuss with children. This discomfort is conveyed in subtle ways; children grasp intuitively that these subjects are not open for discussion. A child's decision to tell a trusted adult about abuse must be met with honesty, support, and belief. A child who senses his or her mother's discomfort about sex will be reluctant to ask for help when Uncle Tony gets "weird"; he or she knows that Mom can't handle the subject. However, if parents admit the stress they feel about the subject, acknowledge that it's their problem, and make it clear that they really do want their children to talk with them about anything, the children will be more likely to approach them for help. Beyond a crisis situation, open communication offers parents an atmosphere that promotes caring, respect, and trust as the foundation for a healthy relationship with children.

Instilling confidence and feelings of self-worth in children are critical aspects of assault prevention. Unintentionally, parents can undermine these qualities. Letting children know they are capable decision makers and problem solvers is crucial to children's ability to respond effectively in a crisis. This means that parents must believe in the child's ability to handle a dangerous situation. Parents must convey this belief through their actions as well as their words, because actions can sometimes belie their words.

For example, parents in one community, responding to the rape and murder of an eight-year-old girl, started carpools to get their children to school safely. Although this measure may have been an effective precaution to take immediately after the crisis, over a longer time it conveyed a second message to the children. It said, "Not only are we afraid for your safety, but we don't believe you could take care of yourselves if you were faced with a dangerous situation." Eight months later, many of the children in this community were still anxious and afraid.

Obviously, such prevention strategies reinforce children's feelings of helplessness and dependence. When we take precautions that limit children's mobility, we must provide them with information about the situation, as well as a reason for our actions that does not deny their capabilities. A parent may say, for instance, "We are going to ride in carpools for a while because of what happened. However, I know if you met up with a dangerous situation, you could handle it well. Let's go over what you would do again, so we all feel safer."

Acting in the Community's Interest

Encouraging adults to confront danger in their communities is the final issue we touch on in this section. Parents will act to protect their own children, but hesitate to act when someone else's children are involved. The CAP Project tries to build parental confidence by encouraging adults to take actions necessary to protect all the children in a community. This may mean calling the police when they see a man hanging around the playground, or asking a neighbor to go with them to confront a stranger. These are simple but effective ways to let offenders know that a community is watchful. However, more complex action may sometimes be necessary. This is an example of what one group of concerned mothers did.

> A mother of a 14-year-old became concerned about a men's gym located up the street from her home when her daughter reported that members of the gym made offensive comments as she and her friends passed by on their way home from school. The mother told her daughter to walk on the other side of the street or to ignore the situation. But since the bus dropped them off on that side of the street, crossing seemed foolish to the young girl.
>
> When the owner of the gym threw a carton of milk at the child, the mother knew that action needed to be taken. She made an appointment with the gym owner, and had seven other women go with her. The mother explained the problem to the gym owner and demanded that it stop immediately. She further stated, with support from the group, what actions she would take if children were harassed again.
>
> First, she would contact other businesses on the block and let them know that she could no longer shop there because of the harassment her daughter and other children faced. She stated that she would also call the city bus system and ask that the bus stop in front of the gym be moved. Finally, she told the owner that she would contact the media and tell her story so that others in the community could be aware.
>
> The gym owner turned pale and apologized profusely, promising that his members would not say another word to the children, or he would cancel their membership. No more incidents or harassment have been reported!

In-Home Prevention Activities

Conclude the parent program by discussing "Suggestions for In-Home Activities" (see Appendix A). Because of the limitations of a one-hour children's workshop, emphasize the need for parents to reinforce assault prevention messages with their children at home. Rarely do parents need to bring up the subject of abuse out of nowhere in order to discuss these issues with their children; opportunities just need to be recognized. TV programs, for example, contain abundant material that parents can use to initiate conversations with children about prevention.

> Optional: Hand out the *Parenting to Prevent Abuse* booklet, which can be ordered from our office.

Commonly Asked Questions in the Adult Workshops

Q: What made you take an interest in this type of work? Were you abused as a child, or raped as an adult?

A: We believe that nearly everyone has had some type of experience that relates to the experience of assault. Harassment on the street or on the job is an example that almost every woman has had to deal with. Men may have to think about their childhood. But we all have felt vulnerable when our rights to be respected and treated as a whole person were violated.

Q: Will this workshop frighten, rather than educate, children? Do children have nightmares following the classroom workshop?

A: Naturally, parents worry that children will become fearful if they are made aware of the danger they face. However, one of the things we have found is that children are already very aware of assault. Watching television and overhearing adults discuss sensitive topics has exposed them to much more violence than they are ever likely to face in their lifetimes. The fear is already there; unfortunately, the skill to handle the fear is not. Just as teaching children to cross the street safely or to get out of a burning building gives them life skills, assault prevention makes children feel safer and more confident. Children have fun and leave the workshop feeling stronger. The evaluations that have been conducted on CAP reveal this very clearly.

Q: Do women sexually assault children?

A: Yes, women *do* assault children, and when this happens we need to treat it as seriously as we treat other types of assault. Recent research in the field suggests that men commit 95 percent of assaults against female children and 80 percent of assaults against male children. One reason for this is that boys and men often learn that aggression is an acceptable way to feel powerful.

Q: Aren't men who assault male children homosexuals?

A: No. The vast majority of same-sex offenders identify themselves as heterosexual, not as homosexual. This includes both incest offenders who assault their sons and molesters who assault unrelated boys. Many offenders are married or have an active heterosexual sex life. Often, people who are afraid of a gay lifestyle or who dislike gay people will blame gay men for child molestation. This attitude encourages people to believe that child abuse is a "homosexual problem." However, in one study, 92 percent of reported child abuse cases involved heterosexual offenders. Offenders violate children. As Linda Sanford says, "A child molester is neither heterosexual nor homosexual, he is a child molester."

Q: If children are taught to maintain their rights, specifically the right to say "no" to an adult, doesn't this undermine parents' (or teachers') authority?

A: Children are capable of differentiating between saying "no" to bedtime and saying "no" to a frightening adult. Blind obedience ("Now, you do whatever the baby-sitter says") is at best undesirable, and at worst downright dangerous! Research on our project clearly shows that children do not refuse to obey adults following the workshop.

Q: I want my children to trust people, especially relatives and close friends. My children are spontaneously affectionate and I'm afraid they will lose that trait if we talk to them about assault.

A: Children choose whom they will be affectionate with, based on their trust of the adult. This does not change because children learn that someone they know may try to touch them in a bad way; it simply gives them the right and the skill to stop that type of touching. Children who have control over how and by whom their bodies can be touched will still be comfortable returning truly affectionate behavior.

Q: Don't children fantasize a lot? How do we know that children aren't lying about a supposed assault?

A: Researchers have concluded that children rarely lie about abuse. For very young children who lack experience, making up a believable story about assault is impossible. Because the media abounds with images of children as liars, it is easy to see why children lack credibility. Older children lie to get out of trouble, not into it.

  Children who are known as liars may be children who have tried to compensate for the behavior of an assaulter or to protect themselves. Often these children are the most likely to be denied treatment. It is up to us, as adults, to ask appropriate questions in a manner sensitive enough to elicit the truth to validate the child's claim.

Q: When I think about talking to my children about sexual assault, I don't know what language to use. How can I describe a potentially dangerous situation without being graphic?

A: Talking about children's rights is a sensitive, nonthreatening introduction to the subject of assault. For the most part, we have found that graphic, highly descriptive language is unnecessary. "A touch that is confusing or frightens you" is a calm yet accurate way to discuss assault. Think of assault as another safety issue, like crossing the street or holding a fire drill. We don't use graphic language to describe these dangers, and we don't need to do so when we discuss assault. The *Parenting to Prevent Abuse* booklet can help you too.

Q: If children fight back, even verbally, won't this make the assaulter angry? Perhaps the children may come to greater harm.

A: Children are taught basic self-defense techniques to enable them to get out of highly dangerous situations, where the chance of their being abducted and seriously hurt is great. Self-defense is not "fighting until no one is left standing." Obviously, a child could never succeed! The techniques we use during the stranger role-play are designed to be used in the first few seconds of an assault. The element of surprise is on the child's side. Using prevention techniques that are not based on height, weight, or strength gives children the ability, with a couple of specific maneuvers, to get free, yell, and run away to safety.

Q: Are we seeing an increase in child sexual assault because it is happening more often, or are people just beginning to report it more?

A: It's difficult to know whether child sexual assault is more common now or whether people are just more likely to report it. Child assault is a topic that is being discussed more in general, and so people feel more comfortable discussing it. There are also more services available for survivors: hotlines, support groups, and shelters. But we do believe that more children are being sexually assaulted each year. Recent movies, television shows, and pornographic literature depict children as seductive. Offenders, therefore, become desensitized to children's feelings and children's rights. Indeed, the National Center on Child Abuse and Neglect estimates conservatively that 100,000 to 500,000 children are sexually assaulted annually, and some studies state that 50 percent to 80 percent of all sexual assaults go unreported. Simply put, we don't know the extent of the problem yet, but even conservative estimates indicate it is epidemic.

Q: Do the workshops change for older children?

A: The general content of the workshop is the same for each grade. However, sixth graders would be bored in a kindergarten or first-grade workshop. This is because we explain ideas more and repeat ourselves for younger children. We ask older children open-ended questions such as "What could you do if this happened to you?" Older children's questions to us are also different because of their life experiences. They ask, for example, "Should I answer the telephone if I am baby-sitting?" Younger children need the same type of information, but it needs to be delivered at a slower pace and with a vocabulary that they will understand.

Q: What can men do about assault? I really feel bad hearing all this information, and I want to do my part to stop assault of women and children.

A: We believe men can help by challenging accepted male behavior. Confronting a man at a party who tells a rape joke or supporting a women who stands up to street harassment are difficult and brave responses for conscientious men, but they need to happen. Professionally, men need to assume much of the responsibility for counseling sex offenders. There are very few effective counseling and treatment programs for offenders. We realize that dealing with assaulters, pedophiles, and incest fathers is a frightening task. However, it is work that desperately needs to be done by men who care about the quality of life for women and children. We also need more men to help us provide workshops, publicize our program, fundraise, and help in other ways. If you are interested, please see me after we are done tonight.

Q: We have two classrooms of "slow learners." Should they get the workshops?

A: Unequivocally, yes. Studies show that children who have been assaulted often have problems in classroom achievement. Some children branded as "slow learners" could be victims of unreported and untreated child sexual assault. In addition, children who are separated from their peers and labeled often have to deal with older children who bully them. Children with learning problems should receive the workshop to help them deal with their special vulnerability.

References

1. David Finkelhor, *Child Sexual Abuse: New Theory and Research* (New York: Free Press, 1984).

7
Responding to Children

Talk Time

Immediately following the children's workshop, all three facilitators spend time with individual children who wish to talk. This component of CAP, called *talk time* or *review time,* takes about 30 minutes. Teachers release children three at a time, until every child who so desires has had an opportunity to visit with a facilitator.

If math immediately follows a CAP classroom workshop, it is not unusual to have 90 percent of the classroom come to the talk time location! Even when recess follows the workshop, we usually talk individually with more than half the students. Children come for a variety of reasons, based on their age, their energy level, their interest in the topic, and their concerns. After 12 years of experience, we believe that most children see us as people they can talk with about any scary situation. Thus, we have talked with children about television programs, divorce, illness in the family, spousal battering, drug and alcohol use and abuse, bullies, sibling rivalry, spanking, strangers, Halloween, and just about any other subject you can think of that a child might consider frightening.

We also talk with children who just liked us and want to thank us for coming to their classroom. "That was fun, when are you coming again?" is a common reaction. Some children also come just to share facts about their lives: "I have a puppy named Shrimp," or "My mom and dad ride bicycles." The CAP facilitator just smiles and thanks the child for sharing, and he or she runs back to the classroom giggling. Some children ask facilitators, "How did you get this job?" or "How do I get a job like this when I grow up?" A brief but honest response is all that's needed. Remember that although talk time can be hard, it is often also a fun time with children. They appreciate us for our energy and honesty, for our role-playing, and for letting them yell in school!

Reviewing CAP Concepts

Although children may come with questions of their own, we always try to use talk time to review and reinforce prevention information and skills. Talk time is a continuation of the learning opportunity that allows children to tailor the information and skills to their own situations. When children ask questions about any potentially threatening situation, whether it's a frightening television program or a bully in the neighborhood, we review specific strategies that help children realize their options in that particular situation and more clearly define their rights to be safe, strong, and free.

Identifying the Abused Child

When most of us have a crisis, chances are we reflect it in our behavior. We may eat too much, get a migraine, sleep a lot, or become insomniac; we may be cranky and irritable or teary-eyed and emotional. The behaviors we display may appear unrelated to our problems. But if a friend stops to listen, he or she can easily understand that the stress, confusion, or fear we are experiencing is manifesting itself in our bodies and our behavior.

Children react to crisis in much the same way. When faced with a problem they can't seem to solve, or when worried and confused, children's bodies and behaviors often display indications that they are suffering.

Researchers and clinicians in the field of child abuse have identified some common key indicators of abuse. Learning to recognize these indicators makes us better able to help children. For this reason, we always provide information about these indicators to parents and teachers during the adult training. A list of common characteristics of children who have been abused is located in Appendix A of this manual so that you may easily reproduce it for the adult presentations.

Adults often find it hard to believe that children who suffer from abuse would not tell someone. We expect that a hurt or frightened child would reach out for help. But Dr. Roland Summit, a physician who has worked with thousands of child victims of abuse, reports in his article "The Child Sexual Abuse Accommodation Syndrome" that the typical child does not tell anyone about abuse.[1] Therefore, we must learn to perceive what is unspoken in children's behavior.

Any time a child is acting in ways that seem inappropriate, the child needs help. If we were simply to follow this belief, we would help children with many life situations. Divorce, illness in the family, moving to a new town, having a pet die, or seeing something frightening on television or at school are all problems that children may not completely understand. Fred Rogers of *Mr. Rogers' Neighborhood* says, "What's mentionable is manageable," meaning that if we take the time to listen to children and talk to them about the confusing things that go on in their world, we could help them to cope more effectively and healthfully.

Nearly every professional in the field of child abuse agrees that children rarely lie about sexual abuse. This does not mean that children *never* lie about sexual abuse but it does encourage us to listen to children carefully. Since, according to Dr. Summit, many adults believe that children who disclose sexual abuse are liars, we must always be careful to stress in adult training sessions the importance of believing children.

As you review the list of common indicators of abuse keep in mind that many of the indicators are natural and normal for nonabused children. Suspicion of child abuse would only be warranted if there were a number of indicators present or if the behaviors were extreme. The following clues are not conclusive evidence of child abuse. They should be seen as signals of *possible* victimization, alerting the adult who notices these behaviors to observe carefully.

Clues to Possible Abuse

Remember, child abuse doesn't restrict itself to any particular group of people. Child abuse happens in every neighborhood and within every racial, ethnic, religious, and socioeconomic group.

Many clinicians have discovered that children who have been abused are often

- fearful *or* overly compliant
- withdrawn *or* aggressive
- irritable *or* listless
- affectionless *or* overly affectionate

If you think about these opposites, they clearly make sense since these same characteristics are often reflected in our own behavior when we feel vulnerable. Each of these four sets of opposites reflects extremes; emotionally healthy children fall in the middle of the continuum.

In one CAP workshop a teacher told us about a kindergarten boy who used to hide under the table during free time and recess. He would pull his body into the shape of a ball and rest on his knees and elbows while he sucked both thumbs. He would reluctantly play with other children only if required to do so. The teacher said that most of the day she didn't feel as if he were really in the classroom; he seemed to be a million miles away. After the CAP workshop the child disclosed physical abuse and anal penetration by his father.

In a sixth-grade classroom a 12-year-old girl always wanted to sit next to the role-players. She held their hands and even tried to kiss them, even though the role-players had never met the child before. During the "Uncle Harry" role-play the girl covered her eyes and turned away from the group. After the workshop she disclosed repeated sexual abuse by her father and other men he brought to the house. She had learned that in order to make people like her, she must be physically affectionate with them.

A young boy in a second-grade classroom was, according to the teacher, "a bundle of trouble." She reported that he destroyed other children's artwork, punched other children, and yelled at people (including the teacher) using harsh tones and language. After the workshop he disclosed that his father punched him, destroyed his toys when drunk, and told he was "no good" all the time.

These three cases illustrate the ways in which children internalize abuse and then manifest it in their behaviors. All three teachers reported difficulty with the children, yet none had suspected abuse. In fact, two of the three teachers had labeled the children as problem students, unwilling to listen to adult authority.

Physical Symptoms

When a child is being physically abused, we can often discover the abuse from looking at the child's injuries and by listening to the child's explanation of those injuries. Bruises, burns, scars, welts, lacerations, and broken bones can all be indicators of physical abuse.

When an object is used to hurt a child, it may leave a mark that tells the story. A belt buckle may leave the imprint of the buckle on the child's skin. An immersion burn (from immersion in scalding water) looks distinctive, and markedly different from accidental burns from hot water faucets. A slap often leaves digital bruise marks on a child's neck, arms, or face. Another clue to physical abuse is explanations for the child's injuries that don't seem to make sense.

A three-year-old child was brought to the emergency room with a burn on the palm of his hand. The parents reported that the child had accidently reached up and touched a burner on the stove. But the fingertips on the child's hand were not burned at all. In fact, all four coils of the electric burner were clearly and evenly imprinted on the child's palm, revealing that the child had to have been above the burner to receive such an injury. Furthermore, pressure would had to have been exerted in order to leave such an even burn. The hospital emergency room called children's protective services, since it was impossible to explain the injury as described by the parents.

Symptoms of Sexual Abuse

Sexually transmitted diseases, of course, cannot be obtained from toilet seats or door knobs; they can result *only* from sexual contact. Sexually transmitted diseases should *always* be reported to protective services and the child must always have medical care. Genital warts, syphilis, gonorrhea, chlamydia, and herpes virus infection in the genital area are indicators of sexual abuse.[2] AIDS also can be transmitted through child sexual abuse. Many types of vaginal infections, as well as vaginal or anal sores and bleeding, are indicators of possible sexual abuse. Young children with urinary infections are also possible victims of sexual abuse.

Activity and Habit Clues

When a child is in crisis, behavior can be disturbed and new activities may be undertaken by the child. Nightmares are a common symptom of children suffering from abuse. Although occasional nightmares are normal for any child, frequent nightmares that result in terror can be a sign of physical or sexual abuse — particularly recurring nightmares of being chased, overpowered, and murdered.[3]

Victims of sexual abuse sometimes masturbate compulsively. Masturbation is normal even in young children, but uncontrollable masturbation, masturbation at school or in other public places, or masturbation that appears to be reenacting some activity should be cause for suspicion.

> Before a workshop a first-grade teacher told of a girl in her classroom who masturbated regularly against the floor or on the corners of desks. The child disclosed sexual abuse after the CAP workshop.

Sometimes children "tell" us about abuse only by revealing their fears. A child who is afraid to go to a particular place, or afraid to be with a particular person, should not be forced to do so without further investigation.

> After a fourth-grade workshop a girl disclosed physical and emotional abuse by both her father and her mother. After the abuse was disclosed the teacher informed us that this girl never wanted to go home. She often came to school when she was sick, and when the school tried to send her home she would cry and beg to stay in the nurse's office until she felt better.

Delinquency

Early childhood sexual abuse has been correlated with running away, delinquency, chemical dependency, and prostitution. Some young people run away in order to leave abusive homes. Unfortunately, running away can be an equally dangerous alternative. Many young runaways are forced into prostitution to support themselves, since their work experience and skills are usually limited. Many teen runaways report that prostitution was the only option open to them for money, protection from the dangers of the streets, and continued independence from home.

Substance Abuse

Drug and alcohol use, abuse, and addiction become problems for a sizable number of abuse survivors. Since drugs and alcohol are easily accessible in American society, and since drugs can blur the conscious mind, many young people use them in order to cope with abuse. Although the research to date on the actual number of abusers among survivors is conflicting, all the research indicates that drug and alcohol use is a significant problem.

Age-Inappropriate Behavior

When children behave in ways that seem inappropriate for their age we should try to determine the cause. For instance, victims of sexual abuse often appear to know a lot about sex. Sometimes we conclude, erroneously, that they obtained this knowledge by watching pornographic movies or by observing their parents during sexual intercourse. Children who have been sexually abused do have an age-inappropriate understanding of sexual acts. It is not unusual to hear from teachers that certain children talk about or try to demonstrate certain sexual acts with other children; these children may well be victims of sexual abuse.

> A third-grade boy was repeatedly reported to the principal by his teacher for trying to pull down other children's pants and for making "lewd" comments to other children. After a CAP workshop, this little boy disclosed sexual abuse by his next-door neighbor.

An onset of bed-wetting or thumb-sucking behaviors that a child has left behind and suddenly reverts to is also cause for concern.

Unfortunately, adults sometimes blame children for behaviors that are the result of abuse. Girl victims of sexual abuse are often labeled "promiscuous" or "seductive." But early childhood sexual abuse can desensitize a child to sex.

> Marsha was 17 when she reported childhood sexual abuse by her father. She said that it had been going on for as long as she could remember. Her father would get out a bottle of wine and encourage his wife to drink with him. When his wife had fallen asleep he would come into Marsha's room and molest her. After he tried to penetrate her she reported his behavior to her mother. Marsha was afraid she would become pregnant and this fear was greater than her fear of telling her mother. In counseling Marsha disclosed having had sex with "lots of guys." She indicated that she hated it but that she knew that "guys wouldn't stay with you if you didn't 'put out'."

Educational Concerns

Many children who are abused do poorly in school. They have a lot on their minds and may find it difficult to concentrate. Sometimes children sleep in class because they've been kept awake at night. Other children use academic achievement to cover up the abuse. An adult survivor reports that she got straight A's in school so that everyone would think she was fine. If she got poor grades, she reasoned, someone might realize that something was wrong.

Emotional Indicators

Sexual, physical, and emotional abuse can cause great emotional turmoil. The professional literature clearly indicates that childhood abuse is traumatic and may have lasting negative results if the abuse remains unreported and untreated. This emotional harm can cause depression, even in young children. It can cause phobias, or fears of certain places or people that remind the child of the abuse. Severely traumatized children may lash out at themselves, like the second-grade victim of abuse we met. He repeatedly hurt himself with any sharp instrument he found in school. At one point he carved his initials in his stomach with a blunt pair of scissors. Sometimes children lash out at each other, hurting other children, or injure animals.[4]

Childhood is supposed to be a time when we can learn, in a safe and loving environment, the information and skills we need to be happy and productive adults. But for far too many children, childhood is something to be left behind as soon as possible. It is a time of great terror, confusion, and hurt. Children need our intervention in order to make the passage into adulthood safely. Too many of us ignore their signals for help; we see the children as the problem rather than seeing children with problems.

We cannot romanticize childhood. It is not an easy time for parents or teachers. Children are incredibly active and inquisitive. They demand great patience and tolerance, as well as great love. One of the most important things we do is to remind teachers and parents that children need our help, not our blame or punishments. Abuse is punishment enough without the child then being labeled as bad. We encourage parents and teachers to become familiar with the clues that might signify abuse, but remind them that not every child who displays these signs is suffering from abuse as we know it. Still, a child who displays many of these characteristics is a child who needs attention.

Helping Children in Crisis

As painful as it is to realize, CAP Projects report many cases of abuse to protective services. Each time we enter a classroom we must be aware that there may be children who have experienced or currently are experiencing some type of abuse. Therefore, even though our primary mission is to *prevent* abuse, we must be prepared to help children reassert their rights to be safe, strong, and free.

Disclosures of abuse come to a CAP Project from a variety of sources. Some children disclose abuse during talk time. Sometimes parents approach the CAP presenter before or after the parent program to describe abuse of their son or daughter. Sometimes teachers inform us of possible abuse of a child in their classroom. Because of the work that we do, our own friends, neighbors, and acquaintances often seek us out to discuss a case of child abuse. For this reason it is important that every CAP role-player and primary facilitator be fully trained in crisis intervention skills, the steps involved in reporting child abuse, and resources in the community that can help families in crisis.

Confidentiality

All the information you gain as a result of your work in CAP is confidential. It cannot be shared in any way that jeopardizes confidentiality. Parents, teachers, and children share personal information with you because they trust you; we cannot violate that trust. Many projects encourage parents to facilitate workshops. However, a parent should never work in the same school that his or her child attends. This policy increases trust that confidential information will not be shared.

Understanding Crisis Intervention

Crisis intervention is helping someone who is emotionally and/or physically hurt. Parents do it all the time. A child runs into the house crying because he or she has skinned a knee. The parent calms the child, examines the injury, and decides what action needs to be taken. A child wakes up in the middle of the night from a bad dream. The parent comforts the child, lets the child know that he or she is safe now, and discusses ways to get back to sleep.

Crisis intervention is not therapy or treatment. It is simply identifying the crisis and discussing options for resolving it. Most of us, adults and children alike, rely on our friends when we are in crisis. Although a victim of abuse has special needs, our goals in crisis intervention are the same regardless of the problem: We identify the crisis and discuss options available to the child for getting help and stopping the abuse.

Listening

Crisis intervention requires good listening skills, or *active listening.* Active listening is an "edge-of-your-seat" activity requiring energy and concentration. In active listening, we are listening not just to the words, but to the *whole child:* his or her body, tone of voice, hand gestures, eye contact, and general demeanor. This helps us more clearly understand what the child is telling us. For instance, a child may not say, "I am very frightened," but the child may tell us this in body movement and tone of voice. This helps us comfort the child and affirm the child's feelings, so it is important for us to "hear" the child's fear. In active listening, we acknowledge our own ignorance of what the child is feeling, and listen completely to the child. We try to retrieve as much information as the child is giving out, not just through the words but from all the ways the child communicates.

We also practice a technique called *reflective listening.* This method of listening means that we communicate, or *reflect back* to the child, what we believe we heard in order to make sure we understand. To listen reflectively is to restate in our own words what we believe the person has told us. For example, we might say to a child, "Are you saying that you are afraid to tell your teacher?"

Active and reflective listening help us to realize our obligation to the child to make sure we understand his or her experience. By doing this we offer the child a safe adult to talk to, one who won't misunderstand him or her or misinterpret the situation. Since we each bring our own experiences and feelings to every situation, we have to be careful that we listen to the child's voice and not to our own inner voice.

Crisis intervention demands that we respect children and their experiences. To the best of our ability, we leave our own judgments behind. We try to be truly present for the child.

Comfort

It is very important to remember that when talking to children, it is their comfort we must protect, not our own. Consider this scenario:

> At the request of the parents, a rape crisis counselor met at the hospital a girl who had been molested by a neighbor. The family was still in the emergency room; doctors had not yet examined the child. The counselor found the child sitting between two very upset adults. The expression on the father's face was pure anger, and the mother was sobbing quietly but continuously. The child looked as though her heart would break. Neither parent was comforting the child; both were stuck in their own pain.

As obvious as it might seem that the child's needs are foremost, it may not be easy to disregard our own comfort. Because we must create a safe place for the child to tell us what has happened, we must concentrate solely on helping the child. Sometimes children will fidget nervously while they talk; we can't tell them to sit still. Sometimes children speak very softly, making it difficult to hear. We don't tell them to speak up unless we honestly can't understand. Sometimes children turn away when they are disclosing the scary part; we don't tell them to turn around when speaking because we respect their needs for comfort.

Some children want to be held or touched, and others want distance from the person with whom they are talking. Your active listening techniques will help you to determine these needs. If you reach out to touch a child and he or she withdraws from your hand, do not touch again. On the other hand, if the child seems comforted by the touch, you know you can continue it. You can also ask a child, "Would you like to hold my hand?" or "Would you like to sit closer to me?"

Crisis intervention is for the child. You may be upset by what you are told. Nonetheless, you must put the child's interests and needs before your own. When you leave the child you may need to seek your own friend, who will be concerned only about your comfort, as you discuss your hurt at talking with a child who is in crisis. Although you must at all times guard the confidentiality of the children, you can take comfort from a co-worker or friend. When you ask a friend to listen to your pain, don't disclose any information that could identify the child or family. In this way you can get the care you need to do this work.

Power and Control

When children have been victimized they often feel powerless, helpless, and out of control. Someone is, or was, doing something to them that they can't or couldn't seem to stop. Victimization makes us all, adults and children, feel powerless.

We certainly don't want to magnify or exacerbate those feelings of powerlessness in children. Therefore, when we offer crisis intervention we are careful not to "take over" or to "rescue." There are opportunities in crisis intervention for children to make some choices. If we take these choices away by making decisions for the child, we reinforce feelings of helplessness and powerlessness. If, however, the child decides which actions to take, we restore some feelings of power and control.

One choice children can make is whom they talk to after the children's workshop. They may want to pick the primary facilitator because for their own reasons they liked that person the best. An African American child may want to speak to an African American facilitator; a male child may want to talk to the man on the team. As we discuss later, someone in the school must also know about the child's situation. We can ask the child to choose whom he or she wants to tell at school.

It is true that in abuse cases children don't have many options. Abuse must be reported, and so the parents must find out. Someone the child doesn't know will come and talk with him or her to gain additional information. Even with these foregone conclusions, children still have some choices. We can help them to make the choices, allowing them some small feelings of power and control in an otherwise overwhelming situation.

Steps in Effective Crisis Intervention

Effective crisis intervention helps children feel empowered to help themselves. We use a four-step crisis intervention process. This four-step process can be applied to any type of crisis, not only abuse. The steps may result in children taking all of the action themselves, or may require adult intervention. Since crisis intervention is "identifying the crisis and determining options for action," these steps support that activity. The four steps are:

1. Identify the problem.
2. Examine all possible solutions.
3. Evaluate each alternative.
4. Prepare a realistic plan of action.

Step 1: Identify the Problem

Sometimes children communicate the problem they want to solve immediately and clearly. In this case you can move promptly to step 2. In other cases, however, children sit silently in front of you or talk around the problem. You must clearly understand the problem if you are to help resolve it.

CAP workshop language gives you a vehicle for questioning the child. Begin the conversation with a couple of icebreakers so that both you and the child can establish comfort. "Did you like the workshop?" "What was your favorite part?" "Do you remember your three special rights?" are good openers. Then you can ask, "Is there something you wanted to talk with me about or ask me about?" If the child doesn't start talking more freely, or if you are getting one- or two-word responses, you can ask, "Do you feel safe, strong, and free at school?" "How about at home?" The answers to these questions will help identify concerns the child may have.

After asking questions that would allow the child to describe the problem, you still may not know if there is something with which the child needs help. You can only do what the child allows you to do. It is possible that the child just wanted to see you one more time, and doesn't have a problem with which he or she needs assistance. Of course, the opposite is also true. A child may really need your help but be unable to disclose the problem. It is the child's right to make this choice. We offer the child a safe place where he or she will be truly listened to, but that is all we can do.

As we conclude our talk time with children about whom we have concerns, but who have not disclosed a problem, it is important to remind them that finding a trusted adult is important: "If you did have a problem, whom could you talk with?" By brainstorming with other adults who might help, we increase a child's choices and encourage him or her to seek help.

You never forget some children, not because of what they told you, but because you fear what they didn't tell. Respecting children who believe they cannot talk about their problems is something we live with.

Step 2: Examine All Possible Solutions

When a child describes a problem to us, it is important to know what actions the child has already taken to solve the problem and what other options the child has. Since the majority of children talk to us about problems that are not abuse-related, many children have lots of options for solving their problems with or without adult intervention.

After you have identified the problem that needs attention, find out what actions the child has taken so far. Ask specific questions, such as: "Have you talked with anybody about this?" "What happened when you told your mom and dad?" "Have you asked your sister to leave your things alone?"

Once you have reviewed actions the child has already taken, you and the child must brainstorm other possible solutions, including ones that require adult intervention. "Who else do you think you could tell who might be able to help?" "How about talking to your teacher?" "What if you asked your mom and dad for help with that problem?" "What if you said 'no' to your friend?"

Step 3: Evaluate Each Alternative

Once the child and you have proposed possible actions that could be taken to resolve the problem, each alternative should be evaluated by the child, with your help. "Does that sound like it would help the situation?" "What do you think she would do if you said 'no'?" Listen carefully to the child's responses so that you can understand the fears he or she has about the particular strategy.

If abuse is the problem, you must, at this juncture, tell the child that there is something that you *must* do. "When abuse happens we must get help. Is there someone in the school whom you can tell?" This is one goal we always try to achieve. CAP facilitators are in the school only for a short period of time. It is important to try to get the child a support system of people who can help after we are gone. Therefore, unless the abuse is happening in the school, we always say a version of the following: "I can't help you with this problem alone. Whom in the school would you like to talk with?" We often help children brainstorm supportive adults. "How about your teacher?" "How about the school nurse?" "How about the counselor?" In the majority of cases the child chooses an adult. If the child refuses to choose, then we must choose an adult we believe will help the child. This is difficult but necessary. We have no way of knowing whether the very child we are talking with today will have an injury from abuse tomorrow. It is simply not our place to decide that the child will not have intervention. We try to convey this to the child by acknowledging that we understand he or she doesn't want us to tell anyone, but that we must because we care for his or her safety. "You have the right to be safe, strong, and free, and I must do what I can to help you have that right."

Step 4: Prepare a Realistic Plan of Action

After the child has identified the problem, thought of possible solutions, and talked about the consequences of each action, then he or she decides what to do. The CAP facilitator helps the child clarify the ideas that were previously discussed. "You said that your mom and dad would help you. Do you want to talk with them? When do you think would be a good time to talk with them?" The plan of action should be very specific, with decisions about what to do, when to do it, and how to do it.

The facilitator reviews the plan before the child returns to his or her classroom. "O.K. You said you want to talk with your teacher during recess today about the book you lost. You want to tell her that you are afraid your mom and dad will punish you. You want to ask her where you can look in case someone at school found your book. Is that right?"

When abuse is the crisis, then you must review not only the child's plan of action, but your own as well. "After you tell your teacher, then she will call the people who try to help children who have been abused. They will want to talk with you and will do it at school or at home, I'm not sure where. It will happen today or tomorrow. Do you understand that they will ask you lots of questions and that the best thing to do is answer them honestly? They will then try to help you."

The four-step crisis intervention process can help you clarify the goals you are trying to achieve with the child. Sometimes this process takes as little as one minute; rarely does it take more than ten minutes, even when a child has a serious problem. Read on for more helpful information that will build your confidence and skills in the area of crisis intervention.

Affirm Innocence

A child is *never* responsible for being abused. One goal in our crisis intervention is to find ways to communicate this to the child. Since bribes and tricks are often part of child abuse, children may judge themselves harshly for taking or not taking some action. They blame themselves and fear that others will blame them for the abuse. Every communication that we have with a child, whether in a children's workshop or in talk time, must contribute to his or her health, not detract from it. We find ways to say, "You are innocent." Sometimes a child will state, "It's all my fault," and you have a ready opportunity to counteract self-blame. But sometimes the CAP worker must find an appropriate time to communicate this message. It may be at the very end of your time together when you say, "I'm so glad you told me. It is not your fault that you have been abused. No one ever deserves to be abused."

Guidelines for Talking with Children

In Columbus a young girl disclosed sexual molestation by a convenience store employee. The man had, over a period of time, given the child soft drinks and candy bars until trust was established. Then he molested her and told her if she didn't come back regularly, or if she told her parents, he would accuse her of shoplifting. During talk time, she disclosed the abuse but expressed guilt since she had repeatedly gone to the store knowing that she would be abused. The CAP worker was careful to affirm her innocence.

Believe the Child

We are not investigators; our role in crisis intervention is to be the child's *advocate*. This means that we *always* believe the child. Those responsible for investigating abuse and determining what evidence exists will assess whether the abuse happened. Knowing this gives us the freedom to talk with the child rather than to "interview" the child.

When children disclose abuse, they may not do it chronologically or include all the facts. Sometimes when children disclose abuse, there are holes in the story or parts that don't make sense to us. There are reasons why children disclose in this manner, but they do not discount the abuse.

Children may be afraid to tell the whole story for fear they will be punished for doing something wrong. They may find parts of the story too hard to talk about, or may fear that they won't be believed. Fear of retribution from the offender may make them reluctant to share all the details.

We are the child's advocate. We take this into consideration and believe the child. Since children rarely lie about abuse, and since an investigation will be performed, we are free to give children the support they need to discuss their problem.

During the parent program and the teacher/staff in-service training, we provide information about crisis intervention. By increasing the number of adults who can respond sensitively to a child in crisis, we increase the likelihood that children will have the support system necessary to act on their own behalf. Often teachers believe that they must determine whether abuse happened before reporting it. In every state in the United States teachers must only "suspect" abuse to report; they need not have proof that it took place. Again, it is the role of authorities to collect evidence and determine whether the abuse took place. Teachers and parents can act as advocates for children.

Assess Safety

Whenever we speak with a child in crisis we must determine the immediate safety needs of the child. For instance, if a child has been abused by a relative whom he or she visits only in the summer, then the child is safe to return home at the end of the school day. But if children are abused by family members living in the home, their safety is in jeopardy.

> A child described physical abuse by a baby-sitter. He went to the sitter's home every day after school until his father was able to pick him up. The CAP facilitator asked whether he would be going to the sitter's home that day. The child replied, "No, she's in the hospital." This information is vital to protecting the child. If the child had been going to the sitter's that day, protective services would have needed to act quickly on the child's immediate safety needs.

Although it may seem improbable to an adult, many children describe abuse without a time frame. The CAP facilitator must ask specific questions in order to determine whether the abuse is current and/or immediate.

Validate Feelings

Children who have been or are being abused may have conflicting feelings. Although they may hate the behavior of the offender, they may also love the person. This is confusing to a child, but normal.

CAP facilitators must affirm the child's feelings: "Yes, I can really understand why you feel that way. I think I would feel the same way." Remember that crisis intervention requires us to hear children and listen to their experiences as they feel them. Our own reactions may well be different from theirs.

Be Honest

It is important not to make promises you can't keep. You may be tempted to tell a child, in order to facilitate disclosure, that you can protect him or her or make the abuse stop. Unfortunately, this is not within your power.

You have the responsibility to be honest with children and to tell them what actions you must take. It is not fair to keep secrets from a child who already feels powerless and out of control. Having a protective services worker arrive at a child's home without warning to investigate the allegation of abuse contributes to feelings of powerlessness. Therefore, we must communicate every action we are going to take as a result of the child's disclosure and discuss the implications of those actions. "I can't help you with this problem alone. I must tell the people who are responsible for helping children about this, and they will want to speak with you. How do you feel about that?" In this way we not only warn the child about what the future holds because of his or her disclosure, but we help prepare the child to face that future.

Occasionally a child says, "Please don't tell anyone about this." Of course, if abuse is the problem, we cannot keep the secret. "I must tell the people who try to help children who have been abused. Abuse is wrong, and I want to make it stop. What are you afraid will happen if I tell someone?" This allows us to understand the child's fears. There may be actions we can take to relieve the fear, and we should certainly communicate the child's fear to protective services workers, giving them insight into the child's situation as well.

> A second-grade girl disclosed sexual abuse by her stepfather to a CAP facilitator. When the child was told that the abuse must be reported, she said, "No, you can't tell anyone." The CAP facilitator asked why not, and the child replied that the stepfather had guns in the house and had threatened to shoot her and her mother if she ever told anyone. The child was assured that this information would be communicated to protective services, alerting them to the possibility of violence. The child replied, "If the people know my dad has guns they will be careful. I don't want anybody to get shot."

Children often understand their own situations much more acutely than we give them credit for. Trusting children's accounts of the difficulties they see is important. We must not trivialize or minimize children's fears; we must instead hear those fears and be honest about our ability to help.

Find Out What the Child Wants

Occasionally a child discloses abuse to a teacher or CAP facilitator and secretly hopes to be rescued. Asking the child what he or she wants to happen allows us to let the child know whether this is possible. For example, a boy in kindergarten asked a CAP facilitator if he could "sleep at your house tonight." The facilitator told the child honestly that this would not be possible, but affirmed the child's feelings. Later, the teacher held the child's hand while a protective services agent interviewed him. He had requested the teacher's presence, and that was a need that could be met.

Use the Child's Language

Children disclose abuse in words that are familiar to them. Because we are not investigators or prosecutors, we can use the same language that is comfortable for the child. This language may be embarrassing or shocking, but our goal is to help the child feel comfortable.

Sometimes children use "street" language (pussy, cock, fuck); and sometimes they use abstract language (it, thing, stuff). Younger children may use family language (pee-pee, wiener, bo-bo). Be sure to clarify what the child is talking about. "Can you point to your pee-pee so I know for sure what you mean?" "What did the stuff look like?" One 12-year-old girl said, "He put his peanuts in my ground." The CAP facilitator clarified that "peanuts" meant penis and that "ground" was the child's vagina. (The offender might have inserted real peanuts, or "ground" could have meant the child's mouth or anus.) Once we establish what the child means, then we can use that language with the child.

Sometimes children simply point to parts of their body. In this case the CAP facilitator should use words to clarify what the child means.

Listen — Don't Interrogate

It is not necessary to have all the facts to report abuse. In fact, at the point at which you *suspect* abuse you must report it (see reporting section, page 127). You don't need to probe for a complete account of the abuse.

The child will be interviewed during a subsequent investigation in order to find out the "who, what, when, where, how many times" of the abuse. For you, it is best to let the child tell his or her story with your support, and for you to clarify information that is unclear to you. For instance, if a child says, "I am hit at home," you need to find out more information, since corporal punishment is not necessarily illegal. "Where on your body are you hit?" "Are you hit with a hand? An object?" "Do you ever have bruises or cuts on your body after you are hit?" This information allows you to ascertain whether the child's disclosure is reportable. Whenever you are in doubt, report.

Special Considerations

Since every child is different, it is impossible to review all the topics that children bring to our attention in order to ask for help. If you follow the four-step problem-solving procedure with each child and pay attention to the other guidelines in this chapter, you will be a great source of support and help. There is no magic to crisis intervention; it just takes your patience, attention, and practice. After you have talked with a number of children you will find that your comfort level rises; the more experience you have, the more comfortable and better skilled you become.

Still, there are a number of situations that come up over and over again, and we have found some useful and creative ways to help children choose a plan of action with which they are comfortable. The following scenarios are regularly recurring areas of concern for children.

Separation/Divorce

The divorce or separation of parents is often frightening or painful for children. Parents handle this in a variety of ways, some better, some worse for the children involved. Children often seem to need someone to tell, someone who will understand that it is hard on them and who will give them a little comfort.

We almost always advocate that children try to talk with one or both parents about how they are feeling. We help them select a good time, such as after dinner, when activity in the house may finally come to a lull. It is our hope that parents will try to help their children if their awareness is raised about how the children are feeling. Talking to a teacher or school counselor can also help, and we offer that alternative for the child's consideration as well.

Some children have specific fears that only a parent can answer. Some children worry that they will never see their fathers again, or that some behavior on their own part has caused the divorce. Again, we suggest that a child find a good time to talk with Mom or Dad and ask, "When you move out, will I still see you?" Whatever the child decides, we phrase in the form of an action plan. "You have decided to talk with your mom after your little brother goes to bed tonight and ask her if you've done something that made Dad so mad that he is leaving. Is that right?"

Spanking

We sincerely hope that someday we will look back at our history of child rearing and see spanking as an unnecessary and abusive practice. In our opinion, spanking is a counterproductive and humiliating act. At the same time that we are trying to teach children to control their impulses and to solve problems with words, we use force to obtain their compliance. Children are often humiliated and angered by the act itself, outcomes that do not teach the lesson we seek. Children are the only group of people for whom hitting is sanctioned by law and by social norms.

Although many of us define "spanking" as swatting a child with an open hand on the buttocks, this is not the only form of corporal punishment that parents and some teachers use with impunity from the law. For parents, hitting a child with an object such as a hairbrush, a belt, or a switch is also sanctioned by law. In some states and school districts, a child can be hit with a paddle or other object, even resulting in bruises to the child, without a report of child abuse. Although we may view these behaviors as abusive, in many states a report of child abuse can only be made if the child is injured by a parent (i.e., marks are left on the child's body) or if a teacher crosses some undefined line (which, in many cases, allows for bruises on the child's body).

Some children come to talk time after a workshop to discuss spanking. We must clarify how much a child is being hurt; therefore, we answer two questions when trying to decide whether a report is justified. First, has the child ever had marks on his or her body after being physically punished; second, is the child truly frightened, so that home or school feels basically unsafe? If either of these criteria is met, we will always make a report to protective services.

But some children who talk to us about spanking are clearly not being injured, and they clearly feel safe at home and at school. They simply hate to be spanked. Again, we recommend a talk with their parents and/or their teacher about how it feels to be spanked. It is our hope that more and more parents and teachers will begin to see spanking as an oppressive and ineffective way to achieve the result they seek.

Many groups across the country are working to change laws that allow corporal punishment in schools. These advocates are winning over many school districts to the belief that corporal punishment is unjustified and possibly harmful. Indeed, many states currently ban corporal punishment in the schools. You need to find out what the law says in your state and each school district in which you provide services. Unfortunately, parents have the right to hit their children, with discretion, everywhere in the United States.

Battering

Sometimes children are worried not for themselves, but for their mothers, aunts, or grandmothers. Spousal abuse is all too common in the American household, and it is not surprising that children want to talk about it. Researchers estimate that three to four million women are beaten in their homes every year by husbands or partners. Battering is rarely an isolated episode; it usually occurs frequently, and the severity of the abuse escalates over time.

In cases where children report battering in the home, it is important to determine whether the child is also being hurt. If this is the case, then protective services can be called. *Children in homes where battering occurs are abused and neglected at a rate 1500 percent higher than the average in the general population.*

When children simply witness violence, it is very difficult to intervene. If an adult woman feels powerless to change her plight, she will most likely see her children as powerless as well. Again, we ask the child whether he or she might like to talk with school counselors or teachers, who may be able to give more consistent support if they become aware of the violence. We also ask the child if he or she could discuss it with the victim. This may be difficult if the victim lives in the home. Most battered women feel frightened and threatened all the time, never knowing when the batterer will unleash his anger at them. Still, children can evaluate whether to communicate to their mother that they feel unsafe. There are many instances where the welfare of her children was the impetus for a mother entering a shelter or moving in with friends. Sometimes an older child requests the telephone number of a shelter, which we provide as we do at all parent programs and teacher/staff in-service training. A school counselor can also send that number to a mother, along with those of other services that might aid the family in finding safety.

When the victim of battering lives outside the child's house, it is a little easier for the child. In these cases we encourage children to talk with one or both of their parents about approaching the victim.

A child who is living with fear that a loved one could be hurt or killed is a child in crisis. We know that some children who witness battering may learn that there is nothing they can do if someone tries to hurt them, leading to a lifetime of hurt and victimization. Other children learn to be violent themselves, and they hurt and victimize others. Clearly, living in a home where violence is witnessed is not healthy for any child. But battering is a learned behavior, and so it can be changed.

Drug and Alcohol Abuse

"I live on a crazy street. I'm scared from gun shooting."

Children often discuss drugs. A family member may have a serious drug or alcohol problem, or their neighborhood or school may bring them into direct contact with drug sellers and users. Children commonly express fear about drugs and request help.

When parents or other family members have drug or alcohol problems, children are often abused or neglected. As in all other cases, when abuse or neglect is suspected, a report should be made.

Visible drug use in the community is harder to resolve. Children can evaluate the help that teachers or school counselors might offer to try to prevent drug transactions on school grounds. Sometimes children can ask for extra help from a parent in getting to school safely. Sometimes the police can help. Reviewing prevention strategies taught in the workshops and applying them to neighborhood danger also helps children feel safer.

Reporting Child Abuse

Every CAP facilitator must become thoroughly familiar with the relevant child abuse reporting law. You can obtain information from your local child protective services agency, at the public library, or at the county prosecutor's office. The law will specify who is mandated to report (doctors, teachers, school counselors, etc.) and under what conditions they must report. Every state requires some professionals to report if child abuse is suspected. The law will also state the penalty if a mandated professional fails to report.

As we noted, we always ask a child who discloses abuse: "Whom in the school would you like to talk with about this?" Once the child talks with this adult, that adult must make a report to protective services.

It is not unusual for the CAP coordinator to offer support and assistance to the principal, teacher, or other school staff member who is calling in the report. First and foremost, we help the adult by providing the phone number and reviewing the information that will be needed by the intake worker at protective services. If the teacher has observed suspicious behavior in the past or has knowledge about who lives with the child or of other siblings who may have been victimized, then he or she should provide this information as well. Everyone who makes a report in "good faith" (with a true belief that child abuse may have occurred) is immune from prosecution.

Dual Reporting

Although we urge the school staff to report child abuse to protective services, we have no way of knowing whether they have done so. Therefore, we also make a report.

In order to avoid confusion on the part of the protective service workers, our office has worked out a cooperative agreement with our local agency about this dual reporting. Every year before the beginning of school, we meet with all the intake workers to explain the process. We inform them that one of our goals is to encourage teachers and other school staff to make reports. But on a number of occasions we found out that school staff did not report, as we recommended. Therefore, in the interests of the children, we also file reports, being careful to mention that the school will be providing a more detailed report that includes the child's full name, address, mother's and father's names, and other information that is accessible in school records. The intake staff understand the reason for the dual reporting, and we acknowledge that at times we may create confusion. However, in order to ensure that reports of all suspected cases are made, we use the dual report method.

School staff sometimes need help in making a report. Even though they may have participated in the teacher/staff in-service training, in the stress of the moment they may not be sure how to report. We offer support and information to make filing a report less frustrating. We review with the school staff members the types of questions that will be asked by the intake worker and encourage them to prepare the information before calling. We also help them sort out their own feelings. Sometimes teachers feel guilty because they did not report abuse before or did not identify a child's problem as abuse. We help them think through their past interactions with the child for any additional information that might be useful to protective services. We encourage them to call us again if they experience problems. We hope that our support makes school staff more likely to report abuse in the future.

School staff members often express frustration because they are never told the outcome of their report. A child may disappear from a classroom, and the teacher does not know whether the family moved, or whether protective services removed the child and that he or she goes to another school because of the change in residence. We certainly appreciate their frustration, for we, too, rarely hear about the outcome of the cases we report. However, confidentiality laws protect this information; protective services is not permitted to share it with the teacher. Explaining this to school staff members often helps to alleviate their anger at the caseworker.

Community Networking

When we look at the problems children may have to face during childhood it can make us angry and frustrated. "Why should children have to learn all this? Why can't adults give children a safer world? Why are we putting the responsibility for safety on children's shoulders? Why can't we stop the perpetrators and allow children their innocence?"

Teaching children prevention information and skills does not make them responsible for preventing abuse; it gives them permission and the ability to resist abuse if at all possible, and to talk about the abuse if it does happen. In fact, as we make clear, abuse is never the child's responsibility. The responsibility lies with the perpetrator and with our society, with often sanctions violence.

Beyond helping individual children, our activities also help the community. If a number of children from a school district, for instance, report drug sales on school property, or a suspicious stranger repeatedly lurks in the school vicinity, there is action we can take. We may suggest that the school call the police to discuss a visible problem that threatens the safety of the children. We might contact a community organization that could offer information on drugs and drug abuse to adults. We might write an article for the community newspaper with information on spousal battering or youth violence. We can participate in community organizing, finding new ways to build a safer community.

Advocacy

Sometimes we must make a report that the school does not want made. A teacher or principal may know a child's family and refuse to believe that abuse is possible. This puts us in a difficult situation, since we want the support of the schools in our work, but we must make the report. Our role is to be the child's advocate, and this requires us always to stand up for the child. This may make us unpopular; in fact, school personnel may be angry with us.

We are careful, when this happens, to explain our role to the school staff involved. We let them know that we suspect abuse and remind them that the law is clear about what actions we must take. We review educational materials, reminding them that abusive parents do not usually appear to be monsters, and that even though the family may be known and respected, they cannot be sure that abuse has not taken place.

Linkage with Protective Services

Before you ever go into a classroom, it is important that you meet with protective services and let them know about your work. Establishing a relationship with protective services in advance makes for a much smoother relationship when reports begin to be generated.

Protective services should be completely familiar with the workshop, the crisis intervention component, and the way in which you will handle reports. In this way you can discuss procedures or agreements that will make reporting easier on you, on school staff, and on intake workers.

Protective services is often one of CAP's biggest supporters. We hear from CAP Projects all across the country who enjoy the support and appreciation of protective services for the work that we do. In fact, CAP Projects have earned the support of many organizations in their communities, including the police, PTAs, hospitals, advocacy organizations, the prosecutors' offices, and schools. CAP becomes part of a local network that strives to help children grow up healthy and strong.

References

1. Roland Summit, "The Child Sexual Abuse Accommodation Syndrome," *Child Abuse and Neglect* 7 (1983): 177–93.
2. Suzanne Sgroi, *Handbook of Clinical Intervention in Child Sexual Abuse* (Lexington, MA: Lexington Books, 1982), 74.
3. Sgroi, 46.
4. Cynthia Crossen Tower, *Understanding Child Abuse and Neglect* (Needham Hts., MA: Allyn and Bacon, 1989), 76.

8
Creating, Implementing, and Running a CAP Project

Introduction

So, you think you want to start a CAP Project? The recipe is simple. You start with an outrageous idea — that abuse can be prevented — you work like an ox, you find a bunch of harebrained people who also believe in this program, you schlep all over your county, you write grant proposals until you're dizzy, and you pray for miracles. Simple!

But it isn't simple or easy or miraculous. It is a lot of hard work, but it is possible. Thousands of people in communities around the world have embarked on the same journey you are about to try. Rural, urban, and suburban projects in diverse communities from Gulfport, Mississippi, to Oakland, California, from Attleboro, Massachusetts, to Choctaw, Arkansas, have shown that communities will support prevention services. Montreal offers culturally appropriate workshops in English and French; Costa Rica, Germany, Ireland, and the Grand Bahama Islands are offering prevention services to children, parents, and teachers much as you will in your own area. You are not alone; you are part of a growing network of prevention professionals who believe that children have the right to grow up safe, strong, and free.

Determining Your CAP Territory

You need to figure out what your territory will be. Are you going to serve a school district, a metropolitan area, a county, several counties, or a province? Many CAP Projects serve a countywide area, but this certainly isn't a rule. Your territory will depend on how many children you believe you can serve, what other CAP Projects exist in your area, and your need for expansion after the first few years as your ability to provide services improves with experience.

When you have determined your territory, we (the national CAP office) need to approve it, so that we can ensure that no other CAP Project is serving the same area and so that we can make appropriate referrals to you. You will find a form called "New CAP Project Information" in Appendix B of this manual. Please keep all of this information updated, so that we can always reach you.

Beginning

In order to begin a project in your community you must first attend a training in the CAP model so that you know exactly what you are doing, and so that you can benefit from our experience and our support. Training in the CAP elementary model is regularly offered at our office at the National Assault Prevention Center in Columbus, Ohio. Trainings are three days in length and are exhilarating and exhausting. You can expect an intense three days wherein we cover every aspect of project philosophy, content, and implementation. If you live in an area with a CAP Regional Training Center, then you may obtain your training from that center. If you're not sure whether there is a center in your area, ask the national office.

Another way to obtain training from our office is to schedule a training in your area. A national trainer from NAPC will travel to you and train a group of people from your area in the model. One of the benefits of this method is that a sizable group of people can all be trained at the same time. This means that you don't have to return to your area and conduct a training in a model you have never implemented. Since you need a pool of facilitators to conduct workshops, this saves you the hassle of organizing a training and ensures that the training is a comprehensive presentation and practice of the CAP Project. To discuss training further, contact our office. We can let you know about existing dates for training or help you figure out whether the best way to be trained is by bringing a trainer to your area.

The benefits of being trained by one of our trainers are numerous. First, you will have a complete understanding of the program and the barriers you may encounter. Second, you can have all your questions answered without having to take on too much trial and error in your own community. Third, our trainers have all been doing CAP for a significant number of years and have trained other groups with great success. Fourth, we maintain high standards for our trainings so that we can guarantee quality and completeness of content. Fifth, once you obtain training from this office you receive technical assistance about project implementation, new information in the field, and new materials available to enhance prevention activities. For instance, April is Child Abuse Prevention month in the U.S., and we offer high-quality public education information so that you can increase your project's visibility and community awareness. Finally, you can share your disappointments and successes with us and the rest of the international CAP network so that all of us benefit from each other's experiences.

Finding Facilitators

Whether you obtain training at our offices or choose to bring a trainer to your area, you will need a pool of people who will become facilitators of the workshops. Many communities obtain facilitators by advertising. We run an employment ad in the newspaper and hire facilitators every year. Here is sample of the ad we run:

> WORKSHOP FACILITATORS to present child assault prevention workshops in Columbus schools. Part-time, Sept.–May, $9.00/hr., 3–10 hrs. per week. Requires good communication skills and experience working with children. Send resume by 8/31 to: National Assault Prevention Center, P.O. Box 02005, Columbus, Ohio 43202. Equal Opportunity Employer.

We also advertise with a flyer (see next page), which we ask to post in a variety of locations. We have posted flyers in senior citizen employment offices, minority employment assistance offices such as the Urban League, churches, university and college social work offices, and Hispanic and African American studies offices. This flyer is used to request resumes and to inform potential facilitators about the nature of the positions. Flyers can also be distributed on cars in church parking lots, at day care centers, in grocery store parking lots, and on any bulletin board that provides community information.

In your first year you may choose not to use this type of advertising. Many CAP Projects ask radio stations to announce an upcoming training in the CAP model and request that interested listeners contact the CAP coordinator. We have also found it useful to call former facilitators, whom we ask to call their friends and acquaintances.

☆ ☆ ☆ NEEDED ☆ ☆ ☆
Child Assault Prevention Facilitators

The National Assault Prevention Center has openings for Task Force Facilitators to do Child Assault Prevention (CAP) workshops with elementary school students.

•

We want to hire a multicultural task force that represents the entire community.

•

Flexible daytime hours. Rate of pay is $9.00/hour.

QUALIFICATIONS:

Candidates must have time available during the day. Workshops will be conducted during regular school hours.

•

Candidates must have good verbal and written skills. Candidates must feel comfortable with role-playing and/or small group facilitating.

•

Candidates should feel comfortable with an empowerment/feminist approach to assault prevention.

•

Candidates must participate in 20 hours of training, September 18–20th, 8:30 a.m. – 4:30 p.m. There is no remuneration for training.

•

Workshops will be scheduled from September through May (3–10 hours per week possible).

Send resume/work experience to:

NATIONAL ASSAULT PREVENTION CENTER
P.O. Box 02005
Columbus, Ohio 43202
Attention: CAP Coordinator

(Equal Employment Opportunity Employer)

Diversity

Each CAP Project should make every effort to recruit a culturally diverse task force of facilitators. This takes a lot of effort for most projects, but it is simply too important to accept failure. Children need safe adults around them. Safety is different for different children. A male child may need a male facilitator; an African American child may need an African American facilitator; a deaf child may need a deaf facilitator in order to feel safe and comfortable enough to participate and learn from the workshops.

Aside from children's needs, our communities have needs as well. The subject matter of abuse needs widespread public discussion so that parents receive the quality information they need to help their children effectively. When our task force is diverse we give our communities permission and safety in talking about abuse.

Interviewing

You will want to interview carefully and thoroughly every potential facilitator. The appendix offers a sample interview form, which our office uses to screen applicants after we obtain their resumes or letters of introduction. Every facilitator should be completely comfortable with the empowerment/feminist philosophy. Since facilitators will be working with a diverse group of co-workers and children, we ask interviewees about their comfort level with diversity and their ability to support and assist diverse children. We are careful to outline work responsibilities, hours when the facilitators will be working, rate of pay, benefits available, the need for transportation, and other information about the job. Generally speaking, we end up with a hardworking and successful group of facilitators.

Volunteers

Some projects use a combination of volunteers and paid staff. The coordinator or co-coordinators may be paid, but the facilitators of the children's workshops volunteer their time. During 12 years of doing this work, we have found that a task force of volunteers is difficult to maintain over time. The emotional and time commitments that CAP demands means that those with only a couple of hours a week to volunteer make scheduling difficult. Furthermore, CAP facilitators go through extensive training and deserve to be paid for their work. In some communities volunteers are not as respected as paid employees. Whatever you decide, make your decision carefully, and be aware that if you choose to use volunteers you will spend many hours ensuring a task force large enough to handle classroom-by-classroom workshops.

Once you have a pool of facilitators, you will need to train them and rehearse the workshops with them. Training takes no fewer than 20 hours, and rehearsals average another ten hours. Workshop facilitators must rehearse role-plays and primary facilitation duties, as well as crisis intervention. Therefore, before anyone has even entered a classroom, you have more than 30 hours of training invested in each individual facilitator. Training is designed to ensure that each facilitator is familiar with all aspects of project content and implementation.

Facilitator Responsibilities

The following responsibilities should be clearly outlined to each facilitator:

1. **Practice the role-plays prior to each workshop.** Workshop leaders should be prepared to tailor role-plays to different age groups. For example, a first-grade class likes animation, whereas a sixth-grade class is more likely to perceive the subtleties of

nonverbal communication. A large task force gives workers the opportunity to work with different people at each engagement. To ensure smooth role-plays, workers should practice with different partners and learn different styles and approaches.

2. **Sign up for workshops.** If a regular task force meeting has not been scheduled, contact the coordinator to sign up for workshops. Always give 24 hours' notice if you find you need to cancel an engagement; trying to find another workshop leader at 7:00 A.M. is one headache that coordinators would rather avoid! Whenever possible, role-players should make arrangements with other task force members to replace them if they are unable to attend a workshop.

3. **Prepare for travel to an engagement.** Task force members meet 30–45 minutes before leaving for an engagement to practice role-plays. This is energy-efficient, and it reduces tardiness to workshops.

4. **Fill out all project forms.** Do this immediately following the children's workshop. If a role-player is concerned about a particular child's reaction, it should be noted on the evaluation form. The place to note these reactions (or any other out-of-the-ordinary happenings, such as constant interruptions, fire drills, etc.) is on this form. Don't discuss these concerns in the school hallways where children or other adults may overhear you.

5. **Inform the coordinator immediately should a crisis arise.** The coordinator and the task force facilitator will work together to find the best way to help a child.

6. **Dress appropriately.** Encourage workshop leaders to wear casual, comfortable clothes that will not inhibit their ability to stoop, bend, sit on the floor, or demonstrate self-defense. T-shirts with political messages are not appropriate for the workshops.

7. **Attend CAP task force meetings.** These meetings offer a forum for information on the community, an opportunity to brainstorm problem situations, and the chance for leaders to reaffirm the good work being done.

Preventing Burnout

Classroom workshops are fun but they also cause exhaustion. The high energy level of the students, coupled with the amount of material to be covered, makes each hour-long workshop a rigorous experience. Because each classroom has its own unique atmosphere and personality, it is sometimes difficult to predict how a workshop will progress. Chaotic classes required a calming influence to help focus the discussion; particularly quiet classes may need higher levels of enthusiasm from workshop leaders to generate participation. Either situation can challenge a leader's creativity.

As primary facilitator, you are "on" for an intense hour. All your energy is directed toward the children: Are they with you? Do they understand? Is the pace fast enough? Are any children showing signs of distress? The primary facilitator continually evaluates these questions while presenting material and guiding discussion.

Although role-players portray passive and assertive roles in each situation, they get breaks between role-plays and are able to watch children when they are not performing. Although they may not get exhausted so quickly, role-playing is also demanding.

"Burnout" ("to become exhausted, marked by excessive demands on energy, strength, and resources") is a popular term used to describe an increasing phenomenon among human service workers, and it can happen to workshop coordinators and leaders. A burned out worker may unintentionally withdraw from a child in crisis, losing the ability to be the caring person the child needs for a productive interaction. When leaders foresee this problem and become aware of the first signs, burnout can be prevented. We offer the following suggestions to help minimize the potential for burning out on the project.

1. The children's workshops are scheduled over a two- to three-week period (depending on the size of the school) at the maximum rate of three workshops a day. Hold classes in the morning or the afternoon, with a break in between. We've found morning workshops work best; the children are most alert. A break of 30 to 45 minutes between workshops helps leaders maintain their concentration and the high energy level needed to conduct workshops. The break also allows time to meet with individual children who have questions or concerns.

2. Following the workshop, share observations with each other. This process not only releases tension, but encourages constructive criticism for refining the program. Such emphasis on growth helps reduce feelings of boredom or stagnation that many workers experience.

3. Primary facilitation responsibilities can be rotated among workshop leaders; it is a very demanding role. The primary facilitator role can also be shared among the three members of the team.

4. Get involved in different aspects of the project. Help to train new leaders or assist with fundraising, public relations, or correspondence.

5. Implement CAP Project workshops in diverse communities. The challenges of adapting the project to new communities has its own rewards.

6. Celebrate your success! Hold a task force potluck, barbecue, or picnic periodically, where task force members can socialize together and where appreciation for their hard work can be the focus.

Establishing Services

The CAP Project was designed to be conducted in elementary schools. This does not mean that a summer camp, YWCA, or scout troop cannot be offered CAP workshops, but you will have to adjust the model to provide high-quality services. Ensuring that there is staff and parent training, as well as a clear format for crisis intervention and reporting cases, will mean some minor adjustments. But CAP can be and is being done wherever there are groups of children.

Working in schools gives access to the greatest number of children with the smallest number of logistical problems and the greatest likelihood of reaching most children. The school is a natural community where children, teachers, and parents come together with children's needs and interests in mind.

Finding schools in which to conduct workshops may initially be difficult, but you will find that once you have successfully implemented the CAP Project in one or two schools demand for the program will increase exponentially.

We recommend that you begin CAP by piloting the workshops in a small number of schools. Many projects take on only two to four schools in their first year. They set up appointments with principals from the schools in which they would like to provide services and thoroughly review the entire CAP model with them. Many projects obtain a grant or other funding to pilot the workshops so that schools are offered project services free of charge under the grant (see "Grants" later in this chapter). A grant is an incentive for school officials. "We've obtained a grant from the _____ Foundation to offer primary abuse prevention services to a few schools in this area. Would you like to discuss the possibility of your school being chosen as one of the pilot schools? Of course, with the grant we will be able to provide services free of charge. After the grant is completed we cannot promise that schools would be offered the same opportunity." In almost every school this opens the door for negotiations. Once you have an opportunity to describe what we do and how we do it, you will find that the overwhelming majority of principals want project services. You're in!

Some CAP coordinators question whether they should begin with the school board, formally requesting an endorsement of the project so that schools will have automatic permission to offer CAP. Although this has worked successfully in a number of communities, we know that it also occasionally backfires. It is difficult for a school board to endorse a project with which it is unfamiliar and which does not have a track record in the community. We believe that for most communities, requesting school board support should happen only after the pilot has been successfully completed. Then the school board members will have some direct experiences on which to base their decision. Many school principals are willing to allow CAP into the school without school board endorsement when you share program information, explain the benefits of using a national model that has worked successfully in many communities across the country, and inform them that you are engaging in a local pilot study to determine the project's success and support in your own community.

Logistics and Scheduling

Once you have a school's permission to conduct CAP, then you will have to work with the school on scheduling and logistics. You will be conducting at least one, maybe two, parent programs, a teacher/staff in-service workshop, and classroom-by-classroom workshops throughout the school. This takes some planning and cooperation on your part and on the part of the school.

Once you have agreed on the dates and times of the adult programs, it is time to advertise the presentations. You will find some materials in Appendix B that will facilitate that process. There is a sample letter to parents, which the school should provide on school stationery to be sent home with children along with a permission slip for their children's participation in classroom workshops. It describes the program and informs parents that any questions they may have can be answered at the adult program. Give the principal this sample parent letter so that he or she can use it as a model for informing parents.

The teacher/staff in-service workshop is scheduled by the principal. Since the teacher/staff in-service program requires approximately 90 minutes, the principal may want you to provide the training on a special day, and then do a shorter, refresher version right before you go into the schools. Sometimes we offer the teacher/staff in-service program on two consecutive days for 45 minutes each day, before school starts in the morning. Sometimes we conduct workshops after school, and teachers are asked to stay late. Scheduling enough time with teachers is a problem. Teachers already feel overworked and underpaid, and being asked to stay late for no pay is not popular. School staff also have other business to conduct during their regular staff meetings. Providing you with the time necessary to present the in-service training may take away time from other school needs. A few CAP Projects have actually provided two teacher/staff in-service programs for school staff. Classrooms were combined to allow some teachers to attend the in-service session while the remaining teachers worked with the children. Then they reversed their duties so that the teachers who had been trained in the morning staffed the combined classrooms in the afternoon. Scheduling these in-service workshops is a challenge that requires you and the school to be creative, flexible, and understanding.

The actual scheduling of children's workshops is handled either by the principal or at the teacher/staff in-service program itself. Classroom workshops should not be scheduled when children normally have other activities such as recess, art, or gym. We don't want children to feel that CAP is a punishment that takes them away from something special that they love to do. Therefore, we set up a blank schedule of workshop times when we are available, and teachers can sign up for times that are convenient for them.

A sample sign-up sheet is located in Appendix B for your use. The calender in Figure 1 is a sign-up sheet that has been filled in as it might look after you have completed the scheduling.

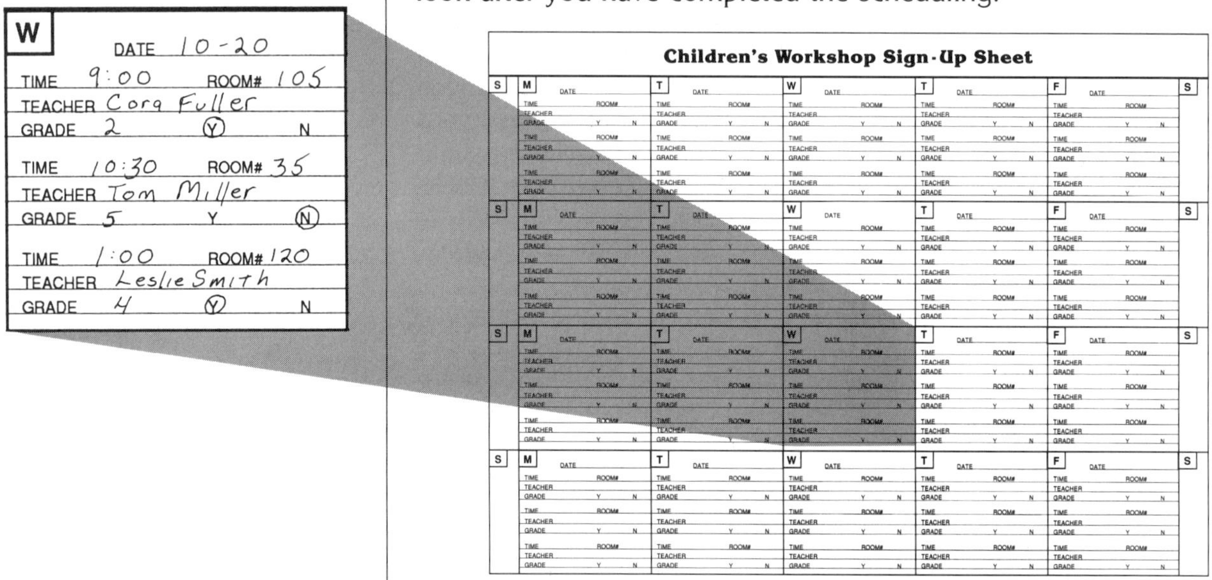

Figure 1

Please note that when teachers sign up we ask them to provide us with their grade, room number, and name. This way, when we copy the calendar for our facilitators, they know where they are going and what grade they are serving. We also ask teachers to confirm their participation in the teacher role-play. If it says "yes," then the teacher agrees to role-play with the facilitators. If it says "no," then we must contact the principal in order to arrange for another adult in the school to role-play with us.

Review Time

Another arrangement you must make with the principal is the location where you will provide review time with the children. In some schools this location is the same each day; in other schools it changes, based on school use of the area. If it is to change daily, then facilitators must be notified of this each day so that at the conclusion of the children's workshop they know where the children are to be sent.

This area, called the safe location, safe space, or review space by many CAP Projects, may be an empty room, an activity center, or the school library. Any room that is large enough to accommodate three facilitators and three children is acceptable. Some schools have limited space available, and finding this location may take some creative thought. The principal's office is not appropriate (it may feel a bit intimidating to the children), whereas the counselor's office may be just fine, depending on its size.

Permission Slips

Some projects use what is called the *positive,* or *active,* permission slip. It must be signed and returned by a parent in order for the child to attend. Some projects use the *negative,* or *passive,* permission slip, which means specifically denying a child permission to attend. An example of each is located in Appendix B.

Whenever a child is denied permission to attend, we ask the school principal to call the parent to determine why. This gives us valuable feedback about the project's reputation and about parental fears, and also allows the school to gain feedback about why a parent does not wish a child to participate. The principal has an opportunity to answer questions about the program, which may alleviate concerns that a parent holds.

> In one community 35 parents refused permission. The school discovered that all 35 parents were Latino and had not received any materials or parent programs in Spanish. The situation was rectified by providing materials and presentations in Spanish for the children as well as the parents.

On some occasions the fact that permission is denied concerns a principal or teacher greatly. When a child who seems to be in crisis or who may have shown signs of abuse in the past is then denied permission to attend, it often causes alarm to school personnel. Calling the parent to determine why the child was denied permission can confirm a problem, allowing a report to be made to protective services, or the alarm can be put to rest. Very few children are denied permission to attend workshops. In Columbus, the rate is less than .015 percent, or about one child in every 200.

Children who are denied permission to attend the workshop by their parents should be included in a fun activity instead. Using a computer, helping in the office, or going to recess with another class are all examples of activities that children will enjoy. Nonparticipation should not feel like a punishment to the child who is denied permission to attend.

Coordinating a Project

Project coordinators, directors, administrators, or whatever you choose to call them can make or break a project. Coordinators must have good oral and written skills, handle details without procrastination, be diplomats, and have a talent for public relations. They answer correspondence, write grants, hire, train, evaluate, supervise (and occasionally dismiss) facilitators, and conduct the parent programs and the teacher/staff in-service workshops. Coordinators are leaders: They must instill confidence in the project among facilitators, school personnel, protective services, the police, and the media. The following advertisement is one our office uses to recruit the coordinator, along with a copy of the job description. Please note that the job description you design may include some or all of these duties, depending on the way your project is set up.

**IMMEDIATE OPENING
ELEMENTARY CAP COORDINATOR**

Coordinator needed to administer Child Assault Prevention (CAP) program in elementary schools. Requires excellent written and verbal skills, experience in supervision, public speaking, working with children. Ten-month position beginning August 1, 1990. Send resume to NAPC, Box 02005, Columbus, Ohio 43202. Equal Opportunity Employer.

Elementary CAP Coordinator Job Description

1. Administration of local contract with school district.
2. Hire, train, and supervise all CAP elementary task force employees.
3. Evaluate task force employees' performance.
4. Set up and conduct parent/teacher in-service workshops, exit interviews with principals, and, where necessary, children's workshops.
5. Keep ongoing statistics on number of people served, using quantitative and qualitative methods.
6. Prepare year-end report for the Columbus City School District, and other reports as requested.
7. Work with NAPC staff to increase communication and lessen isolation of individuals within NAPC.
8. Work with NAPC staff to develop a long-range plan for continuing elementary services.

Requirements

Skills, knowledge, experience: Must have experience and ability in public speaking and working with children, and administrative and supervisory skills. Previous child assault prevention experience desirable.

Personal attributes: Must have an interest in and respect for people who have experienced assault, and belief in personal empowerment. Must be able to work closely with staff and handle conflict in an open, respectful manner. Must be self-directed and have ability to work independently. Must believe in human rights. Must possess the ability to seek assistance, support, and feedback, both personally and professionally.

Evaluations and Exit Interviews

As we have stated, when you use the CAP model you gain all the benefits of working with a tested model. We know that the CAP model, when implemented as designed, teaches children new information and strategies for preventing abuse.

Since evaluation of any program is an expensive and labor-intensive process, you will want to decide carefully what type of program evaluation to conduct. Chapter 9, "CAP Program Evaluation," will fully inform you about the evaluations done to date on CAP and offer suggestions for program evaluations that you may want to try.

When you are working with limited resources, research into program effectiveness is almost impossible. You will, however, want to monitor your project carefully so that you ensure quality services and implementation. If you provide a quality program, you can safely assume that the evaluations done on CAP as a whole will apply to your project as well.

There are a number of forms located in Appendix B that can help you monitor your project's services. Following every parent program and teacher/staff in-service training you should hand out an evaluation form in order to gain feedback about the quality of the in-service workshop and the usefulness of the program. This will let you know whether your presentations to parents and teachers are perceived as beneficial.

Each facilitator should fill out a form that monitors the quality of each children's workshop. This form, called "Evaluation of Children's Workshops," gives the coordinator some basic information about each workshop conducted, and provides a place for facilitators to note any problems or unusual situations that may have occurred.

There is also an "Exit Interview" form (see Appendix B), which is given to the principal of the school for his or her feedback on a wide variety of subject matters including program implementation, quality of program, and parent or teacher feedback to the principal. The exit interview should be given to the principal within a week or two following completion of children's workshops. This interview allows the principal to offer his or her feedback on the project and also allows the CAP coordinator the opportunity to discuss any concerns he or she may have about individual children.

These forms also gather important data for your statistics. They tell you how many children, parents, and teachers you have served, how many children were denied permission to attend, how many children participated in crisis intervention, how many cases of abuse were reported to children's services, and what type of cases they were. This information will be helpful when you write an annual report on your project's work, send in your data to our office for national and international tabulation, and report to the funders of your project.

Disclosures of Abuse

Every facilitator must carefully fill out the form called "Disclosure and/or Suspected Abuse" (see Appendix B) when he or she talks to any child who discloses abuse. Every detail of the interaction with the child can be captured on this form, which then is given to the coordinator. With this form the coordinator can call in a report of abuse with all the information necessary at his or her fingertips.

We keep these forms in the office, and when a team reports back from a school all facilitators immediately fill one out if they've spoken to a child who has disclosed abuse. After filling out the form they review the information verbally with the coordinator for clarity. Completed forms are kept in a locked file cabinet at all times.

In some states the facilitator who actually spoke with the child must make the report. In this case the facilitator still provides all information to the coordinator and fills out the same forms.

Disclosures of abuse must be handled with the utmost care. Children depend on us when they confide in us, and we have an obligation to act quickly and professionally in this regard.

School Responsibilities

The school is responsible for a number of tasks, which should be clearly defined during the negotiation phase. Here is a checklist of the school's responsibilities.

1. To send a letter on school stationery to all parents, informing them that CAP will be providing workshops in their school.
2. To distribute and collect permission slips, and to follow up on children who were denied permission to attend.
3. To host the parent program, providing space and informing parents of the date and time.
4. To arrange for the teacher/staff in-service workshop, providing space and encouraging all school staff to attend.
5. To arrange a "safe space" or "review space" for children who participate in crisis intervention after the classroom workshop.
6. To arrange for children who are denied permission to attend the workshop to participate in some other activity.
7. To be available to discuss and to have a commitment to reporting all suspected cases of child abuse.
8. To provide feedback about the project and to participate in an exit interview with the CAP coordinator when classroom workshops have been completed.
9. To help and support children who have been abused or who have other issues or problems that are identified as a result of the CAP workshops.
10. To maintain confidentiality about victims of child abuse, disclosing information only to those with an absolute need to know.
11. To understand and support CAP's efforts in the school, despite the disruption of our presence, and to encourage follow-up activities that reinforce child abuse prevention lessons.

Teacher Responsibilities

Teachers also have specific responsibilities. They are:

1. To attend the teacher/staff in-service training.
2. To accept their responsibilities under the law to report suspected cases of abuse.
3. To spend five minutes before and after the children's workshop with a CAP facilitator. Before the workshop we review the role-play that most teachers will be participating in and also ask about children who may be in crisis. After the workshop we ask that the teacher tell us about any children he or she is concerned about as a result of the workshop.
4. To participate enthusiastically in the last role-play, if agreed to during the teacher/staff in-service workshop.

Teachers and principals should also be aware that:

- We will rearrange their classrooms, pushing tables and chairs off to the side so that we can sit together on the floor.
- We will handle all discipline problems unless we specifically request their assistance.

- We will need one-half hour at the end of the workshop for children to meet with us individually to review the workshops.
- We will provide name tags for children in their classroom.
- Children get excited and CAP is a disruption (a fun disruption) in the routine. It may take some time for children to settle down again after we have left.

Nonprofit Status

Are you starting a CAP Project under the auspices of another nonprofit agency, or are you part of a group of individuals who are starting a CAP Project? If the latter, you will want to get nonprofit status so that you can receive grants and tax-deductible charitable donations.

Starting a nonprofit and getting all the paperwork in order is a lengthy process. Nonprofit status in the United States requires incorporation as a nonprofit corporation in one of the 50 states. To incorporate as a nonprofit agency, you'll need first to find out what the requirements are in your state. You must file Articles of Incorporation and produce nonprofit bylaws that specify the structure and regulations of your CAP Project. Although the process can be cumbersome, it also helps you consider and think through your new organization comprehensively. An attorney must advise you on this process, but the Secretary of State's office (for projects in the U.S.) is a good place to start since staff there can offer general information on setting up a nonprofit organization.

Most grants require that if you are a nonprofit organization, you are also tax-exempt under the Internal Revenue Service (IRS) 501(c)(3) guidelines. To obtain 501(c)(3) status, you need to acquire and then painstakingly complete the IRS form for requesting tax-exempt status. A lawyer might help here, too, although you can do it on your own. The process takes several months.

Insurance for CAP Projects

There are many different types of insurance that CAP Projects have to consider. Your insurance needs depend to some extent on the size and scope of your project and whether you are operating independently or as part of another nonprofit organization. If you are operating as part of a nonprofit agency, you must coordinate your insurance plan with that of the agency.

Directors and officers liability insurance, called *D&O* in the business, protects your board members and directors. Professional liability, also known as malpractice, insurance provides coverage for damages that come about from negligence, error, or omission. Some liability policies also cover personal injury. Premises liability insurance can cover many incidents such as fire and theft that may happen at your office.

Contact a good insurance agent, preferably one who is recommended by another nonprofit, to get some advice. Carefully consider the coverages you need to protect your CAP Project.

Fundraising

Every CAP Project, even those who use volunteers exclusively, has to do some fundraising to cover costs associated with the project. Raising the necessary money to provide CAP training can be done in a variety of ways. If you are inexperienced in fundraising, this information will help you get started.

CAP Brochure

Every CAP Project should put together a brochure that describes its work in general terms. This brochure can be used for a variety of purposes, fundraising being only one of them. Your project's brochure should include a brief description of the children's workshop, parent program, and the teacher/staff in-service program; some significant statistics on child abuse; and your project's name, address, and phone number. We recommend that you find someone in your community who is experienced at creating public relations tools to work with you. A local university or art school might be a source of ideas and assistance. At the very least, gather brochures from other agencies to give you some ideas that you might adopt for your own brochure.

Fundraising Events

Many CAP Projects raise charitable contributions by hosting an event. A wine and cheese party, golf tournament, or walkathon are examples of events that can raise $50, $500, or $5000. Collect invitations or notices of events from other nonprofits to give you some ideas and then get creative! We have held a '60s celebration with golden oldies, dancing, and pizza, as well as open houses at the office, an antiques and collectables auction, and a party in an art gallery, with a cash bar and string quartet. The donations you ask should cover your costs plus raise the dollar goal you have set. You may have to pay for a graphic artist to design your invitation, typesetting, printing, postage, refreshments, space rental, and decorations. Prepare a budget of your estimated costs and your estimated donations. Then draw up timelines and a list of people needed to meet your goals. This will help you predetermine whether your plan can be successful. For instance, if you need to sell 5000 tickets at $25 each, but think you can only sell 500 tickets using your volunteers, you'll need to rethink your plan.

Conferences and Seminars

Some CAP Projects have raised needed dollars for their project by bringing an expert into town and charging a fee for an in-service workshop. In this case you might have airfare, lodging, and a speaker's fee as expenses in addition to space rental, refreshments, printing for the announcement, and postage. If you find a speaker who has strong appeal among a wide variety of helping professionals or who is popular with some other large segment of your community, this can be an effective fundraiser and public relations event. By bringing an expert into town, you not only make your project more visible, but you educate your community, too!

Risks

Whatever event you plan, there are risks. Think your event through carefully. Overestimate costs and underestimate revenue. You'll be spending money with the hope, not the guarantee, of making money. But carefully planned events usually make some money, even if it doesn't meet the original goal.

Grants

Many CAP Projects provide services through a grant. Grants also require careful planning. There is almost always an application process, wherein you must carefully and concisely describe exactly what you will do with the grant dollars, if awarded.

Some grant applications require lots of information, including your project's history, goals and objectives, budget, and plan for evaluating your success. If you've never written a grant before, it is wise to obtain help the first time around. You may be able to find an individual who has written other grants to help you, or the place to which you are applying may give technical assistance. Keep your eyes open for workshops on grant writing that are offered in your community. These can be really helpful to both the novice and the pro.

The library is a good place to start. There you can find books on grant writing and on foundations that give money to specific causes. Most foundations have priority areas they fund, so look for foundations interested in youth, human services, prevention education, and abuse. If you live near a large city, your library may sponsor grant-writing seminars and may have a Foundation Collection (provided by The Foundation Center in New York City).

Government agencies also award grants. Talk to people at departments of health, human services, mental health, and criminal justice for information on state and federal dollars available. Your state may have a Children's Trust Fund, which might provide grants in child abuse prevention.

Talk to people in the field, legislators, other child advocates, and government employees. Writing a grant is a skill that, with a little practice, can become routine. Like everything else in life, the first time it may be scary, but it gets easier.

Budgeting

"How much does it cost to do CAP?" That's a question our office hears frequently. The answer is: "It depends!" For instance, if you use a volunteer task force of facilitators, instead of a paid task force, your costs will be lower. If you need a half-time coordinator rather than a full-time coordinator, the same is true. The costs of providing CAP services vary widely from project to project and region to region. The less you pay for rent, utilities, salaries and benefits, insurance, postage, printing, long distance phone service, and a variety of other costs, the less it will cost you to provide CAP services.

This section of the manual will provide general information on budgeting for a CAP Project. However, you will need some assistance from an auditor or certified public accountant (CPA), and it is best to find someone from whom you can gain advice. A budget is a useful tool in planning and in ongoing management; learning to use it as a tool will help you manage an efficient project.

The following provides an easy overview of staffing costs associated with running a CAP Project.

Salaries
Program Coordinator
Most CAP Projects have a program coordinator to adminster the project (see job description on page 142). Some coordinators work full-time for 12 months per year; some work half-time for ten months, or any

combination of the above. A full-time, 12-month position involves a standard 2080 hours a year. Therefore, a 50 percent position would involve 1040 hours. A 10-month position at full time would involve 1733 hours (2080 ÷ 12 months per year × 10 months). Once you determine the time it will take the coordinator to administer the project, you compute your costs by using the rate of pay. For instance, we pay our CAP coordinator 12 months per year at 80 percent of full time, at $10.41 per hour (1664 hours × 10.41/hour = $17322.24).

Task Force Facilitator

(See job description on pages 135-137.) Many projects pay facilitators an hourly wage; we pay our facilitators $9.00/hour. For every children's workshop provided, we pay facilitators for two hours; this covers travel time and review time after the workshop. In order to compute your costs, you must know the actual number of classrooms (not schools!) in which you will provide workshops. For discussion purposes, let's say you have 100 classrooms. The formula for detemining costs is:

100 classrooms × 3 facilitators × 2 hours × $9.00/hour = $5400.

If facilitators also provide teacher/staff in-service workshops and parent programs, you must compute this time as well. If you will be working in five schools, you will be providing ten parent programs (two per school) and five teacher/staff in-service programs, or 15 adult workshops. If two facilitators copresent for two hours at each adult in-service program, here's the formula:

15 adult in-service events × 2 facilitators × 2 hours × $9.00/hour = $540.

In our office the program coordinator provides all adult in-service programs as part of the 80 percent full-time position, so this line item is unnecessary in our budget.

Benefits

The following benefits need to be considered in preparing your budget.

FICA

FICA is an acronym for Federal Insurance Contribution Act, in the U.S. Both employees and employers pay into this social security fund. The amount is based on a percentage of the employee's gross wages. The employees pay their share by having it deducted from each paycheck, and the employer matches the amount as required by law. At the beginning of each year the Internal Revenue Service provides a booklet, Circular E, Employer's Tax Guide. This booklet states the percentage to be charged for employees and employers, in addition to other federal tax requirements. An accountant or CPA firm can assist you with this tax-filing requirement, but you need to budget for this expense. The present FICA rate is 7.65 percent. If your CAP Project is part of a city, state, or federal organization, then you may be exempt from paying this social security tax.

Unemployment Insurance

In the U.S. this expense is usually mandated by state governments. It requires that you pay into a fund to provide for unemployment benefits for employees who are laid off from work. The procedures and method of computation will vary from state to state. An accountant or CPA firm can assist you with this tax-filing requirement for your state. It is important that you allow for this type of expense in your budget projections.

Worker Compensation Insurance

In the U.S. this is the insurance that pays workers for injuries received in the course of their employment, and it is handled by the states. Therefore, the procedures and computation methods for this expense vary from state to state. An accountant or CPA firm can assist you.

Employee Health/Dental/Life Insurance

This expense represents the amount of premium the employer pays an insurance company to provide medical, dental, and life insurance coverage for each eligible employee. It is an asset for any organization to provide insurance coverage to employees because it helps in recruiting well-qualified staff. It is also expensive. You will have to research insurance programs for small organizations before you can determine whether your CAP Project can pay all of the premium for each employee, or only a percentage of the premium, with the employee paying the difference. Most insurance plans have guidelines regarding providing coverage to full-time staff and part-time staff. Some require that you purchase the life and dental insurance for all employees, and then provide medical coverage for those who desire it. We recommend that you talk with a local independent insurance agent about group insurance plans, costs, and special provisions. Decide what will work best for your CAP Project.

Direct Program Expenses

What kind of supplies do you need to run an effective CAP Project? Pens, pencils, staples, file folders, letterhead, envelopes, name tags, typing paper, desk organizers, calendars, standard forms, and maybe some office cleaning supplies will be needed. You should also plan to budget for the following expenses:

Postage: This covers the purchase of stamps as well as the costs to ship items via postal or parcel services.

Advertising (Help Wanted): The only way to estimate this cost accurately is to call your local paper for an estimate of what it will cost to run help wanted ads for a stated period of time. If you pull a figure out of the air, you could shortchange yourself and your budget. These costs vary greatly, so call first.

Conference/seminar costs: New research brings new information; new legislation may dictate how disclosures and reporting requirements are to be handled, and as the topic of abuse becomes more open to discussion, statistical data are updated and changed. Attendance at conferences and seminars is one effective way to make sure your CAP Project staff is up-to-date in the field of child abuse.

Local mileage expenses: The task force is not the only group who will be incurring mileage expenses. The program coordinator will be traveling to schools to provide exit interviews with the principals. In addition, attendance at conferences or seminars will mean some mileage expense. Try to think of all the reasons for which mileage expenses will be incurred, and then calculate what should be budgeted for the entire project.

Equipment: Do you need to purchase a desk, file cabinet, typewriter, computer, or other equipment?

Program Supplies

Costs of Doing Business

Insurance: After you have determined your insurance needs (see pages 145 ff. and 149) and obtained quotes for your coverage, include these costs in your budget.

Accounting/CPA/audit fees: Instead of hiring an accountant or bookkeeper, some organizations contract with a CPA firm to handle the fiscal accounting and reporting requirements. This includes everything from handling the payroll to entering accounting transactions and producing monthly or quarterly financial statements. Most CPA firms can help you set up your internal accounting system and assist in hiring an accountant. If you have established a nonprofit corporation, we recommend that you seek out a CPA firm that is knowledgeable in nonprofit fund accounting and audit requirements for entities covered under OMB circular A-133. If you are part of a larger organization, then the CAP Project's share of the cost of an annual audit should be included in your budget. Most grantors and foundations require copies of the annual audit as part of their application guidelines. Many require that an annual audit be performed and the results submitted to the granting agency at the close of the grant period.

Direct and Indirect Costs

If your CAP Project is supported in some way by a larger organization, then only a portion of the total operating expenses (such as rent and utilities) will be charged directly to the CAP Project. If you have established a nonprofit corporation 501(c)(3), and perform fundraising activities to help support the cost of running the nonprofit, in addition to providing CAP program services, then the operating costs need to be allocated to each activity. Generally acceptable accounting principles (GAAP) and procedures will determine how operating costs are prorated and allocated to each activity. In addition, there are other costs, called indirect costs, which most grantors and foundations allow under their grant guidelines. An accountant or CPA firm can determine appropriate treatment of these costs based on your particular situation. The following general definitions can serve as a guide to distinguish between direct and indirect costs.

Direct costs are those that can be identified specifically with a particular program or other direct activity of an organization. Costs that benefit more than one activity are prorated by using the most appropriate distribution base; e.g., percentage of salaries, percentage of space. For example: If a person spends 50 percent time providing CAP Project services and 50 percent time working on a different activity, and these are the only two activities the organization is involved in, then 50 percent of the total rent can be charged to each activity. If an expense relates completely to the CAP Project, such as a help wanted advertisement for a program coordinator, then 100 percent of the cost can be charged to the CAP Project.

Indirect costs are those that are incurred for common or joint purposes and cannot be readily identified with a specific project. Indirect costs are those costs remaining to be allocated after direct costs have been determined. For example: The salaries and expenses of executive officers, personnel administration, and accounting benefit all activities of the organization. They may not be readily identified with a particular grant award or project. Using an appropriate allocation method, these costs can be distributed to each project, such that each contributes a fair share toward paying for the administrative expenses incurred. The allocation of indirect costs and the computation of an indirect cost rate should be left to an accountant or CPA firm. For the most part, grantors, contractors, and foundations allow for the charging of indirect costs, but it is not unusual for the rate to be limited to a certain percentage.

This sample budget illustrates the costs described, along with estimates for expenses such as postage and mileage.

CAP Project Annual Budget

Program Coordinator		
(80%, 1664 hours at $10.41/hr)	17,322.24	
Task Force Facilitators (100 classrooms)	5,400.00	
Subtotal employee salaries	22,722.24	
FICA (@ .0765 of total salaries)	1,793.20	
Unemployment Ins. (est. .0250 of total sal.)	586.01	
Worker Comp. Ins. (est. .03 of total sal.)	703.22	
Employee Health/Dental/Life Insurance	2,500.00	
Subtotal employee benefits	5,582.43	
Total Salary and Benefits		**28,304.67**
Program Supplies	500.00	
Postage	150.00	
Advertising/Help Wanted	300.00	
Conference/Seminars	300.00	
Local Mileage	528.00	
Subtotal direct program expenses	1,778.00	
Rent (12 mos. @ $300 per mo.)	3,600.00	
Utilities — electric (12 mos. @ $50 per mo.)	600.00	
Utilities — gas (12 mos. @ $30 per mo.)	360.00	
Office maintenance —		
(12 mos. @ $50 per mo.)	600.00	
Telephone — local line charges		
(12 mos. @ $40 per mo.)	480.00	
Telephone — long distance calls	50.00	
Insurance — property and equipment	250.00	
Insurance — professional liability	2,000.00	
Accounting/CPA/Audit fees	2,500.00	
Legal retainer fees	1,500.00	
Subtotal operating expenses	11,940.00	
Total direct program and operating expenses		**13,718.00**
Total CAP Project Budget		**42,022.67**

Finalizing the Budget

As you can see, some research needs to be performed and some experts consulted before you can prepare a budget. However, when you've finished your research you should feel confident that the budget you have prepared is an accurate estimate of all of your costs. Each year you'll become more and more accurate in your estimates as you become familiar with the budgeting process.

9
CAP Program Evaluation

Introduction

Since CAP was created in 1978, it has won the appreciation and support of communities throughout and beyond the United States. Much of the evaluation to date has examined whether child sexual assault prevention programs accomplish what they set out to do. Efforts to understand the strengths and weaknesses of prevention programs can lead to better, more effective programs. Additionally, program evaluations are becoming increasingly important for obtaining support from social service administrators, funders, and the general community. As you work toward a successful project, you will need to determine what role program evaluation will play from year to year.

Evaluating Your Project

If you are just starting a CAP Project in your area, the thought of performing an evaluation in addition to the other challenges awaiting your group may seem somewhat overwhelming. Relax. It is not necessary for you to launch into comprehensive or complex program evaluation early in your project's career, and it is unlikely that even the most skeptical funders will require you to do so. However, with moderate amounts of planning and coordination, even new projects can begin to accumulate useful feedback about their quality.

Program evaluations can take different forms and can entail various degrees of sophistication. Two different types of program evaluations, formative and summative, are discussed. Additionally, we present several different designs for both types of evaluation. A design basically dictates when and from whom measurements will be gathered during the course of an evaluation. One of these evaluation designs, or a combination of them, may meet the needs of your project at different times in the future.

The first part of this chapter focuses on various ways to evaluate your project; the second part reviews research studies on the effectiveness of CAP and other child abuse prevention programs over the past several years.

Formative Evaluation

Formative evaluation focuses on measuring the extent to which the CAP program is presented in the manner and style in which it was intended. This evaluation is used to gain information about program implementation. The purpose, therefore, of the formative evaluation is to monitor your project continually to assure high-quality performance.

The elementary CAP model has been developed in precise detail, and adherence to all program components and to the written curriculum is necessary to maintain the program's integrity and effectiveness. If the elementary model is presented as it is scripted in *Strategies for Free Children,* a growing body of research suggests that the program will be effective. This research is discussed later in the chapter.

One of the advantages of using the CAP national model is that your project is a beneficiary of ongoing research and evaluation. It is important for you to be able to communicate to funders that a growing body of scientific literature indicates that the CAP model is effective. Knowing this, many funders will not find it necessary to demand independent evaluations, although they will want to know that the program is being implemented as designed.

Formative Design 1: Evaluating Program Implementation

It is possible that primary facilitators and role-players sometimes forget some of the script, or that occasionally program staff extemporaneously supplement the program with personal insights or points of view. For example, during an evaluation of a prevention program created by the Cook County (Illinois) Sheriff's Department, researchers found that the program facilitators strayed significantly from the script, using horror stories to exhort children to avoid strangers.

One method you can use to keep your project's staff sharp and effective is to ask them to evaluate themselves and each other at the end of a day's program. This process will not take much time and can be completed when the staff members complete their postworkshop paperwork. A standard form should be used for this evaluation (see Appendix A, "Evaluation of Children's Workshop").

Your team members should be encouraged to be candid, to discuss the observations with each other, and to support and assist one another. Generally, problems can be resolved by repeated practice.

Formative Evaluation 2: Descriptive Statistics

Another type of formative evaluation requires that your project keep detailed records on your accomplishments and the services you provide. You should keep accurate records on:

- the number of children who receive CAP workshops
- the number of adults served (teachers/parents)
- the number of workshops provided
- the number of disclosures of abuse that occur
- the number of cases referred to child protective services or other public agencies
- the number of general public presentations made

You will find that keeping these records will be valuable both for internal planning and budgeting and for documenting your project's activities for funding agencies.

Occasionally you will hear of a child who participated in a CAP workshop in your area and later used CAP strategies when faced with a threatening situation. Be sure to document these situations as well as you can. Write them up and share them with the national office in Columbus. These documented reports serve to affirm the work of your project, and the success of CAP strategies is important to include whenever you are promoting your project.

Summative Evaluation

Whereas the first type of evaluation deals with ensuring sound program implementation and monitoring, the second type determines whether the program accomplishes what it sets out to do. Attempts to evaluate program effectiveness are more difficult to undertake and can range from fairly basic to complex. Most research in this area has tried to determine whether parents, teachers, and students have actually learned what CAP set out to teach them.

Summative Design 1: Measurement of School Personnel's Perceptions of Program Effectiveness

This evaluation design asks teachers, counselors, and administrators to share their perceptions about the program after you have completed workshops at a particular school. One evaluation of this type was conducted on the CAP Program by the Dade County (Florida) Public School System, but this type of evaluation can also be effectively handled by CAP Projects themselves. In Dade County, a questionnaire was developed by the Office of Educational Accountability and sent to professional staff at the schools receiving CAP. The questionnaire solicited perceptions of the program in both formative and substantive areas. The teachers reported their perceptions of such items as the postworkshop level of awareness of how to deal with bullies, how to respond to strangers, and how to deal with uncomfortable touching. A variation of that questionnaire, entitled "School Personnel Evaluation," is presented in Appendix C.

This type of evaluation is valuable because it deals with the perceptions of school personnel, whose opinions are usually well regarded in their communities and who work directly with children. Their perceptions may highlight potential problems in staff performance. Positive perceptions by school personnel may also influence funders and help garner additional community support.

Planning and cooperation are required to perform a successful school personnel evaluation. Permission must be obtained from key school administrators; busy teachers and other school personnel must take the time to respond. Questionnaires must be copied, disseminated, collected, and analyzed. Experience suggests that several follow-up attempts may be necessary before all, or most, of the questionnaires are completed and returned. Analysis of the completed questionnaires, however, need not be complicated. Just counting responses and determining percentages is usually adequate. However, even this relatively uncomplicated type of evaluation can be time-consuming, so be sure to plan ahead and make sure your project has adequate resources and staff time to perform it.

Summative Type 2: Measurement of Teacher/Parent Knowledge Acquisition

This type of summative evaluation is more sophisticated in that, instead of dealing with *perceptions* of program effectiveness, this design focuses on direct *measurement* of program effectiveness. However, since this design involves the measurement of participant knowledge and attitudes, several ethical considerations have to be discussed. First, teachers and parents should be given the option of declining participation in the evaluation. So, although you should request their participation and explain the purpose and value of the evaluation in general terms, you should also be prepared to accept refusals. Second, because participants should remain anonymous, you should instruct them not to put their names on the questionnaires. You are not interested in how specific individuals respond, but rather in how the group as a whole responds, and anonymity will facilitate honest responses.

In this type of evaluation, parents and teachers should be asked to take a few minutes after the workshop is over to answer a brief series of questions covering the most important points addressed in the workshop. These responses are then analyzed to ascertain the degree to which the group has acquired the workshop content. This type of design is commonly referred to as an *after-only* design, in that measurement of participant knowledge is undertaken only at the conclusion of the workshop.

Although this type of evaluation is useful and relatively easy to administer, you cannot be sure that the evaluation measures what the participants learned from the program, rather than information they already knew before it began. One way to get around this problem is to ask the participants to take a few minutes before the workshop to answer the questions (pretest) and then to repeat the procedure after the workshop is over (posttest). Arguably, changes in the respondents' answers from pretest to posttest can be attributed to the workshop. You will gain valuable information, but it will cost you in terms of time and resources.

In order to perform a pre- and postworkshop measurement of participant knowledge you will need to allot additional time for adult workshops. You must have double the number of questionnaires on hand, with half labeled *preworkshop* and half labeled *postworkshop*. Additionally, the analysis will become somewhat more complex after counting responses and determining percentages for both pre- and postworkshop responses. You may find that the participants answered differently, but you may not know whether the differences in the responses are more than what could have occurred by chance. We recommend that you consult someone with skills in statistical analysis to assist in the interpretation of your results.

With the preceding considerations of time, resources, and energy in mind, your project will have to decide upon the type of adult evaluation that both meets your needs and is affordable. Although they have shortcomings, after-only designs are widely used and provide important information about the level of participant knowledge.

For a suggested questionnaire, see the form titled "Adult Questionnaire" in Appendix B.

Summative Design 3: Student Evaluations

Evaluation of the effectiveness of the children's workshops can also be done by your project, but again, several important ethical issues must be addressed. First, before children participate in the CAP workshops, their parents must be informed about the intended program evaluation and given the opportunity to request that their children not be participants. This requires that parents be given detailed information about the evaluation process — who will do it, where it will be done, what types of questions will be asked, and so forth. Parents should also be informed that their children will remain anonymous if they participate in the program evaluation, since only information about the effect of the program on the group is important. If you plan ahead adequately you can include information about the evaluation on the same correspondence that notifies parents about the workshops. Be sure, however, that if a parent requests that a child not be included in the evaluation that the child is still given the opportunity to participate in the workshop.

Once parents have been informed and provided the opportunity to withdraw their children from the evaluation, the children must also be given the right to decline participation. Children should be told in advance about the evaluation and, if they agree to participate, should also be given the right to refuse to answer any questions they choose and to end the evaluation process whenever they prefer. In addition to these ethical issues concerning participation and confidentiality, any evaluation method should be designed so that children are not put in a situation that makes them uncomfortable or fearful. For example, if children are to be interviewed, they should have had some previous contact with the interviewer, and the interviews should occur in a place where the children feel safe, preferably within sight of their teacher and classmates.

The first type of children's evaluation you may want to attempt is the after-only measurement of prevention knowledge acquisition. Within a few days after the workshop has been completed, return to the classes that received workshops and perform brief interviews to ascertain what the children learned from the program. Each child should be interviewed individually. An important question for you to answer at this juncture is, What questions should be asked? You should confine your questions to those that directly reflect the CAP workshop. That is, prepare questions that focus specifically on what CAP teaches to children. One type of question that has been used focuses on student acquisition of prevention strategies. Questions based on scenarios that correspond to workshop material can be used to measure student knowledge of prevention strategies. For example, students can be asked the following:

> Chris was walking to school. A bigger, older student came up to Chris and said, "Give me all your lunch money, and give it to me now." What should Chris do?

After recording a child's response, ask, "Is there anything else Chris could do?" Keep asking this until the student offers no further response. By carefully recording the student's responses, you can later analyze them and count the number of responses that reflect what was taught in the CAP workshop.

Although this design can be useful in ascertaining children's acquisition of prevention concepts, it is very time-consuming, requiring hours of project staff time to coordinate the interviews, conduct them, and analyze students' responses.

A major weakness of this design is one that was discussed regarding the adult evaluation. After-only designs cannot control for what the students knew before they participated in CAP workshops. That is, if students already were aware of some basic prevention information — and many are — you may mistakenly credit all of their knowledge to the CAP program. If you decide that it is important for your project to address this weakness of the after-only design, you will have to conduct a preworkshop interview with each child to determine what he or she knows before the workshops begin. The obvious problem with this approach is that it requires even more project staff time and resources. Pretesting must be coordinated, performed, analyzed, and later statistically compared to the posttest responses. Due to the logistical problems of performing all these tasks, you may be forced to conduct an after-only design.

One method of conducting a preworkshop and postworkshop measurement of student knowledge in a less cumbersome fashion is to provide students with written surveys to complete at their desks. Although this method is infinitely more manageable, you will lose some of the richness and detail that you can obtain in an interview. Additionally, this method is only appropriate for older children who are able to understand the survey questions and to give adequate written responses. If you use this method, ask the children not to write their names on the surveys, but instead to write a special code that only they will know (for example, the last four digits of their telephone number). By asking them to remember and use this code again on the postworkshop survey, you can match individual pre- and postworkshop surveys while still ensuring anonymity (see "Children's Evaluation Form" in Appendix C).

Evaluation Performed by Non-CAP Personnel

An evaluation performed in-house can be very useful for self-assessment by program administrators and staff. However, such an evaluation may have limited credibility among funding sources and others not connected with the project. Evaluations that have the most credibility are those whose designs closely follow scientific guidelines. By using a carefully selected sample of respondents, a control group, more sophisticated measurement instruments, and so forth, experienced researchers are able to perform a more credible evaluation.

In order to obtain the assistance of people with evaluation expertise, your project must have the necessary funds available. If funders or administrators push hard for program evaluation, you should make it clear that evaluation money has to accompany that desire, whether the evaluation is to be in-house or performed by outside researchers. Although it is possible that an interested graduate student at a nearby university might evaluate your project for a thesis or dissertation, at his or her own cost, it is probable that a more scientific evaluation will occur only if funders allocate appropriate funds. Be sure to get estimates from researchers, since quality evaluations can easily run into thousands of dollars.

Hiring or working with people with research and evaluation expertise, however, will not guarantee a quality evaluation. Although they have knowledge of the best way to conduct credible evaluations, most outside researchers will not be familiar with the issue of child abuse and the specific goals of your project. You will want to have adequate staff time budgeted to work with the researchers. They will have to incorporate your knowledge and expertise about CAP and its goals, and you will have to work closely with them to construct interview schedules or surveys that ask the right questions.

Experience suggests that caution should be exercised when working with outside evaluators. The issue of child abuse and its prevention is one that stirs the emotions of many people. Researchers are not immune to these emotions, and it is possible that their personal attitudes can exert strong influence on their work. For example, a university researcher in California conducted a federally funded evaluation of the CAP preschool model and six other preschool abuse prevention programs. Although the results of the evaluation indicated that significant gains were made in the CAP preschoolers' prevention knowledge, the researcher minimized those gains. Instead, he expressed disapproval of child abuse prevention programs such as CAP by suggesting that these programs undermine the participants' childhood. The researcher concluded that it was the parents who should be responsible for protecting children from abuse. He warned that childhood should not be encumbered with awareness of sexual abuse, and of prevention information or strategies in particular. The researcher recommended discontinuing public funding for preschool prevention programs.

In light of the possibility of an experience like this, you should acquaint yourself with the past work and relevant issue positions of potential outside researchers. You will want to work with objective evaluators who are capable of conducting an unbiased evaluation of your program. These researchers should welcome your participation and input in the evaluation process. Work closely with them in the construction or consideration of research designs and instruments for measuring program effects.

Finally, we strongly suggest that your project work with the national CAP office so that we can assist in the review of designs and instruments and contribute to a quality evaluation.

Review of the Literature

Over the past several years, a body of research has accumulated on the effectiveness of child sexual abuse prevention programs. Several of these studies have focused on CAP. Others have looked at different programs or have created prevention curricula for the purpose of measuring children's response to prevention materials. We first review studies that have focused on CAP, and then review research on other child abuse prevention models. Interpretation of these studies has been facilitated in part by a review conducted by David Finkelhor and Nancy Strapko. Their work, "Sexual Abuse Prevention Education: A Review of Evaluation Studies," is included in *Child Abuse Prevention,* edited by Diane Willis, E. Wayne Holder, and Mindy Rosenberg.[1]

Before reading this material, you should be aware of two key issues that are tied to many of the research studies to date. First, most studies have focused on whether children actually learn the prevention strategies taught by CAP and related programs. As part of this question, prevention program providers and researchers alike have wondered to what extent the increase in children's prevention knowledge is actually carried over into their behavior. That is, if children learn about ways to deal with a bully who takes their lunch money, will they actually use these strategies in a real-life situation?

Although there have been many individual success stories of children using CAP strategies to defend themselves, it is difficult to conduct a scientific study that measures actual behavioral change. To date, only one study has been done that has actually placed children in videotaped, simulated abductions to see how children would respond after having participated in a prevention program. However, that study is controversial due to the obvious ethical issues that arise over subjecting children to the experience. So, although questions remain about the actual impact of program participation on children's behavior, most studies are confined to measuring increases in children's prevention knowledge, with the assumption (supported by success stories) that such knowledge can be carried over into actual behavior.

A second important issue that has surfaced recently asks whether children's participation in CAP and other prevention programs has detrimental effects on children, such as increased fear of strangers, nightmares stimulated by awareness of abuse, misinterpretation of affectionate touches by benevolent adults, and so forth. Years of experience in primary abuse prevention for children on the part of CAP and other providers has revealed little cause for concern. Still, some in society, especially those who already oppose primary prevention efforts to reduce child assault, continue to raise the question. Consequently, many of the following studies address that question and, as you will see, most have found few negative effects.

Research on CAP

In 1986 Rene Binder and Dale McNiel from the University of California at San Francisco conducted a comprehensive study of the effects of CAP on 88 children aged five to 12 years. They found that children's knowledge of how to cope with potentially abusive situations increased significantly after CAP training. Interviews with the children's parents revealed that parents were significantly more likely to discuss the issue of sexual abuse with their children as a result of the CAP training. Neither parents nor teachers noticed any signs of increased emotional distress in the children following CAP training. Parents did report a significant decrease in fighting, physical complaints, and clinging behavior by their children after CAP training. After the program the children reported that they felt safer and better able to protect themselves.[2]

In 1987, a doctoral dissertation at the California Graduate School of Marital and Family Therapy, written by Jeri Smock, focused on the effects of CAP on children's levels of anxiety and trust. Eighty fifth and sixth graders and 19 parents participated in the study. The research revealed that children who participated in the prevention program showed significantly less anxiety in general and about strangers in particular after CAP training than before. Parents' anxiety regarding their children's safety was also lessened after CAP training.[3]

In 1987 Mary Kenning and associates at the University of Nebraska conducted research on the CAP model and its effects on children's knowledge and skills related to preventing sexual abuse. In their study of 72 first and second graders, the researchers found significant increases in children's knowledge about how to help a friend in need, telling a trusted adult, and behaving assertively in situations involving exploitive touch by either strangers or familiar people. The most significant behavioral gains were in situations involving familiar people, both children and adults.[4]

David Nibert of the National Assault Prevention Center conducted an evaluation of our own CAP in Columbus in 1987. Participants were 413 elementary school students in kindergarten through fifth grade. This study revealed a significant increase in students' knowledge about how to behave in an assault situation. CAP students were more likely to report that they would behave assertively in an assault situation than children who had not had CAP. For example, students who had CAP training were less likely to report that they would give in to inappropriate demands by peers and adults, and they were less likely to report that they would respond to aggression with violence. Finally, CAP graduates were significantly more likely to report that they would get detailed descriptions of assaulters.[5]

In 1985 Yvonne Lutter and Andrea Weisman evaluated a program that combined CAP, Illusion Theatre, and other prevention materials. The study participants were a group of Camp Fire Girls. This study revealed that the children who attended the program knew more about possible offenders and about what to do if confronted with an assault situation. The children who attended the program were also more likely to perceive their peers as a support resource and were more comfortable discussing sexual abuse.[6]

In 1985 Horace Leake conducted an evaluation of CAP for the Women's Center of San Joaquin County in Stockton, California. Studies were conducted with first, second, third, and fifth graders. His findings indicated that CAP was effective in significantly increasing students' ability to recognize and avoid abuse and assault situations. Leake also found that the CAP model was more effective in teaching children prevention knowledge than was another program that centered on a prevention film. Leake suggested that the active and experiential nature of the CAP model was a more effective learning method than was film viewing.[7]

In sum, research focusing on the elementary CAP program has indicated that the program is successful at increasing children's awareness of prevention strategies. Little evidence has emerged to indicate that CAP has any adverse effects on elementary school children. These studies should be shared with funders, parents, educators, and others who are interested in research findings on the elementary school program. A handout titled "Research on the CAP Elementary Model" is located in Appendix A, and can be given out at parent programs, teacher/staff in-services, or included in grant applications or reports to funders.

The CAP Preschool Model

In 1989 the staff of the National Assault Prevention Center examined whether children aged three to five were capable of learning information contained in the CAP preschool model. One hundred sixteen children from diverse social backgrounds were included in the study. The results indicated that young children have a high capacity to learn basic prevention knowledge, as measured by their application of prevention concepts to concrete "what if" scenarios. A large percentage of the children were capable of suggesting correct prevention responses in scenarios involving a luring stranger, a stranger attempting abduction, and a known adult abuser. However, there was a tendency for children to suggest aggressive or violent responses in a scenario involving peer abuse. These results suggest that even very young children have the ability to learn basic prevention concepts for concrete threatening situations.[8]

NAPC staff also asked the parents of preschoolers receiving the CAP preschool program to report whether their children were upset or harmed in any way because of their participation in the program. Very few of the responding parents reported postprogram behavior problems, and 26 percent reported observing positive behavior changes in their children. This finding has helped to alleviate fears about teaching young children about the possibility and prevention of sexual abuse.[9]

The CAP Special Needs Model

An adaptation of the CAP elementary model for children with developmental disabilities (CAP special needs model, by the National Assault Prevention Center) was studied by Lori Greene at The Ohio State University in 1986. Participants in this study were 23 students aged 13–18 from special needs classes of a public school system. Students were pre- and posttested on their knowledge of prevention concepts, and they participated in role-plays as a measure of how they might behave in an abuse situation. The students who attended the CAP program performed significantly better than did the control group on both knowledge and behavior measures. One area where learning did not increase substantially was in the differentiation of good and bad secrets. Greene suggested revised approaches to teaching this concept to children with special needs.[10]

The TeenCAP Model

An evaluation of the CAP program for teens (TeenCAP) was conducted by Mary Hess at the CAP national office in 1987. Six hundred thirty-seven teens from 12 to 18 participated. Before and after TeenCAP training, these teens completed written surveys focusing on their knowledge of prevention strategies. The survey also focused on knowledge about the causes of assault behavior and attitudes toward circumstances under which assault would be justified. After training, 75 percent of the teens were able to list three assertive strategies for dealing with assaults perpetrated by adults or peers. This performance was statistically significant when compared with pretest responses. There were also significant changes from pretest to posttest on questions about the definition of abuse and about prevention awareness.

Teen attitudes about the appropriateness of violence in several areas were not significantly altered. For example, many male teens believed that in some situations there are no alternatives to physical violence, especially if one's "honor" is threatened. This finding suggests a need for more research and program development to deal with the apparent inclination of some teens to be violent in certain situations.[11]

Research on Other Prevention Programs

Research on other child abuse prevention programs has also found that children can learn prevention concepts. At North Dakota University, Raymond Miltenberger and Ellyn Thiesse-Duffy evaluated a prevention booklet, designed to be used at home, called *Red Flag, Green Flag*. They found that the book alone was unsuccessful in teaching children prevention concepts. However, when the book was supplemented by role modeling, role-plays, and rehearsals developed by the researchers, a significant increase in children's prevention skills occurred. Follow-up measures two months later revealed that older children had maintained the skills they acquired. Parents reported no signs of behavioral or emotional problems following the program.[12]

A prevention program in the form of a play, *Bubbylonian Encounters*, was evaluated in 1984 by Helen Swan and associates. Sixty-three Kansas children aged eight to 11 participated in the study. The researchers found that the 30-minute play did not significantly increase the children's knowledge of abuse. They did note, however, that the children were significantly more likely to indicate that they would report sexual assault after attending the play.[13]

In 1985 University of Chicago researcher Jon Conte and associates conducted a study of a sexual assault prevention program developed by the Cook County (Illinois) Sheriff's Department. The program was presented on three consecutive days and lasted one hour each day. The curriculum utilized role-plays to teach assertiveness skills, used the terms "ok" and "not ok" touch, and differentiated between good and bad secrets. Forty children whose ages ranged from four to ten participated in the study. Results revealed that children showed significant improvement on the prevention knowledge questionnaire after the program. However, the older children showed greater improvement than the younger children.[14]

In 1984 University of Washington researcher Ann Downer evaluated the "Talking About Touching" personal safety curriculum developed by the Seattle-based Committee for Children. Eighty children, aged nine and ten, participated in the study. Downer found that the children demonstrated increased prevention knowledge after the program. Children were more likely to answer correctly such questions as: Do you know any rules of personal safety? Whose fault is it if a child is molested? What should children do if they have a touching problem? In addition to their increased prevention knowledge, trained students demonstrated more competence in assertiveness skills, especially verbally assertive responses to pressure.[15]

Also in 1984 Carol Plummer conducted a study of the prevention curriculum used by Bridgework Theatre in Michigan. The three-day program, consisting of discussion, role-plays, and a film, was tested on 112 fifth-grade students. Use of a 24-item prevention knowledge questionnaire revealed that significant learning had occured on 14 items. Plummer found that after the training children were more prepared to cope with stranger assault than with an assault by a known adult. Follow-up measurement eight months later, however, did not indicate that learning had been retained at significant levels.[16]

In 1986 University of Western Ontario researcher David Wolfe and associates evaluated the effects of a brief prevention program created and implemented by medical students in a community in the Southeastern United States. The participants were 290 school children in grades four and five. The program consisted of two skits followed by group discussion. The study demonstrated that fourth- and fifth-grade children showed an increase in prevention knowledge and were more aware of possible actions to take if confronted with an assault situation. Children showed significant increases in the knowledge that they could yell for help if they were afraid of an adult, that they could tell someone in the event that someone tried to abuse them, and that not all people who could hurt them are easily recognizable by appearance alone. However, after the program many children expressed the belief that someone they trusted would not believe them if they reported an adult was hurting them.[17]

Several interesting studies have been conducted at Washington State University. In 1986 Sandy Wurtele and associates conducted a study that compared the results of the prevention film *Touch* with a behavior skills training program that involved role-plays and behavior rehearsal. Participants in the study were 28 kindergarten and first-grade students and 43 fifth and sixth graders. The researchers found that the behavior training was more effective than the film in increasing children's prevention knowledge. Children's skills were measured by asking them how they would respond in several vignettes that were read to them. Only modest increases in children's skills were found, prompting the researchers to emphasize the need for more concentrated behavior training with children. Surprisingly, a three-month follow-up found that the knowledge scores of students who only attended the film had also increased.[18]

In 1986 Sandy Wurtele and Cindy Miller-Perrin researched children's conceptions of sexual abuse. They studied 48 children, whom they separated into two groups by age. Roughly half of the children were five to seven years of age; the other half were ten to 12. Their findings revealed that the two groups of children differed in their conceptions of sexual abuse, descriptions of abusers, and perceptions of the consequences for the abuser. Most of the younger children were unable to directly define the term *sexual abuse*. However, half of the older children were fairly accurate in their descriptions. Older children were likely to describe an abuser as a teenager or an adult, whereas the younger children described an abuser as someone their own age or slightly older. The majority of the children believed that an abuser should be punished for the deed; however, older children were more likely to suggest that the abuser receive some type of mental health services.[19]

Additionally, Wurtele and Miller-Perrin researched parents' perceptions of problem behaviors demonstrated by their children after they attended prevention programs. The prevention programs were the film *Touch* and behavior skills training. Parents reported observing relatively few changes in their children's behavior as a result of the programs. Only 7 percent of the sample reported that their children experienced any problems, and no parents reported that the program had a prolonged negative effect. The researchers found that the program stimulated discussions of assault between parents and their children, and they concluded that the program was not harmful to children.[20]

These studies indicate that prevention training has positive effects and that children learn prevention concepts. However, are these programs effective in actually reducing children's vulnerability to assault? Although anecdotal information continually supports prevention programs, quantitative information is difficult to obtain. One controversial research project did directly examine the effectiveness of a prevention program. A 1987 study conducted at the University of Colorado by George Fryer and associates involved students in a simulated abduction. Participants in the project were 44 Denver children who were in kindergarten and first and second grades. Parents and school officials gave permission for the study and cooperated closely with the research staff.

Before receiving training, children's prevention skills were measured by their responses in the following situation. They were sent, individually, to another part of the school for reasons fabricated by school staff. Alone in the hall, the child was approached by a stranger who asked the child to accompany him to his car to help bring in treats for his son's birthday party. Children who agreed to help were told by the stranger that he would come back later to get their help. Children's reponses were audio- and videotaped.

After the pretest, half of the children had eight days of prevention training in daily 20-minute presentations. Following the prevention program, children were again approached by a stranger who asked each child to accompany him to his car to help bring in puppets for a school show. Each simulation was carried out without the child's awareness. The children were not informed that they had participated in a simulated encounter. Findings revealed that most children participating in the pretest simulation agreed to leave the school building with the stranger. After prevention training, however, children were significantly less likely to agree to leave the building with the stranger than children who had not had training. This finding was repeated at a follow-up simulated abduction six months later.[21]

In 1981 Cheryl Poche and associates at Western Michigan University conducted preschool research that also used a simulated abduction. Nine preschoolers, aged three to five, were approached by a stranger who asked them to leave the school with him. Eight of the nine children agreed to leave. Three of the eight children were then given safety training. The researchers developed training that consisted of modeling, behavior rehearsal, and social reinforcement. The training lasted approximately 90 minutes and was broken down into five sessions. After the training, the three children displayed a substantial improvement in verbal and behavioral skills in a subsequent abduction simulation. They were significantly less likely to agree to leave with the stranger after training. The children's self-protective responses were maintained in yet another simulated abduction, involving a different stranger, in a community location. One of the three children was tested by the same method three months later and the improvement was fully maintained.[22]

Although simulated abductions can provide useful information about knowledge and skills children learn from prevention programs, this method of evaluation raises serious ethical questions about the appropriateness of the approach. Research that presents children with realistic and potentially frightening situations may have implications for children that are unknown to researchers.

Since the Poche study of preschoolers in 1981, additional studies have examined prevention training with preschoolers. In 1986 University of Cincinnati researchers Joyce Borkin and Lesley Frank created a puppet show and coloring book to teach prevention concepts to 83 preschoolers, aged three to five. Four to six weeks after the training, these children were asked what to do if someone touched them in a way that was "not okay." Out of 25 three-year-olds, only one child (4 percent) spontaneously offered a correct response. Out of 30 four-year-olds, 13 children (43 percent) spontaneously offered a correct response. Borkin and Frank noted that the three-year-olds had difficulty learning prevention rules.[23] This finding was similar to Jon Conte's (see note 14).

In February 1988 a study was released by Neil Gilbert and associates at the University of California. The project tested seven different preschool curricula, including CAP, and approximately 95 children participated in the study. In this study children's prevention knowledge and skills were measured by a new method. Potentially dangerous scenarios were presented to children; however, bunnies were substituted for children in the stories. Children were asked, for example, whether the little bunny should go with a big bunny she does not know. This method was used primarily because of the researchers' concern about scaring child participants.

Children did demonstrate improved knowledge abilities after attending one of the seven trainings. They were better able to distinguish between good and bad touches, to offer strategies on how to stop a bad touch, and to demonstrate knowledge about avoiding risk situations. The researchers, however, did not believe the amount of learning was substantial, and they recommended discontinuing prevention training with preschoolers.[24] This highly publicized study has been viewed by prominent researchers as troublesome in both its methodology and its recommendations. The use of bunnies to determine children's knowledge and skill may not have tested the children's own abuse resistance. In addition, the recommendations provided by the researchers are not substantiated by the results of the Borkin and Frank study or by the Poche study. Clearly, more research is needed to determine the effectiveness of prevention programs for young children.

Summary of Major Findings

- Children learn prevention concepts after exposure to CAP and other programs. Children can learn prevention concepts and acquire skills that can be used to reduce their vulnerability to abuse and assault.
- CAP does not cause emotional or behavior problems in children. Some people have feared that prevention training may cause children to misunderstand physical affection by their parents and family, or that prevention programs may cause children to develop an unhealthy fear of strangers or create other problems. Although some short-term problems have occurred among a small number of children, research results reveal that the vast majority of children experience no problems after their exposure to CAP and other programs. Children become less aggressive and more assertive in their reports of how they would deal with peer and adult abusers.
- Parents and children talk more about the topic of child sexual abuse as a result of their exposure to prevention programs.

Constructive Information Gained from Research

Although quantitative research supports the use of primary abuse prevention programs for children, it has also provided information on areas in which prevention programs can improve their efforts. Some of the most important findings are:

- Programs that get children actively involved (such as CAP) are more effective in teaching concepts than are passive programs or efforts limited to films, books, and discussion. This appears to be especially true for preschool-aged children.
- Children's prevention knowledge should be reinforced periodically after training, especially for prevention knowledge pertaining to abuse from known adults.
- Children appear to comprehend concrete concepts more readily than more abstract ones.
- Children learn facts and concrete information more readily than skills.

- Even after participation in one prevention program, some children felt that someone they trusted would not believe them if they reported an adult was hurting them.

Research conducted to date has provided a great deal of support for the continuation of efforts to reduce children's vulnerability to sexual abuse by increasing their prevention knowledge. Valuable information about what works and what does not work continues to be integrated into program curricula.

Your project will need to perform in-house formative evaluations, and it is likely that questions will be raised about the effectiveness of your project. Should you develop questions or problems concerning project evaluation or if you desire further information on the topic, you should contact the CAP national office.

References

1. D. Finkelhor and N. Strapko, "Sexual Abuse Prevention Education: A Review of Evaluation Studies," in *Child Abuse Prevention,* eds. Diane J. Willis, E. Wayne Holder, and Mindy Rosenberg (New York: Wiley, in press).

2. R. Binder and D. McNiel, "Evaluation of a School-Based Sexual Abuse Prevention Program: Cognitive and Emotional Effects" (Paper presented at the 1986 Annual Meeting of the American Psychiatric Association, Washington, DC, 1986).

3. J. Smock, *Missing Children: A Study of the Effects of a Public School Prevention Program on Children and Their Families* (Ph.D. diss., California Graduate School of Marital and Family Therapy, 1987).

4. M. Kenning et al., "Evaluation of Child Sexual Abuse Prevention Programs: A Summary of Two Studies" (Paper presented at the National Conference on Family Violence, Durham, NH, 1987).

5. D. Nibert, "Evaluation of the Child Assault Prevention Project in the Columbus Public Schools" (Unpublished, Columbus, OH: National Assault Prevention Center, 1987).

6. Y. Lutter and A. Weisman, "Sexual Victimization Prevention Project" (Final Report to the National Institute of Mental Health, Grant R18 MH39549, 1985).

7. H. Leake, "A Study to Compare the Effectiveness of Two Primary Prevention Programs in Teaching Children to Recognize and Resist Child Sexual Abuse and Assault" (The Women's Center of San Joaquin County, 1985).

8. D. Nibert et al., "The Ability of Young Children to Learn Abuse Prevention," *RESPONSE: To the Victimization of Women and Children* 12, no. 4 (1989): 14–20.

9. D. Nibert, S. Cooper, and J. Ford, "Parents' Observations of the Effect of a Sexual-Abuse Prevention Program on Preschool Children," *Child Welfare* 68, no. 5 (September/October 1989): 539–46.

10. L. Greene, *The Effects of an Intervention Training Program to Prevent Child Assault on Children with Developmental Disabilities* (Master's Thesis, The Ohio State University, 1986).

11. M. Hess, *Evaluation of the TeenCAP Project* (Unpublished, Columbus, OH: National Assault Prevention Center, 1987).

12. R. Miltenberger and E. Thiesse-Duffy, "Evaluation of Home-Based Programs for Teaching Personal Safety Skills to Children," *Journal of Applied Behavior Analysis* (Forthcoming).

13. H. Swan, A. Press, and S. Briggs, "Child Sexual Abuse Prevention: Does It Work?" *Child Welfare* 64, no. 4 (July/August 1985).

14. J. Conte et al., "An Evaluation of a Program to Prevent the Sexual Victimization of Young Children," *Child Abuse and Neglect* 9, no. 3 (1985): 319-28.

15. A. Downer, *Evaluation of Talking About Touching* (Committee for Children, Seattle, WA, 1984).

16. C. Plummer, *Preventing Sexual Abuse: What In-School Programs Teach Children* (Paper presented at the National Conference for Family Violence Researchers, 1984).

17. D. Wolfe et al., "Evaluation of a Brief Intervention for Educating School Children in Awareness of Physical and Sexual Abuse," *Child Abuse and Neglect* 10 (1986): 85-92.

18. S. Wurtele et al., "Teaching Personal Safety Skills for Potential Prevention of Sexual Abuse: A Comparison of Treatments," *Journal of Consulting and Clinical Psychology* 54, no. 5 (1986): 688-92.

19. S. Wurtele and C. Miller-Perrin, "Children's School Based Sexual Abuse Prevention Programs: Reassure the Parents" (Presented at the 94th Annual Convention of the American Psychological Association, Washington, DC, August, 1986).

20. Wurtele and Miller-Perrin, "Children's School Based."

21. G. Fryer, S. Kraizer, and T. Miyoshi, "Measuring Actual Reduction of Risk to Child Abuse: A New Approach," *Child Abuse and Neglect* 11, no. 2 (1987): 173-85.

22. C. Poche, R. Brouwer, and M. Swearingen, "Teaching Self-Protection to Young Children," *Journal of Applied Behavior Analysis* 14, no. 2 (1981): 169-76.

23. J. Borkin and L. Frank, "Sexual Abuse Prevention for Preschoolers: A Pilot Program," *Child Welfare* 65, no. 1 (January/February 1986).

24. N. Gilbert et al., *Child Sexual Abuse Prevention: Evaluation of Educational Materials for Preschool Programs* (United States Department of Health and Human Services, Grant #90-CA-1163, 1988).

10
Working Together: NAPC and You

What's in the CAP Name?

One question that comes to the minds of many who decide to start a CAP Project is "What will be my relationship with your office?" In order to clarify your rights and responsibilities and ours, in this section we examine the issues that often emerge. We are your friends and colleagues, and we believe that the basis of our relationship should be respect for one another's work. With that basis and with mutual goodwill, we believe that you will find our office helpful as you work toward the prevention of abuse.

The CAP network across the globe comprises a number of different entities, all of which are doing at least one CAP curriculum. Most projects start out with the elementary model, and add models as their project receives requests to serve new populations. Therefore, you may see CAP Projects that are providing the preschool model, the special needs model, the TeenCAP model, the hearing impaired model, and the elementary model, or any combination of the five.

Some CAP Projects are part of a larger agency such as a mental health center, battered women's shelter, health department, or rape crisis center. Some stand alone, having prepared and filed all of the paperwork necessary to become a nonprofit organization.

We recognize CAP Projects that have been trained by our offices, which entitles them to a number of benefits that we are committed to increase over time. Currently recognized CAP Projects receive new materials at low cost and technical assistance from our office. We also make referrals to recognized CAP Projects and help to protect the territory in which they work. For instance, if someone from Durango, Colorado, contacts our office about setting up a CAP Project, we refer him or her to the existing local project. We will not provide training in any CAP model to an area already served without express permission of the existing CAP Project. In this way we avoid duplicating services in an area, because resources to provide prevention services are always limited. We also encourage cooperation rather than competition, since CAP Projects are always looking for people who are committed to prevention to join their efforts.

There are also Regional CAP Training Centers (RCTC). An RCTC usually serves a state or province and provides training and technical assistance to that area with our permission. Currently there are five RCTCs, serving Quebec, New Jersey, Rhode Island, Massachusetts, and California. Our office in Columbus also serves the entire state of Ohio, so we are the RCTC for Ohio, as well as the International Office for CAP. Figure 2 shows the relation-

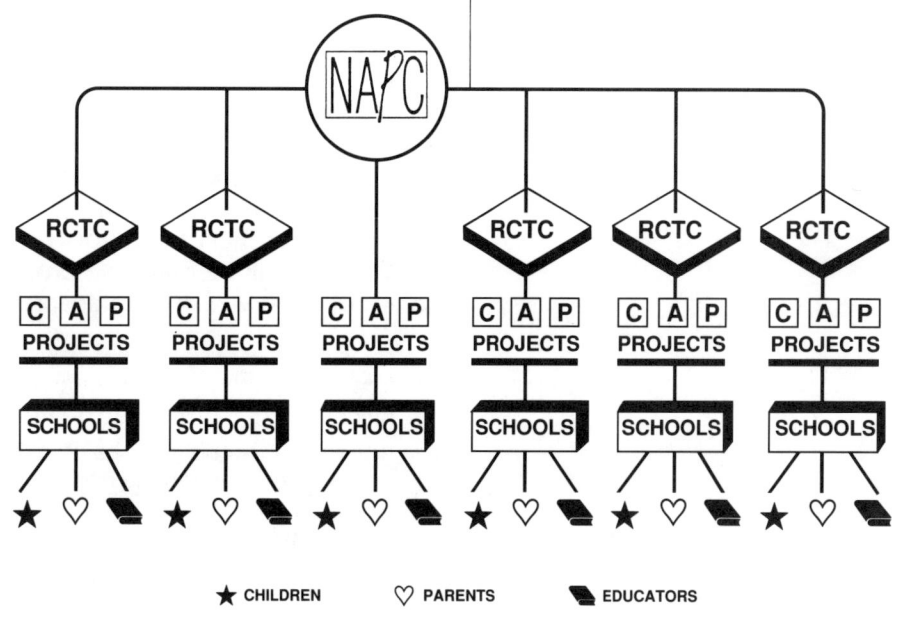

Figure 2

ships among the members of the CAP network from the community to the international level. An RCTC is set up after a particular project has run a successful program for a number of years and has a track record in service provision. When any project indicates an interest in becoming an RCTC, we negotiate this new identity with the project.

What It Means to Call Yourself a CAP Project

CAP has come to stand for something special in the field of child abuse prevention. Our concept and programs have earned the respect of writers, researchers, feminists, clinicians, police officers, protective services workers, educators, and parents from all across the United States and in many other nations. That reputation for excellence is something each of us must protect for every CAP Project.

When you call your project CAP, you receive all of the benefits that come with the name. If you are going to call yourself a CAP Project, then you must make a commitment to the principles and the curriculum. Although minor adaptations can be made to the curriculum in order to increase cultural competence in your area, other changes in the curriculum should not be made. When someone says, "This is a CAP Project," it should mean the same thing in every community.

Even a good program can live or die by the media exposure it receives. There are many risks in working with children about such sensitive subject matter, and this is why we have invested so much in the development and evaluation of our curriculum. If you want to take additional risks by designing new materials, we wish you success, but we can't assume or share your risks. You should call your project by a name other than CAP if you intend to operate on a different theoretical model or use a different curriculum.

We could all be hurt by a project whose members have good intentions, but whose curriculum adaptation backfires. Consider this scenario:

> A CAP Project in a certain city decides to change a few things in the CAP curriculum. They decide that "Uncle Harry" should touch his niece directly on the crotch during the role-play, so that children more clearly understand what Uncle Harry's intentions are.
>
> On the same day he had CAP workshop in school, one little boy discloses abuse to his mother, who makes a report to the authorities. The boy states that he was touched by his uncle in the groin area.
>
> When the case goes to trial the defense attorney subpoenas the CAP coordinator and asks her many questions about the CAP model. The defense attorney twists her comments to make it sound as though the only reason the little boy disclosed was because he had seen a role-play on molestation by an uncle, and this "put ideas in his head."

> The next day the headline in the local paper reads: "Boy Lying, Says Jury." The story publicizes the defense's allegation that CAP's presentation caused the child to invent a story.

In seeking to provide clear information, this fictitious CAP Project made a mistake that could cost all of us dearly. One good reason to use a national model such as CAP is that it has already been researched, and we can defend each element of our program with that research (see Chapter 9, "CAP Program Evaluation"). Although we can't promise you that using CAP will mean hassle-free operation, existing research on the model protects us all by confirming what our program does and does not do.

The theoretical framework of CAP is just as important as the curriculum content. Misguided efforts to be "nonsexist" or to accommodate adults, rather than children, can disrupt or subvert the learning experience in unforeseen ways, as this real-life example illustrates.

> One CAP Project decided that there was no good reason why men on their task force should not provide the primary facilitation for workshops. Following their first workshop done in this manner, they realized the problems they were creating. In talk-time after the workshop, several female children said they would "get a big man to kick the stranger." One girl was upset because she lived alone with her mother and did not believe either one of them could protect herself.

Our intention is not to stifle innovation and curriculum improvements, but to protect the reputation we all share. *Please help us do this.* If you have suggestions about ways to change the CAP model, we invite you to send them to us for consideration.

"Safe, Strong, and Free"

Every CAP curriculum is copyrighted, and the slogan "Safe, strong, and free" is registered and service-marked. This service mark gives NAPC exclusive rights to use those words, and we give CAP Projects the right to use all of our materials. Consider the following true story.

> An anonymous woman in Montana sent us a pamphlet that advocated sex with young children in order to "help them appreciate their young sexuality." The pamphlet said that if children could experience sex with a "trusted adult," then they would truly be "safe, strong, and free."

The service mark and the copyright helped us protect the intent of our program by blocking an organization that works *against* the goals of NAPC from exploiting our materials. We wrote this organization a letter explaining our legal rights to the language they were using and were able to stop them from using our materials to further their own aim of rationalizing sex with children.

Your Responsibilities to NAPC

Whenever you conduct a presentation for adults or a media interview, or write about CAP in a brochure, pamphlet, or other written material, you must credit NAPC and provide our address in the credit. Different projects have credited us in different ways, depending on the materials in question. Here are several examples.

> ©1983, National Assault Prevention Center, P.O. Box 02005, Columbus, Ohio 43202. Used with permission. All rights reserved.

> The CAP Project of _____ County gratefully acknowledges the National Assault Prevention Center, whose staff trained us in the

CAP model. We are proud to be a member of the CAP Network, composed of more than 240 CAP Projects around the world. For more information about CAP, contact the National Assault Prevention Center, P.O. Box 02005, Columbus, Ohio 43202.

The CAP materials are copyrighted by the National Assault Prevention Center, P.O. Box 02005, Columbus, Ohio 43202. We gratefully acknowledge the center's work to help our community become a safer place for all of us. We use these materials with their permission.

Designing a Logo

The use of the NAPC logo (the "safe, strong, and free" kids) located on the back cover of this manual is prohibited, although you are welcome to revise the logo in some way. Some projects have put balloons in the hands of the kids or added other twists to the basic logo. Here are a few examples of revised logos.

Newark, OH

South Florida

Washoe County, NV

New Jersey

Media Relations

We encourage you to seek the attention of your local newspapers and radio and television stations in order to help publicize the work of your project. However, all national media (CBS, NBC, ABC, CNN, NPR, *The New York Times, USA Today,* etc.) should be referred to our office for response. Every CAP Project wants to know that when we gain national media coverage, we are represented with the best and most current information about our work. By referring national inquiries to our office, you ensure that a well-informed professional from our office will represent us all.

News inquiries from outside your state or territory should also be referred to our office. If there is a CAP Project operating in the area in question we will make a referral. If not, we will refer the reporters to the nearest project or provide information from our office.

Communication

We request that every CAP Project send us copies of their brochures and other public relations materials. When your project is featured on local TV news or in the newspaper, send us a video or print copy. We like to share the success of CAP Projects in our quarterly newsletter, *RECAP.*

We also require that each CAP Project compute and send to us annual data on the number of children and adults served by the project. We are often asked how many children CAP has served, and we want to include your work in our response. We will provide a data collection format to your project annually.

Finally, we need to be informed of changes in address, personnel, and phone numbers so that we can contact you and make referrals to you.

When you need something, ask; we'll provide all possible assistance. We welcome your suggestions about what would help you do a better job of serving your area. We all share the same goal, to prevent child abuse. Our cooperation and communication bring our goal closer to attainment.

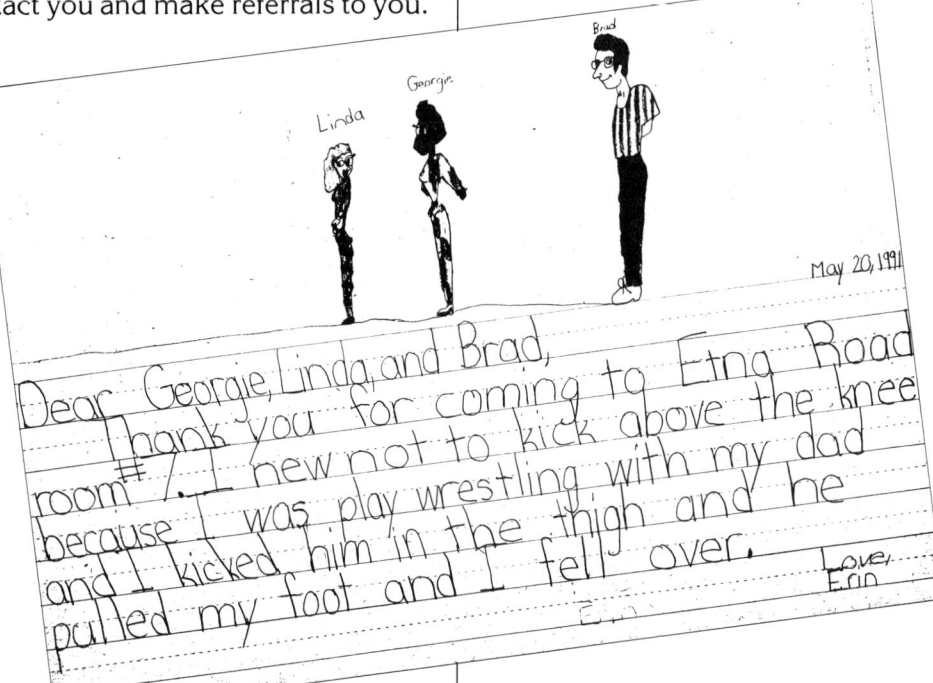

Handouts for Adult Presentations

- Defining Abuse and Neglect
- Myths and Facts About Child Abuse
- Prevention of Abuse: Theory of Vulnerability
- Clues to Possible Victimization
- Responding to Abuse or Neglect
- Reporting: Rights and Responsibilities
- Talking with a Child
- For Parents: Suggestions for In-Home Activities
- Research on the CAP Elementary Model

Appendix A

Defining Abuse and Neglect

Child Physical Abuse
A wide range of behaviors that physically injure or harm a child's body. Some behaviors include burning, punching, shaking, kicking, and throwing a child.

Child Neglect
Failure to provide nutrition, clothing, shelter, supervision, or medical care for a child. Neglect is different from poverty.

Child Sexual Assault
Any forced, exploitive, or coercive sexual contact or experience with a child. Child sexual assault includes:

- molestation
- rape
- incest
- voyeurism
- exhibitionism
- pornography
- forced prostitution

There are three types of force: physical, emotional, and authoritative.

Emotional Abuse
A pattern of behavior that impairs a child's emotional development and positive sense of self.

Emotional abuse includes the presence of a pattern of denigrating language and/or behaviors directed at the child, including:

- profanity
- belittling
- criticism
- rejection
- threats

Emotional abuse also includes the absence of a pattern of supporting language and/or behaviors directed at a child, including:

- pride in the child
- praise
- expressions of love and concern

©1991 National Assault **Prevention** Center • P.O. Box 02005 • Columbus, Ohio 43202 • 614-291-2540

Myths and Facts About Child Abuse

Rare

Myth: Child abuse is a rare occurrence.

Fact: Statistics indicate that child abuse and neglect occur frequently.

- 74,000 cases of suspected child abuse and neglect were reported in Ohio in 1986. (Ohio Department of Human Services)
- An estimated three children died every day of 1987 because of child abuse and neglect. (National Committee for the Prevention of Child Abuse)

Poor

Myth: Abused and neglected children almost always come from poor, minority, and/or inner-city families.

Fact: There is no evidence that links socioeconomic status, race, or educational level to abuse and neglect. Child abuse occurs within every neighborhood and school community across the country.

Girls

Myth: Sexual assault only happens to girls.

Fact: We may not know the full extent of sexual assault against boys because of their tendency not to report. Current research, however, estimates that one of three to four girls and one of four to six boys will be sexually assaulted before their eighteenth birthday.

Strangers

Myth: Most children are sexually assaulted by a stranger.

Fact: It is estimated that 80-85 percent of all child sexual assaults are perpetrated by an adult known and trusted by the child. Only a small percentage of assaulters fit the stereotype of the "stranger."

Easily Identified

Myth: Child abusers are easy to identify.

Fact: Child abusers cannot be easily distinguished from other people. They usually are not adults with mental illness or mental retardation. In fact, many offenders are upstanding community citizens.

Ask for It

Myth: Most children who are abused do something to cause the abuse to occur.

Fact: The child is always the victim. The responsibility for the abuse lies solely with the adult. In the case of child sexual abuse, many offenders try to shift the blame for their actions by accusing the child of being "seductive" or "promiscuous."

©1991 National Assault **Prevention** Center • P.O. Box 02005 • Columbus, Ohio 43202 • 614-291-2540

Prevention of Abuse: Theory of Vulnerability

Traditional Approaches
Traditional approaches to prevention
- prosecution
- avoidance

Effective Prevention
Reduction of vulnerability
- Increase information
- Lessen powerlessness and dependence
- Lessen isolation

Community Approach
Everyone contributes to safety

©1991 National Assault **Prevention** Center • P.O. Box 02005 • Columbus, Ohio 43202 • 614-291-2540

Clues to Possible Victimization

Sometimes children don't *tell* us they are in crisis, they *show* us. A change in a child's behavior could be due to the stress of being abused. These changes in behavior can alert adults to their problem.

Abuse and neglect can also sometimes leave physical marks on a child's body that adults can observe. Knowing both the physical and behavioral clues to abuse can help adults intervene on behalf of children.

Keep in mind that some clues can be normal behaviors for a given child at a given time. Therefore it is important to be aware of new behaviors, extreme behaviors, or combinations of the following characteristics. **Abused children cannot be identified by racial, ethnic, religious, or socioeconomic class. Abuse crosses these lines.**

Abused Children Are Often
- fearful of interpersonal relationships *or* overly compliant
- withdrawn *or* aggressive, hyperactive
- constantly irritable *or* listless, detached
- affectionless *or* overly affectionate (misconstrued as seductive)

Physical Symptoms
- bruises, burns, scars, welts, broken bones, continuing or inexplicable injuries
- urinary infections (particularly in young children)
- sexually transmitted diseases
- chronic ailments, stomachaches, vomiting, eating disorders
- vaginal or anal soreness, bleeding, or itching

Activity and Habit Clues
- nightmares
- inappropriate masturbation
- fear of going home or to some other location
- fear of being with a particular person
- running away
- delinquency
- lying
- prostitution

Age Inappropriate Behavior
- thumb sucking
- sexual activity or awareness
- promiscuity
- bed wetting
- alcohol/substance abuse
- assaulting younger children
- takes on adult responsibilities

Educational Concerns
- extreme curiosity, imagination
- academic failure
- sleeping in class
- inability to concentrate

Emotional Indicators
- depression
- phobias, fear of darkness, public restrooms, etc.
- chronic ailments
- self-inflicted injuries
- injuring/killing animals
- excessive fearfulness
- lack of spontaneity, creativity.

©1991 National Assault **Prevention** Center • P.O. Box 02005 • Columbus, Ohio 43202 • 614-291-2540

Responding to Abuse or Neglect

Responding to a child who has been abused or neglected is never easy. Children, depending on their age and developmental stage, may not be able to explain fully what has happened to them. Researchers report that children have difficulty disclosing abuse because they fear adult anger, disappointment, or disbelief. The following guidelines will help you respond sensitively and appropriately to a child who has been abused.

Guidelines

- Remain calm. Your calm reaction to a child will help him or her talk about the problem.

- Always let the child know that you believe and support him or her. Too often children lack credibility. Listen and receive the child's information in a nonjudgmental way.

- Use whatever language the child uses to describe the assault. Children may use explicit terminology when discussing abuse. Be prepared for this. Try to use this language, too, when talking with the child.

- Do not avoid embarrassing subjects. Let the child know that everything can be talked about.

- Do not project or assume anything. Let the child tell the story without interjecting your own assumptions.

- Know the reporting law; if a report needs to be made, be prepared to do so.

- Do not make promises you cannot keep. You cannot promise not to tell anyone else.

Goals

- Validate the child's feelings.
- Assure the child that you care, that you are still a friend, and that he or she is not to blame.
- Let the child know he or she has a right to be safe.
- Let the child know what action you will take to ensure his or her safety.

©1991 National Assault **Prevention** Center • P.O. Box 02005 • Columbus, Ohio 43202 • 614-291-2540

Reporting: Rights and Responsibilities

In the state of Ohio school personnel are required to report suspected child abuse and neglect. The following information will assist you in understanding this reponsibility.

- School personnel are required to report suspected abuse immediately. You do not need to have proof or evidence of abuse. If you have "reason to believe" a child is being abused or neglected you are mandated to report.

- A report may be made by phone or by correspondence to the children's services agency in your county.

- School personnel should provide the names of the child and the parent(s), the address of the parent(s), the age of the child, and the reason(s) for suspecting abuse or neglect. If you know the name of the person you suspect is abusing the child, this information should also be provided.

- Reporters of child abuse and neglect are immune from any civil or criminal liability.

- All child abuse and neglect reports and investigations are confidential, including the identity of the person making the report. The reporter's name cannot be released without his or her written consent.

- Failure to report child abuse and neglect by any mandated reporter is a fourth degree misdemeanor. It is punishable with a maximum of 30 days imprisonment and/or a $250 fine.

Talking with a Child

Crisis intervention is not counseling or therapy. Crisis intervention is giving assistance to a child in crisis, in a supportive manner, which helps the child determine his or her options available for help and support.

Four Steps of Crisis Intervention

Effective crisis intervention involves four steps:

1. Identify the immediate problem.
   - "An older kid stole my bike."
   - "The baby-sitter made me do things I don't like."

2. Examine possible solutions.
   - "Give up my bike and buy a new one," "Confront the bully with my friend," or "Tell my mom or the police."
   - "Tell my mom I don't like that baby-sitter," or "Tell the baby-sitter 'no'," or "Tell my mom," or "Tell the police."

3. Evaluate each alternative.
   - "I'd be afraid I'd get hurt by the bully," "A friend would help me feel stronger."
   - "If I told my mom, she'd probably talk to the baby-sitter," "The police might arrest the baby-sitter."

4. Prepare a realistic plan of action.
   - "I'm going to tell the bully to give me my bike back and take a friend with me."
   - "I want to talk to my mom and then talk to the baby-sitter with my mom."

Note

If a child discloses abuse you are mandated to report that abuse. Reporting abuse should be a part of the "plan of action" so that the child will not be surprised.

©1991 National Assault **Prevention** Center • P.O. Box 02005 • Columbus, Ohio 43202 • 614-291-2540

For Parents

Suggestions for In-Home Activities

1. Discuss children's rights: the right not be touched in ways a child feels are uncomfortable, the right to say no, and the right to get help.

2. Let your children know that you believe in their ability to stay safe and that you will always be there to help.

3. Answer children's questions about nightmares, television programs, real-life tragedies, and "what if's" positively and creatively without ridiculing their feelings or denying reality.

4. Practice the yell with your children on a regular basis.

5. Encourage children to help other children.

6. Discuss "good" and "bad" secrets, "safe" and "unsafe" touching, and how to tell the difference.

7. Tell your children about bribes: what they are and what they seek to accomplish.

8. Evaluate children's regular walking routes, noting spots of potential danger (abandoned houses, wooded areas, etc.). Discuss these potential dangers with your children.

9. Incorporate the words "safe, strong, and free" into your family's vocabulary.

10. Confront suspicious people and question suspicious events in the community.

11. Read books on building children's self-esteem, preventing child assault, children's rights, and assertion as a family. Make children's good self-esteem and safety a family project.

12. Role-play or play "what if" games with your children. "What if you get lost at the mall?" "What if you thought someone was following you?" Focus on what children can do to stay safe.

©1991 National Assault **Prevention** Center • P.O. Box 02005 • Columbus, Ohio 43202 • 614-291-2540

Research on the CAP Elementary Model

In 1986 Rene Binder and Dale McNiel from the University of California at San Francisco conducted a comprehensive study of the effect of CAP on 88 children aged five to 12 years. They found that children's knowledge of how to cope with potentially abusive situations increased significantly after CAP training. Interviews with the children's parents revealed that the parents were significantly more likely to discuss the issue of abuse with their children as a result of the CAP training. Neither parents nor teachers noticed any signs of increased emotional distress in the children following CAP training. Parents did report a significant decrease in fighting, physical complaints, and clinging behavior by their children after CAP training. After the program, the children reported they felt safer and better able to protect themselves.[1]

In 1987 a doctoral dissertation at the California Graduate School of Marital and Family Therapy, written by Jeri Smock, focused on the effects of CAP on children's levels of anxiety and trust. Eighty fifth and sixth graders and 19 parents participated in the study. The study revealed that children who participated in the prevention program showed significantly less anxiety in general and about strangers in particular after CAP training. Parents' anxiety regarding their children's safety was also lessened after CAP training.[2]

In 1987 Mary Kenning and associates at the University of Nebraska conducted research on the CAP model and its effects on children's knowledge and skills related to preventing sexual abuse. In their study of 72 first and second graders, the researchers found significant increases in children's knowledge about how to help friends in need, telling a trusted adult, and behaving assertively in situations involving familiar people, both children and adults.[3]

Also in 1987, an evaluation of CAP was performed in Columbus, Ohio, by David Nibert of the National Assault Prevention Center, the CAP Project's national office. Participants were 413 elementary school students in grades kindergarten through five. This study revealed a significant increase in students' knowledge about how to behave in an assault situation. CAP students were more likely to report that they would behave assertively in an assault situation than children who had not had CAP. For example, students who had CAP training were less likely to report they would give in to inappropriate demands by peers and adults, and they were less likely to report that they would respond to aggression with violence. Finally, CAP graduates were significantly more likely to report they would get detailed descriptons of assaulters.[4]

In 1985 Yvonne Lutter and Andrea Weisman evaluated a program that combined CAP, Illusion Theatre, and other prevention materials. The study participants were a group of Camp Fire Girls. This study revealed that the children who attended the program knew more about sexual abuse than untrained children. They were more aware of identifying a possible offender and of what to do if confronted with an assault situation. The children who attended the program were also more likely to perceive their peers as a support resource and were more comfortable discussing sexual abuse.[5]

In 1985 Horace Leake conducted an evaluation of CAP for the Women's Center of San Joaquin County in Stockton, California. Studies were conducted with first, second, third, and fifth graders. His findings indicated that CAP was effective in significantly increasing students' ability to recognize and avoid abuse and assault situations. Leake also found the CAP model was more effective in teaching children prevention knowledge than another program that centered on a prevention film. Leake suggested that the active and experiential nature of the CAP model was a more effective learning method than film viewing.[6]

In sum, research focusing on the elementary CAP program has indicated that the program is successful at increasing children's knowledge of assault prevention strategies.

References

1. R. Binder and D. McNiel, "Evaluation of a School-Based Sexual Abuse Prevention Program: Cognitive and Emotional Effects" (Presented at the 1986 Annual Meeting of the American Psychiatric Association, Washington, DC, 1986).

2. J. Smock, *Missing Children: A Study of the Effects of a Public School Prevention Program on Children and Their Families* (Ph.D. diss., California Graduate School of Marital and Family Therapy, 1987).

3. M. Kennings et al., "Evaluation of Child Sexual Abuse Prevention Programs: A Summary of Two Studies" (Paper presented at the National Conference on Family Violence, Durham, NH, 1987).

4. D. Nibert, "Evaluation of the Child Assault Prevention Project in the Columbus Public Schools" (Unpublished, Columbus, OH: National Assault Prevention Center, 1987).

5. Y. Lutter and A. Weisman, *Sexual Victimization Prevention Project* (Final Report to the National Institute of Mental Health, Grant R18 MH39549, 1985).

6. H. Leake, "A Study to Compare the Effectiveness of Two Primary Prevention Programs in Teaching Children to Recognize and Resist Child Sexual Abuse and Assault" (The Women's Center of San Joaquin County, CA, 1985).

Tools to Help Implement CAP

- Children's Workshop Sign-Up Sheet
- Sample Letter to Parents with Parental Permission Slip
- Evaluation of Children's Workshops
- Disclosure and/or Suspected Abuse Form
- Adult Questionnaire
- Exit Interview Questionnaire
- New CAP Project Information Form

Appendix B

Children's Workshop Sign-Up Sheet

S	M	DATE		T	DATE		W	DATE		T	DATE		F	DATE		S
	TIME	ROOM#		TIME	ROOM#		TIME	ROOM#		TIME	ROOM#		TIME	ROOM#		
	TEACHER			TEACHER			TEACHER			TEACHER			TEACHER			
	GRADE	Y N		GRADE	Y N		GRADE	Y N		GRADE	Y N		GRADE	Y N		
	TIME	ROOM#		TIME	ROOM#		TIME	ROOM#		TIME	ROOM#		TIME	ROOM#		
	TEACHER			TEACHER			TEACHER			TEACHER			TEACHER			
	GRADE	Y N		GRADE	Y N		GRADE	Y N		GRADE	Y N		GRADE	Y N		
	TIME	ROOM#		TIME	ROOM#		TIME	ROOM#		TIME	ROOM#		TIME	ROOM#		
	TEACHER			TEACHER			TEACHER			TEACHER			TEACHER			
	GRADE	Y N		GRADE	Y N		GRADE	Y N		GRADE	Y N		GRADE	Y N		
S	M	DATE		T	DATE		W	DATE		T	DATE		F	DATE		S
	TIME	ROOM#		TIME	ROOM#		TIME	ROOM#		TIME	ROOM#		TIME	ROOM#		
	TEACHER			TEACHER			TEACHER			TEACHER			TEACHER			
	GRADE	Y N		GRADE	Y N		GRADE	Y N		GRADE	Y N		GRADE	Y N		
	TIME	ROOM#		TIME	ROOM#		TIME	ROOM#		TIME	ROOM#		TIME	ROOM#		
	TEACHER			TEACHER			TEACHER			TEACHER			TEACHER			
	GRADE	Y N		GRADE	Y N		GRADE	Y N		GRADE	Y N		GRADE	Y N		
	TIME	ROOM#		TIME	ROOM#		TIME	ROOM#		TIME	ROOM#		TIME	ROOM#		
	TEACHER			TEACHER			TEACHER			TEACHER			TEACHER			
	GRADE	Y N		GRADE	Y N		GRADE	Y N		GRADE	Y N		GRADE	Y N		
S	M	DATE		T	DATE		W	DATE		T	DATE		F	DATE		S
	TIME	ROOM#		TIME	ROOM#		TIME	ROOM#		TIME	ROOM#		TIME	ROOM#		
	TEACHER			TEACHER			TEACHER			TEACHER			TEACHER			
	GRADE	Y N		GRADE	Y N		GRADE	Y N		GRADE	Y N		GRADE	Y N		
	TIME	ROOM#		TIME	ROOM#		TIME	ROOM#		TIME	ROOM#		TIME	ROOM#		
	TEACHER			TEACHER			TEACHER			TEACHER			TEACHER			
	GRADE	Y N		GRADE	Y N		GRADE	Y N		GRADE	Y N		GRADE	Y N		
	TIME	ROOM#		TIME	ROOM#		TIME	ROOM#		TIME	ROOM#		TIME	ROOM#		
	TEACHER			TEACHER			TEACHER			TEACHER			TEACHER			
	GRADE	Y N		GRADE	Y N		GRADE	Y N		GRADE	Y N		GRADE	Y N		
S	M	DATE		T	DATE		W	DATE		T	DATE		F	DATE		S
	TIME	ROOM#		TIME	ROOM#		TIME	ROOM#		TIME	ROOM#		TIME	ROOM#		
	TEACHER			TEACHER			TEACHER			TEACHER			TEACHER			
	GRADE	Y N		GRADE	Y N		GRADE	Y N		GRADE	Y N		GRADE	Y N		
	TIME	ROOM#		TIME	ROOM#		TIME	ROOM#		TIME	ROOM#		TIME	ROOM#		
	TEACHER			TEACHER			TEACHER			TEACHER			TEACHER			
	GRADE	Y N		GRADE	Y N		GRADE	Y N		GRADE	Y N		GRADE	Y N		
	TIME	ROOM#		TIME	ROOM#		TIME	ROOM#		TIME	ROOM#		TIME	ROOM#		
	TEACHER			TEACHER			TEACHER			TEACHER			TEACHER			
	GRADE	Y N		GRADE	Y N		GRADE	Y N		GRADE	Y N		GRADE	Y N		

Sample Letter to Parents

Dear Parent,

During the next few weeks, _____ Elementary School will be participating in the Child Assault Prevention Project (CAP). As parents concerned about the safety of your children, we hope you will join with us in participating in this program.

The CAP Project seeks to prevent child abuse by training children to recognize and deal with potentially dangerous situations, and by preparing adults in the children's community — both teachers and parents — to help children in this endeavor.

The program has three components: a parent program, a teacher/staff in-service for school personnel, and individual classroom workshops for children in kindergarten through sixth grade.

The adult workshops include information on child abuse, identification of child assault victims, reporting of abuse, and crisis intervention skills. There will also be a detailed description of the children's workshop.

The classroom workshop combines guided group discussion and a series of role-plays focusing on situations children frequently encounter: a child-to-child assault; adult stranger-to-child assault; and an assault involving an adult the child knows. Discussion helps children identify what options they have to protect themselves. The strategies focus on self-assertion, peer support, and telling a trusted adult.

The success of the CAP Project depends on the support of the school community. Because we encourage children to share their experiences and concerns with adults, it is important for parents and school staff to be willing and able to respond to these concerns. As part of the _____ Elementary School Community, we invite you to attend the CAP parent program on _____ (date) at _____ (time).

Following this presentation, we will be conducting classroom workshops at _____ Elementary School. We request your written permission for your child to attend. Please sign the permission slip and return it to the school. If you have any questions about the project, please call _____.

Sincerely,

Principal

_____

Parental Permission Slip

I give my permission for my child _____ to participate in the

Child Assault Prevention Project workshops at_____School.

_____
(parent's name)

_____
(date)

| School Name _____ Date _____
| Teacher _____ Grade _____
| Primary Facilitator _____ Role-Player _____
| Your Name _____ Role-Player _____

Evaluation of Children's Workshops

1. How many children are in this class? _____

2. How many children in this class were denied permission to attend the workshop? _____

3. What was the quality of the primary facilitator? General performance (circle one)

   Excellent   Good   Adequate   Fair   Poor

4. How well did the primary facilitator adhere to the script?

   Excellent   Good   Adequate   Fair   Poor

5. How would you rate the primary facilitator's enthusiasm and ability to relate to the children?

   Excellent   Good   Adequate   Fair   Poor

6. What was the quality of the role-playing? General performance (circle one)

   Excellent   Good   Adequate   Fair   Poor

7. How well did the role-players adhere to the script?

   Excellent   Good   Adequate   Fair   Poor

8. How would you rate the role-players' enthusiasm and ability to relate to the children?

   Excellent   Good   Adequate   Fair   Poor

9. List the children you spoke with following the workshop. What, specifically, did you discuss? What instructions or suggestions did you give the child? Quote the child accurately. NOTE: If you have reason to suspect that a child is being abused or at risk of being abused, use separate form entitled "Disclosure and/or Suspected Abuse Form."

1) _____
   _____
   _____
   _____

2) _____
   _____
   _____
   _____

OVER PLEASE

3)

4)

5)

6)

7)

8)

9)

10)

11)

Disclosure and/or Suspected Abuse Form

Please fill out this form for each child whom you have concern about and/or for each child who discloses fear of, or actual, abuse.

Name of Child _____ Date _____

Name of School _____ Teacher _____

Grade _____ Your Name _____

Sex of Child _____ Race of Child (circle one)   Black   White   Asian   Hispanic   Native American Indian   Other _____

Type of incident disclosed. (please describe) _____
_____
_____
_____
_____

Identity of the perpetrator: _____

Are you the first person the child has told? _____

If no, whom did the child tell first? _____

Is children's services already involved? _____

We are interested in how children disclose. Please circle the letter of whichever is applicable.

(a) The child revealed this information at the beginning of our conversation.

(b) The child revealed this information as we were reviewing the workshop concepts and strategies.

(c) The child revealed this information only after we had finished the review and asked if he or she felt safe, strong, and free.

Please describe your conversation with the child and any actions taken on your part. Please use the language the child used. Thanks.

_____
_____
_____
_____
_____
_____

OVER PLEASE

Project Coordinator Notes

Coordinator's Name _____ Date _____

Was contact made with a school official? If no, why? If yes, who? What was discussed and what action was taken?

_____
_____
_____
_____
_____
_____
_____
_____

Was contact made with children's services? If no, why? If yes, who? What was discussed and what action was taken?

_____
_____
_____
_____
_____
_____
_____
_____
_____

Follow-Up Notes: What is the last known status of the child's situation and actions by the school and/or children's services?

Date: _____

Contact: _____

NOTES: _____
_____
_____
_____
_____
_____
_____
_____

Adult Questionnaire

I. Please rate the information presented in the following six areas of the workshop. (Circle the appropriate rating)

	Not at All Useful	Somewhat Useful	Very Useful
A. Myths and Facts about Assault	1	2	3
B. Prevention Approach: Empowerment	1	2	3
C. Description of the Children's Workshop	1	2	3
D. Identification of Children in Crisis	1	2	3
E. Legal Rights and Responsibilities	1	2	3
F. Crisis Intervention Skills	1	2	3
G. Community Resources and Referrals	1	2	3

II. Please provide as much feedback as possible on the following questions:

1. Do you feel the presenter was well prepared and comfortable with the information provided?

   _____
   _____
   _____

2. Has the material presented made you feel better informed and prepared to deal with the prevention of child abuse?

   _____
   _____
   _____

3. What expectations did you have about the CAP Project?

   _____
   _____
   _____

4. What did you find to be the most useful part of the CAP presentation?

   _____
   _____
   _____

OVER PLEASE

5. What did you find to be the weakest part? How could we change that?

_____
_____
_____

6. Did you feel comfortable with the discussion of children's rights?

_____
_____
_____

7. Do you feel that the hand-outs are sufficient for the purposes of the presentation?

_____
_____
_____

8. Do you feel that there is adequate opportunity for questions and discussion?

_____
_____
_____

9. Do you plan to follow up with the prevention information in the classroom or at home? How?

_____
_____
_____

Thank you for your participation!!! Please use the remaining space and/or another sheet of paper for any additional comments/remarks.

_____
_____
_____
_____
_____
_____
_____
_____

Exit Interview Questionnaire

School _____
Principal/Other _____
Date _____
CAP Interviewer _____

1. What expectations did you have about CAP workshops? Have we met your expectations?

   _____
   _____
   _____

2. Are you comfortable with the discussion of children's rights?

   _____
   _____
   _____

3. What issues, if any, did the children seem to have a difficult time understanding? What issues seemed particularly important to the children?

   _____
   _____
   _____

4. Have you heard the children talking about their CAP workshop? What are they saying?

   _____
   _____
   _____

5. Have any parents contacted you concerning the information their children received in the CAP workshop? What feedback are you receiving?

   _____
   _____
   _____

6. Do you think that children should be given information on assault as part of their classroom experience?

   _____
   _____
   _____

OVER PLEASE

7. How will you follow up on the children that were identified as possible victims of assault? How can CAP assist you? (Discuss any reports made to protective services and any other issues that emerged that the principal was made aware of, or that he or she needs to be made aware of.)

_____
_____
_____
_____
_____
_____
_____
_____
_____
_____
_____
_____
_____
_____
_____
_____

8. Do you have any suggestions or comments that might help us improve the CAP Project?

_____
_____
_____
_____
_____
_____
_____
_____
_____
_____
_____
_____
_____
_____
_____

New CAP Project Information Form

The National Assault Prevention Center (NAPC), as part of its effort to maintain current information about each CAP Project, requests that you complete the following form.

Coordinator's Name _____

Name of CAP Project _____

Address _____

_____

_____

Name of Affiliating Agency (if any) _____

_____

Phone Number ( ) _____

FAX Number ( ) _____

Territory Served _____

Populations Served (check all that apply)

☐ Preschool _____

☐ Elementary _____

☐ Teen _____

☐ Special Populations _____

_____

CALL US!!   WRITE TO US!!

National Assault Prevention Center
P.O. Box 02005
Columbus, Ohio 43202
(614) 291-2540 — Office
(614) 291-9206 — FAX

Tools to Help You Conduct Evaluations

- School Personnel Evaluation Form
- Children's Evaluation Form — Interview Format
- Children's Evaluation Form — Questionnaire Format

Appendix C

School Personnel Evaluation Form

School _____ Date _____

Name _____ Position _____

1. I was adequately oriented to the purpose and objectives of the CAP Project.

    Strongly Agree   Agree   Undecided   Disagree   Strongly Disagree

2. The parent or teacher/staff in-service workshop was presented effectively.

    Strongly Agree   Agree   Undecided   Disagree   Strongly Disagree

3. The children's workshops were presented effectively.

    Strongly Agree   Agree   Undecided   Disagree   Strongly Disagree

4. The CAP facilitators were well prepared for the workshops.

    Strongly Agree   Agree   Undecided   Disagree   Strongly Disagree

5. The role-playing format of the children's workshop was effective.

    Strongly Agree   Agree   Undecided   Disagree   Strongly Disagree

6. Students appeared more aware of how to deal with strangers as a result of their CAP training.

    Strongly Agree   Agree   Undecided   Disagree   Strongly Disagree

7. Students appeared more aware of how to deal with bullies as a result of their CAP training.

    Strongly Agree   Agree   Undecided   Disagree   Strongly Disagree

8. Students appeared more aware of how to deal with sexual abuse as a result of their CAP training.

    Strongly Agree   Agree   Undecided   Disagree   Strongly Disagree

9. In general, the CAP Project provided a valuable experience for students.

    Strongly Agree   Agree   Undecided   Disagree   Strongly Disagree

10. The services provided by the CAP Project are needed by this school.

    Strongly Agree   Agree   Undecided   Disagree   Strongly Disagree

Children's Evaluation Form

Interview Format

I am going to tell you about some things that happened to Chris. Chris is a boy/girl just like you, in the _____ grade.

1. Chris was given a new book for his/her birthday and he/she is taking it to school to show some friends. An older student, bigger than Chris, comes up to Chris and says, "Give me that book, I want it." What should Chris do? (After a response is given, ask "Is there anything else Chris could do?" until no further response is forthcoming. Do this for each of the scenarios.)

2. The next day Chris is walking to school. A person Chris does not know pulls up next to Chris in a car. This person offers Chris a ride to school. What should Chris do?

3. What should Chris do if the stranger grabs Chris?

4. What should Chris do if the stranger puts his hand over Chris's mouth?

5. Later, when Chris tells an adult what happened, what things should Chris tell the adult?

6. When Chris tells an adult about what happened, what should Chris do if the adult does not believe him/her?

7. It is Saturday and Chris is home watching TV. A friend of Chris's father comes into the room and sits next to Chris. He starts to touch Chris in ways that Chris does not like. What should Chris do?

Thank you for your help!

Questionnaire Format

Chris is a student your age and goes to a school just like yours.

1. Chris was given a new book for his/her birthday and he/she is taking it to school to show some friends. An older student, bigger than Chris, comes up to Chris and says, "Give me that book, I want it." What should Chris do? List as many things as you can think of.

   _____
   _____
   _____

2. The next day Chris is walking to school. A person Chris does not know pulls up next to Chris in a car. This person offers Chris a ride to school. What should Chris do? List as many things as you can think of.

   _____
   _____
   _____

3. What should Chris do if the stranger grabs Chris? List as many things as you can think of.

   _____
   _____
   _____

4. What should Chris do if the stranger puts his hand over Chris's mouth? List as many things as you can think of.

   _____
   _____
   _____

5. Later, when Chris tells an adult about what happened, what things should Chris tell the adult? List as many things as you can think of.

   _____
   _____
   _____

6. When Chris tells an adult about what happened, what should Chris do if the adult does not believe him/her? List as many things as you can think of.

   _____
   _____
   _____

7. It is Saturday and Chris is home watching TV. A friend of Chris's father comes into the room and sits next to Chris. He starts to touch Chris in ways that Chris does not like. What should Chris do? List as many things as you can think of.

   _____
   _____
   _____

Thank you!

Children's Evaluation Form

Bibliography

Adams, Karen, and Jennifer Fay. *Nobody Told Me It Was Rape: A Parent's Guide for Talking with Teenagers About Acquaintance Rape and Sexual Exploitation.* San Luis Obispo, CA: Network Publications, 1984.

_____, and Jan Loreen-Martin. *No Is Not Enough: Helping Teenagers Avoid Sexual Assault.* San Luis Obispo, CA: Impact Publishers, 1984.

Bass, Ellen, and Laura Davis. *The Courage to Heal: A Guide for Women Survivors of Child Sexual Abuse.* New York: Harper & Row, 1988.

Bear, Euan, and Peter T. Dimock. *Adults Molested as Children: A Survivor's Manual for Women and Men.* Orwell, VT: Safer Society Press, 1988.

Benedict, Helen. *Safe, Strong and Streetwise.* Boston: Little, Brown and Co., 1987.

_____. *Recovery.* Garden City, NY: Doubleday, 1985.

Bolton, F., L. Morris, and A. MacEachron. *Males at Risk: The Other Side of Child Sexual Abuse.* Newbury Park, CA: Sage Publications, 1989.

_____. *A Sourcebook on Child Sexual Abuse.* Newbury Park, CA: Sage Publications, 1989.

Burgess, Ann Wolbert. *Child Pornography and Sex Rings.* Lexington, MA: D.C. Heath & Company, 1984.

Butler, Sandra. *Conspiracy of Silence.* San Francisco: New Glide Publications, 1978.

Child Welfare League of America. *Child Welfare.* Washington, DC, published bimonthly.

Crewdson, John. *By Silence Betrayed: Sexual Abuse of Children in America.* Boston: Little, Brown and Co., 1988.

Daugherty, Lynn B. *Why Me? Help for Victims of Sexual Child Abuse.* Racine, WI: Mother Courage Press, 1984.

Davis, Laura. *The Courage to Heal Workbook (for Men and Women).* New York: Harper & Row, 1980.

Family Violence Research and Treatment Center. *Family Violence Bulletin.* Tyler, TX, published quarterly.

Finkelhor, David. *Child Sexual Abuse New Theory and Research.* Newbury Park, NY: Free Press, 1984.

_____, and Linda Meyer Williams, with Nanci Burns. *Nursery Crimes: Sexual Abuse in Day Care.* Newbury Park, CA: Sage Publications, 1988.

_____. *Sexually Victimized Children.* New York: Free Press, 1979.

_____. *Sourcebook on Child Sexual Abuse.* Beverly Hills: Sage Publications, 1986.

Garbarino, James. *The Psychologically Battered Child.* San Francisco: Jossey-Bass Publishers, 1986.

Groth, A. Nicholas. *Men Who Rape: The Psychology of the Offender.* New York: Plenum Press, 1979.

The Guilford Press. *Response to the Victimization of Women and Children.* Washington, DC, published quarterly.

Hale-Benson, Janice E. *Black Children: Their Roots, Culture, and Learning Styles.* Baltimore: Johns Hopkins University Press, 1986.

Herman, Judith Lewis. *Father-Daughter Incest.* Cambridge, MA: Harvard University Press, 1981.

Hillman, Donald, and Janice Solek-Tefft. *Spiders and Flies: Help for Parents and Teachers of Sexually Abused Children.* Lexington, MA: Lexington Books, 1988.

Hindman, Jan. *Just Before Dawn.* Ontario, OR: Alexandria Associates, 1989.

Horton, Anne L., and Judith A. Williamson. *Abuse and Religion: When Praying Isn't Enough.* Lexington, MA: Lexington Books, 1988.

Hunter, Mic. *Abused Boys: The Neglected Victims.* Lexington, MA: Lexington Books, 1989.

Jaffe, Peter G., David A. Wolfe, and Susan Kaye Wilson. *Children of Battered Women.* Newbury Park, CA: Sage Publications, 1990.

Levinson, David. *Family Violence in Cross-Cultural Perspective.* Newbury Park, CA: Sage Publications, 1989.

Lew, Mike. *Victims No Longer: Men Recovering from Incest and Other Sexual Child Abuse.* New York: Harper & Row, 1990.

Maltz, Wendy, and Beverly Holman. *Incest and Sexuality: A Guide to Understanding and Healing.* Lexington, MA: Lexington Books, 1987.

McKay, Matthew, Peter D. Rogers, and Judith McKay. *When Anger Hurts: Quieting the Storm Within.* Oakland, CA: New Harbinger Publications, 1989.

McNaron, Toni A. H., and Yarrow Morgan. *Voices in the Night: Women Speaking About Incest.* San Francisco: Cleis Press, 1982.

Mechler, David. *Battle and the Backlash: The Child Sexual Abuse War.* Lexington, MA: Lexington Books, 1988.

Miller, Alice. *The Drama of the Gifted Child: The Search for the True Self.* New York: Basic Books, 1981.

_____. *For Your Own Good: Hidden Cruelty in Child-Rearing and the Roots of Violence.* New York: Farrar, Straus, 1983.

_____. *Thou Shalt Not Be Aware: Society's Betrayal of the Child.* New York: New American Library, 1984.

Porter, Eugene. *Treating the Young Male Victim of Sexual Assault.* Syracuse, NY: Safer Society Press, 1986.

The G. Allan Roeher Institute. *Vulnerable: Sexual Abuse and People with an Intellectual Handicap.* Ontario, Canada: G. Allan Roeher Institute, 1988.

Rush, Florence. *The Best Kept Secret: Sexual Abuse of Children.* Englewood Cliffs, NJ: Prentice-Hall, 1980.

Russell, Diana E. H. *Sexual Exploitation: Rape, Child Sexual Abuse and Workplace Harassment.* Newbury Park, CA: Sage Publications, 1984.

_____. *The Secret Trauma: Incest in the Lives of Girls and Women.* New York: Basic Books, 1986.

Sage Publications. *Journal of Interpersonal Violence.* Newbury Park, CA, published quarterly.

Salter, Anna C. *Treating Child Sex Offenders and Victims: A Practical Guide.* Newbury Park, CA: Sage Publications, 1988.

Sandberg, David. *Child Abuse-Delinquency Connection.* Lexington, MA: Lexington Books, 1989.

Sanford, Linda. *The Silent Children: A Parent's Guide to the Prevention of Child Sexual Abuse.* New York: McGraw-Hill, 1980.

_____. *Strong at the Broken Places.* New York: Random House, 1990.

_____. *Top Secret: Sexual Assault Information for Teenagers Only.* Seattle, WA: King County Rape Relief, 1982.

Sgroi, Suzanne M., M.D. *Vulnerable Populations Volume 1, Evaluation and Treatment of Sexually Abused Children and Adult Survivors.* Lexington, MA: Lexington Books, 1988.

Smith, Sandra Butler. *Children's Story: Sexually Molested Children in Criminal Court.* Walnut Creek, CA: Launch, 1985.

Stringer, Gayle, and Dianna Rauts-Rodriquez. *So What's It To Me? Sexual Assault Information for Guys.* Renton, WA: King County Rape Relief, 1987.

White, Evelyn. *Chain, Chain, Change: For Black Women Dealing with Physical and Emotional Abuse.* Seattle, WA: Seal Press, 1985.

Wiehe, Vernon R. *Sibling Abuse: Hidden Physical, Emotional, and Sexual Trauma.* Lexington, MA: Lexington Books, 1990.

Zambrano, Myrna M. *Mejor Sola Que Mal Acompanada: For the Latina in an Abusive Relationship.* Seattle, WA: Seal Press, 1985.